THE LIFE

AND

LETTERS

OF

THOMAS À BECKET

NOW FIRST

GATHERED FROM THE CONTEMPORARY

HISTORIANS

BY THE REV.
J. A. GILES, D.C.L.
LATE FELLOW OF CORPUS CHRISTI COLLEGE, OXFORD.

Est pro justitia casus in ecclesia.

IN TWO VOLUMES.
VOL. I.

LONDON:
WHITTAKER AND CO., AVE MARIA LANE.

1846.

LONDON:
GILBERT & RIVINGTON, PRINTERS,
ST. JOHN'S SQUARE.

TO HIS EXCELLENCY

SIR G. HAMILTON SEYMOUR, G.C.H.

&c. &c. &c.

AMBASSADOR OF HER BRITANNIC MAJESTY

AT THE COURT OF BRUSSELS,

𝕮𝖍𝖎𝖘 𝖂𝖔𝖗𝖐

IS RESPECTFULLY DEDICATED,

IN ACKNOWLEDGMENT

OF THE POLITE ATTENTION AND KINDNESS

WHICH THE AUTHOR RECEIVED

FROM HIS EXCELLENCY,

DURING A SHORT RESIDENCE IN THAT CITY.

OXFORD,
SEPTEMBER, 1843.

PREFACE.

THE English reader who has studied the history of his country in the writings of our popular historians, cannot be unacquainted with the name of Thomas Becket; but he knows him most probably either as a fanatic or as an impostor, certainly as a saint, and therefore as belonging to a class of men who are supposed to have no personal history like other men, or are considered so dangerous in all that concerns them, that their history had better be buried in oblivion. This is not only the case with Becket but with many others, who, perhaps, may in their turn find a biographer that will bring them down from their pedestals, and show them to have been moved by the same passions, and to have aspired, perhaps, after the same virtues as the rest of their species. It is our object in the present work to effect this in the case of Thomas Becket, one of the most extraordinary characters in English history, and whose life, divested of its wonders and its miracles, would furnish matter for a romance, or for an epic poem. The almost unprecedented rapidity of his rise to the highest dignity in the kingdom next to the throne, his versatile abilities, whereby he filled and adorned stations of life so different, his familiarity with one of our ablest monarchs, and subsequently their bitter enmity, followed up by his tragical and barbarous murder, committed at the hour of prayer and in his own Church, are surely of sufficient interest to attract the notice of the public. They were thought to be of sufficient importance to be recorded by the writers of his own time, and a host of biographers came forward to relate what they had seen and heard of so wonderful a character. In this respect he was fortunate; for the reign of Henry II. is one of the golden periods of English literature. The bloody wars which had so long desolated the kingdom had subsided, like a fire which ceases to burn for want of fuel, and a rich and luxuriant crop arose in a singularly short time over the ashes. In this reign begins that crowd of chroniclers, which give us almost the only knowledge we possess of preceding times. Every department of learning was speedily filled, and it was not likely that the "new event," which happened in their own times should be left without an historian. There is indeed no dearth of documents relating to the quarrel between Becket and the king; for, in addition to the limited notice which the writers of our larger chronicles of England have taken of it, at least twenty authors, living in that or the next generation, have written at length the history of the Life and Passion of St. Thomas. Some of these memoirs have either ceased to exist, or have not yet been discovered amid the thousands of ancient volumes which fill our public libraries. Others however are in existence, some mutilated, some still entire, though no systematic attempt has been made before this to ascertain their authors, or the historic authority which may be conceded to them. Though the art of printing has been now four hundred years in full action, one only authentic life of Becket, that by William Fitz-Stephen, his clerk, has yet been printed, and even to this some curious additions may be made from an older and more valuable manuscript copy. The Quadrilogus of Paris, 1495, that of Lupus, printed at Brussels, 1600, consist of extracts only from four or five of the principal of Becket's biographers; and in the different collections of the Lives of the Saints we find no other than meagre abridgments put together at a much later date, and none of them furnishing that minute and intimate information which so important an event demands. Under these circumstances, it is hoped that the following account of the contemporary writers, from whom our knowledge of Becket's life and character is derived, may not be unacceptable to the reader.

In the Royal Library at Paris is a manuscript life of Becket, [No. 5371.] written apparently about the year 1300, or earlier. The preface, literally translated, begins as follows:—

"Jesus Christ, the same yesterday, to-day, and for ever, hath in these our days revealed things which have been hidden from mankind from the beginning of the world," &c. &c.

After a little more of this preliminary matter, the writer continues:—

"Wherefore I have thought fit to reduce into one compact narrative all the different, and yet not contradictory, accounts which have been written about him [St. Thomas], and so to regulate the size of my book, that it may neither be excessively diffuse, nor defective from its brevity: thus the varied nature of the work may counteract the fatigue of the reader, until, from being fatigued, he comes to feel an interest in the narrative. Thus we read in Tully of the sculptor, who is said to have made an image of exquisite loveliness by culling different points of grace from different female beauties. St. Hilary also, in making his book of Synods, extracted in the same way the best parts of various other writers; and he calls himself, not the author, but the compiler of the work in question. In like manner also the author of the Tripartite history acknowledges that he had extracted his sentences from the writings of others. May the Spirit of truth inspire me worthily to set forth the grace of God! Without that Spirit my mind can conceive nothing of high enterprize. May my tongue achieve, in language of purity and of truth, the object which I cherish in the honest purpose of my heart!

"It is not to be doubted that truth will be found in those whom we have taken for our models, and pre-eminent among these is the finger of him whose arm was wounded in protecting the martyr that was to be slain. He left a record, from which I have copied; and I saw him once, when he was an old man and I a young one. Those therefore who wish it, and have it in their power, can read the separate accounts of preceding writers, and my compilation will be no prejudice to their doing so. It was the intention of those persons to omit some facts in drawing up their histories, but in writing my work I have studied only to follow truth, and to introduce what the others had omitted; for we are informed by St. Luke that several points had been passed over even in our Lord's history, which yet are strong bulwarks of our faith. But inasmuch as it is difficult to follow the track of another, and not sometimes step out of the way, if I have done so here, I may ask pardon for having unwittingly offended. However, as Pliny tells us, it is always a mark of an ingenuous mind to give one's authorities; I shall therefore here briefly enumerate my authors for the following work.

"First in rank, because he was a bishop, is John of Chartres: second, Herbert de Bosham, also an eminent doctor: then Edward, surnamed Grim, who was wounded in the arm, as aforesaid, when the martyr was slain. The fourth was another writer of the name of Edward. Then come two others, distinguished for their learning and virtuous lives, namely, Benedict and Alan, both abbats; and next, their abbreviator, the abbat of Clay. Then come two monks, William and Roger, the former of Canterbury, the latter of Pontigny. The last of these attended on the holy man whilst he was in exile at Pontigny. Surely none but an infidel could disbelieve the testimony of such men as these. After these writers am I the tenth, and I have gathered up the pips and grains which have fallen from their hands," &c. &c.

After several pages more of matter irrelevant to our present purpose, the writer proceeds:—

"To these reasons may be added, that I was impelled to write this history by that excellent man Giles, Abbat of Aulne, in the district of Liege, who gave me a plan for the work, requesting me to mark in the margin the name of the author from whom I made the several extracts, &c. &c."

From this quotation it will be evident to the reader, that the manuscript from which they are taken must be of the greatest value for authenticating the histories of Becket's life which are preserved in different libraries. The following list of such works has indeed been drawn up principally on the authority of this very valuable manuscript.

1. By John of Salisbury, afterwards Bishop of Chartres, and intimate friend of Becket. His short work is rather a character than a detailed life of the archbishop; copies of it exist in the Bodleian, the British Museum, at Cambridge, and I believe many other libraries. This work is identified with that of John of Salisbury, by the quotations in the Quadrilogus.

2. By Herbert de Bosham, the secretary of Becket: he wrote his voluminous history fifteen years after the martyrdom. A mutilated copy exists at Arras, a second, which has lost the first three books out of the seven, is preserved at C.C.C. Oxford; the author calls himself Herbert de Bosham in the preface.

A volume of letters, by Herbert de Bosham, and written in the course of the quarrel with the king, is preserved at C.C.C. Cambridge.

3. By Edward Grim, a monk who went to Canterbury, out of curiosity, to see Becket, after

his return from exile: he was present at the murder, and received a severe wound in the arm, in attempting to protect the archbishop. These facts we learn from the work of Herbert de Bosham, and the work, which remains in three MSS. at the British Museum, is ascertained to be his by the words *eodem ictu præciso brachio hæc referentis*, "the same stroke wounded the arm of the writer of this history," which occur in the account of the martyrdom.

4. The fourth writer, also named Edward, we have not been able to identify.

5. By Benedict, abbat of Peterborough, of whose work I have not yet been able to discover a single copy in existence, unless a copious collection of Miracula Sancti Thomæ, found at Paris, Lambeth, Brussels, Douay, and less perfect in the Bodleian, be the latter part of the work in question. There are also extracts from Benedict's work in the Quadrilogus.

6. By Alan, abbat of Tewkesbury, whose short work, embodying that of John of Salisbury, and touching principally on the events which followed the council of Clarendon, occurs in the Bodleian, the British Museum, the hotel Soubire at Paris, and possibly in several other libraries, it is identified by the quotations which occur in the Quadrilogus.

7. By the abbat of Clay, who abbreviated the

works of Benedict and Alan. Of this abbreviation I have not met with the slightest trace, nor from its necessary brevity is the loss of it to be regretted.

8. By William of Canterbury, perhaps the prior of that name, whose letters occur in the collection of Becket's letters. Extracts from this work occur in the Quadrilogus, and are of very little importance.

9. By Roger, a monk of Pontigny, and the attendant on Becket during the two years which he passed in that monastery. His work, which is identified by the allusion which he makes to that fact, is preserved in a single MS. belonging to the Royal Library of Paris, a transcript of which occurs among the Gale MSS. at Trinity College, Cambridge.

10. By the anonymous author of the life, from which we obtain all the details respecting the preceding nine biographers. The work of this tenth biographer is compiled entirely from extracts of the preceding. Its principal value, therefore, consists in the preface.

Besides these ten biographers, there are others, of great historical value, not mentioned in the above list. The principal of these are,

11. Elias of Evesham. With this writer I am entirely unacquainted, having met with the name

by accident in a book which I have forgotten. I am, however, induced by this accidental circumstance to infer, that he is the writer of a life of Becket, preserved in the British Museum [MS. Vesp. B. xiv. f. 33.], who calls himself E., a monk of Evesham, and who addresses his work to Henry, abbat of Croyland. The manuscript above indicated is the only one in existence containing this preface, but it is also probably the earliest which contains the work itself, which, with the exception of the preface, and an account of the translation of the saint's body, added at the end, is verbatim the same as the printed Quadrilogus of Lupus. It is the earliest manuscript copy I have seen of that Quadrilogus. We learn from the preface, that the author extracted from John of Salisbury; Alan, abbat of Tewkesbury; William, sub-prior of Canterbury, and Herbert de Bosham; also that Benedict, abbat of Peterborough, wrote only of the latter part of Becket's life, and of the events which happened after his martyrdom.

12. William Fitz-Stephen, a clerk of Becket, who attended his master through a great portion of his public life. The fullest MS. of his work is in the Douce collection, in the Bodleian library; other less perfect copies occur in the British Museum, and at Lambeth. Though Fitz-Stephen was from Canterbury, his work is certainly dif-

ferent from that of William, the monk of Canterbury, (No. 8.) of which quotations occur in the Quadrilogus.

13. By Guarinus de Ponte Maxentii, a French metrical life, written between two and five years after the martyrdom. It is preserved in a MS. of the British Museum and elsewhere, and is valuable on many accounts, besides the authenticity derived from its antiquity. Part of this life has been printed by Bekker from an imperfect copy.

14. By Henry, abbat of Croyland, assisted by Roger, a monk of Croyland: a work preserved in a single MS. at Paris. It contains two prefaces, one of which is by Henry, inscribing the work to Stephen Langton, archbishop of Canterbury, whom Henry thanks for having invited him to the translation of Becket's body, which happened A.D. 1220. The other preface was written by Roger, offering his revision or second edition to abbat Henry, by whose orders he revised it. In this preface Roger also gives us dates which ascertain the year in which the work was written. He says that abbat Henry had it first compiled (i. e. by his monks), in the last year of the reign of king Richard, A.D. 1199, and that he himself had completed his second edition in the fourteenth year of king John, A.D. 1213. Seven years later

it would seem abbat Henry presented his work to Stephen Langton, with the addition of his own preface before mentioned. The year 1220 was a year of great excitement among the clergy of England, in consequence of the saint's body being removed that year from the grave. It is not unlikely that Elias, the monk of Evesham, whose life stands eleven in our list, wrote that work in consequence of having been present at the ceremony.

15. An anonymous life of Becket is preserved in the archbishop's library at Lambeth, distinct from any of the former; and followed by the Miracula Sancti Thomæ. The author says he was an eye-witness of many of the events of the saint's life.

16. Another anonymous life of Becket is found in a single MS. [Brit. Mus. Lansd. 398,] written about the year 1200, and therefore, of contemporary authority. It is short, and intended apparently for the service of the Church, but it has some curious passages.

17. A life of Becket was also written by Grandison, bishop of Exeter, at a much later period, but of no value whatever, as it is a meagre compilation, written apparently for no other reason than to supply the deficiency of manuscripts. Three copies of it are found in C.C.C. Cambridge.

18. A metrical life of Becket in Latin, by Maurinus Monachus, occurs in the Bodleian Library, a dull composition and of no value.

19, 20, 21. Three other biographies in French verse are found in the British Museum, but apparently of little value.

22. A compilation similar to that of Elias of Evesham, but containing additional chapters from the work of Edward Grim, was published at Paris, fol. 1495. A manuscript copy, very nearly corresponding with it, exists at St. Omer. It is generally quoted by the name of the first Quadrilogus.

23. Another compilation, made by the order of Gregory XI., and corresponding identically, except the preface, with the work of Elias of Evesham, was printed by Lupus, Brussels, 4to. 1682. Manuscript copies occur in the British Museum, Douay and C.C.C. Oxford. It is generally quoted as the second Quadrilogus.

From these authorities, with occasional reference to the chronicle of Ralph de Diceto, the present work is compiled, and it has been my endeavour to make it as far as possible an epitome of all the preceding biographies. If I have succeeded in giving the reader a portrait of the great man whose life is the subject of the narrative, it will be a source of satisfaction, nor shall I be disposed to complain if the patchwork nature of the work, or quaintness of the style, shall attract the censure of critics: the former quality was unavoidable in a book not merely compiled from so many ancient sources, but compiled almost in their very words: for the quaintness of the style my only apology is, that those whose life is spent in old libraries, must not complain if their minds as well as their clothes contract some portion of the dust which is there accumulated. If, however, I am charged with partiality, or with having perverted facts, I shall feel little annoyance at so unjust an accusation: for it has been my wish to begin and end this work with no other guide than truth; and as the book, in almost every page, gives the words of the contemporary writers, it will be in the reader's power, in every case, to form an opinion for himself.

There is, however, one other caution which it is necessary to give, and this concerns a subject which would force itself on the notice of any one who should venture to write a life of Thomas Becket. He died in supporting the Church against the state. If the same question were to occur in the present day, the man who should sacrifice his life in endeavouring to exempt ecclesiastics from the jurisdiction of the civil courts, would be justly considered not a saint and martyr, but a madman. It is necessary to make this statement, lest a prejudice should be raised against a work in which the subject is handled on principles which apply to the twelfth, and not to the nineteenth century. Nor is this a question between the Church of England and the Church of Rome. Protestants and Catholics may agree in their judgment of this work: for it concerns a time when no such distinctions existed; and few, if any, of the points at issue between Henry II. and the archbishop, are identical with those which now harass and divide the rival Churches.

The letters which occur in the course of the narrative are taken from the collections known by the names of "*Epistolæ divi Thomæ;*" "*Epistolæ Joannis Sarisburiensis;*" and "*Epistolæ Gilberti Foliot.*" An enlarged edition of the Latin original of these letters, and also of the contemporary biographies, will soon be published by the author of this work.

J. A. G.

The reader is requested to correct the following errors, which have escaped detection:—

Page 32, note, *read* A. D. 1138 to 1161.
—— 37, line 11, *for* priory *read* provostship

CONTENTS

OF

VOL. I.

CHAPTER		PAGE
I.	Historical Introduction	1
	LETTER I. Lanfranc to William the Conqueror	3
	II. The same to the same	4
	III. William the Conqueror to Pope Gregory . . .	5
II.	Of the Birth and Parentage of Becket	10
III.	Of Becket's Childhood and Early Years	23
IV.	Of Becket's Advancement at the Court of Archbishop Theobald	32
V.	Of his Introduction to the King's Court, and appointment to be Chancellor	40
VI.	Of the Reformation effected in the Government by Becket's Influence—Anecdotes of his Chancellorship	48
VII.	Of his Military Abilities at Toulouse, and in the War with France	66
VIII.	Of the Chancellor's Embassy to the French King	72
IX.	Letters to Becket as Chancellor—Further Remarks on his Character—Charges brought against him refuted	80

CHAPTER		PAGE
LETTER IV.	Arnulf of Lisieux to Becket	81
V.	Peter of Celles to Becket	84
VI.	Peter of Treca to Becket	87

X. Theobald's Death—Of the Events which followed it, and of Becket's Election to the Archbishopric of Canterbury 100

XI. Becket Archbishop—Public opinion of his Election—His purity of life, and many virtues . . 112

XII. His changed mode of life—First acts—Resumption of illegal Grants—The King's Return and Interviews with Becket 127

XIII. The Archbishop attends the Council of Tours . . 140

XIV. Gilbert Foliot, the rival of Becket—His origin—Is first Prior of Clugny, then of Abbeville—Abbat of Gloucester, Bishop of Hereford, and finally of London 143

LETTER VII.	Becket to Gilbert Foliot, Bishop of Hereford	145
VIII.	King Henry to the same	146
IX.	Pope Alexander to the same	148
X.	Gilbert Foliot, Bishop of London, to King Henry (of a later date)	154

XV. Dedication of Reading Abbey—Translation of Edward the Confessor—First Misunderstandings between the King and Becket—Council of Woodstock—Sheriff's Dues—Church of Eynesford—Clerical Offenders—Filling up of the sees of Hereford and Worcester 159

LETTER XI. John of Poitiers to Becket 171

XVI. Council of Westminster—King's measure rejected by the Clergy—His anger—He leaves London—Statement of the question at issue—Power of the Church 176

CONTENTS. xxiii

CHAPTER		PAGE
✓XVII.	John of Salisbury banished—Correspondence with the Papal Court	195
	Letter XII. Becket to the Pope	196
	XIII. Master Henry to Becket	198
	XIV. Abbat of St. Remy to John of Salisbury .	202
	XV. John of Salisbury to Becket, Oct. 1163 . .	203
	XVI. John of Poitiers to Becket, Sens, Nov. 1163	208
XVIII.	Cabals and attempts to shake the Archbishop's Resolution—Interview with the King at Woodstock—Council of Clarendon	210
XIX.	The Archbishop sends Intelligence to the Pope —Twice attempts to leave the kingdom—Unsuccessful attempts to effect a reconciliation	226
	Letter XVII. The Pope to Becket, Sens, Feb. 27, 1164 .	232
	XVIII. The same to the same	234
	XIX. To Becket from his Envoy, Sens, after Easter, 1164	234
XX.	Council of Northampton	237
XXI.	The Archbishop escapes by night to Lincoln, and from thence to Canterbury—Gravelines— St. Omer's—Soissons	268
XXII.	Embassies from both parties to the Pope and the French King	278
XXIII.	The Archbishop's Interview with the French King and the Pope—He becomes an Inmate of the Monastery of Pontigny	289
XXIV.	The harsh Proceedings of the King of England —Exile of the Archbishop's friends	295
	Letter XX. The King to the Bishops, Dec. 24, 1164	298
	XXI. The same to the Sheriffs	298
	XXII. The Archbishop to the Pope, Jan. 1165	299

CHAPTER			PAGE
	LETTER XXIII.	The Pope to the brethren of Clairmarais	302
	XXIV.	The Archbishop to the Queen of Sicily	303
	XXV.	The same to the Bishop of Syracuse	304
XXV.	Inactivity of the Archbishop in 1165—Letters written during that year and the early part of 1166		306
	LETTER XXVI.	Hervey to the Archbishop	307
	XXVII.	John of Salisbury to the same	308
	XXVIII.	John of Poitiers to the same	313
	XXIX.	King Henry to the Archbishop of Cologne	316
	XXX.	The Pope to the Bishop of London	317
	XXXI.	The Bishop of London's reply	320
	XXXII.	The Pope to the Archbishop	324
XXVI.	The Pope returns to Italy		325
	LETTER XXXIII.	The Archbishop to the King of England	327
	XXXIV.	The Pope to the Bishops of the province of Kent	334
	XXXV.	The Archbishop to the Bishop of London and Bishops of the province of Kent	335
	XXXVI.	The Bishops' reply	340
	XXXVII.	To the Clergy of England	347
	XXXVIII.	Gilbert, Bishop of London, to the Archbishop	376
	XXXIX.	John of Salisbury to the Bishop of Exeter	399

LIFE AND LETTERS

OF

THOMAS À BECKET.

CHAPTER I.

HISTORICAL INTRODUCTION.

THE Anglo-Saxon dynasty, which was so securely established in England by the subjection, or extirpation, of the native tribes, rose, within a singularly short period, to the enjoyment of all the privileges of learning and general civilization. But this growth was as short-lived as it was rapid, and for many years before the Norman conquest there was a general dearth of intellect throughout the whole country. This circumstance served to aid the views which William of Normandy formed on the English throne; for even during the reign of the Confessor, who had himself received his education abroad, large numbers, both of ecclesiastics and of laymen, had flocked to the court of England, as to a harvest where all might reap honours and emoluments, without much opposition or rivalry from the degenerate natives. The battle of Hastings put the finishing stroke to the power, and almost to the existence, of the Anglo-Saxon nobility; and when the Conqueror, in the year 1070, raised Lanfranc, prior of Bec, to the archiepiscopal see of Canterbury, the appointment was not merely the election to the first spiritual dignity in the kingdom, but served in fact to create a second power in the state, equal, and occasionally superior, to the throne of the king himself. The influence of the archbishop of Canterbury had indeed been great from the first moment that Christianity was introduced into the island, and the several kingdoms of the heptarchy were each too weak to throw off a certain degree of thraldom in which they were held by the successors of St. Augustine: but this state of things had been much modified in later times: we read of no successful opposition made by the Church to the plans of the great Alfred, Egbert, Edward, and many others. It was only when the spiritual weapons were wielded by the able hands of St. Dunstan and a few others, that we read of such struggles between the Court and the Church, as those which afterwards occurred so frequently under the government of the Anglo-Normans. If the Conqueror could have foreseen the hostilities which were in after years to arise between the king and the archbishop, and which, in more than one instance, converted bosom-friends into the most bitter enemies, he might have hesitated, in the completeness of his newly-acquired sovereignty, to place in the hands of Lanfranc such ample powers, as rendered him the second person in the kingdom, both in Church and State.

History informs us, that William the Conqueror took advantage of an insurrection of the English to reduce the whole kingdom more thoroughly under his subjection. Stigand, the former archbishop of Canterbury, was deposed on account of the informality of his election, and Lanfranc was substituted in his place. When William, on a subsequent occasion, visited his Norman dominions, the government of England was committed to the sole charge of the archbishop. The following letters, addressed to the king whilst he was in Normandy, will serve to illustrate the history of the period.

LETTER I.

"TO MY LORD WILLIAM, KING OF THE ENGLISH, HIS FAITHFUL LANFRANC, LOYAL OBEDIENCE, AND HIS SINCERE PRAYERS.

"WE would as gladly see your face amongst us as if you were an angel sent from God, but we do not wish you to cross the sea at present; for it would be a great shame to us all, if you should take the trouble of coming over to put down such disloyal thieves. Count Rodolph, or rather that traitor Rodolph, has been routed with all his army;

and our men are pursuing him in large numbers, both French and English. Before many days, as our chiefs have informed me, the rebels will be driven into the sea, or taken prisoners, dead or alive. The monk who bears this letter will inform you of other matters: you may place implicit confidence in him, for he has pledged his faith to me. May Almighty God bless you."

LETTER II.

"TO MY MOST ILLUSTRIOUS LORD WILLIAM, KING OF THE ENGLISH, HIS FAITHFUL LANFRANC, LOYAL SUBMISSION AND PRAYERS FOR HIS HEALTH.

"GLORY in the highest to God, by whose mercy your kingdom has been purified from the filthy host of the Britons: Norwich Castle has surrendered, and the Britons who were in it, and held lands in England, have sworn, on condition of being safe, both in life and limb, to leave the kingdom within forty days, and never again to enter it without your permission. But those who, without holding lands, served for pay under that traitor Rodolph and his companions, have prevailed upon us by many entreaties to allow them to do the same within a month.

"Bishop Geoffrey, William de Warenne, Robert Mallet have remained in the castle with three hundred men-at-arms, engine-men, and numerous makers of military machines. The din of weapons has, by God's mercy, totally ceased throughout all England. May Almighty God bless you!"

The good understanding which prevailed between the two chief persons in the state was calculated to delay, for a time, the disputes which were sure, sooner or later, to arise in a community divided into two classes so distinct as the clergy and laity, each owing obedience to a different superior and a separate jurisdiction. But we may perceive symptoms of this tendency beginning to show themselves, even under the firm administration of the Conqueror. The following letter has been preserved among the historical records of that period, and its tone is well calculated to show the spirit with which the victorious sovereign of England would have treated any bolder attempt on the part of the Church to deprive him of that temporal supremacy which he claimed by his royal prerogative. The pope's letter, or message, which elicited this forcible reply has not come down to us.

LETTER III.

"TO GREGORY THE MOST EXCELLENT SHEPHERD OF THE HOLY CHURCH, WILLIAM, BY THE GRACE OF GOD KING OF THE ENGLISH AND DUKE OF THE NORMANS, HEALTH AND FRIENDSHIP.

"YOUR legate Hubert, most holy father, coming to me on your behalf, has admonished me to profess allegiance to you and your successors, and to think better regarding the money which my ancestors were used to send to the Church of Rome. I have consented to one, but not to the other. I would not consent to the allegiance, nor will I now, because I never promised it, nor do I find that my ancestors ever promised it to your ancestors. The money has been negligently collected during the last three years, when I was in Gaul; but now that I have returned, by God's mercy, into my kingdom, I send you, by the hands of the legate aforesaid, what has already been collected; and the rest shall be forwarded by the messengers of our trusty archbishop Lanfranc, when an opportunity of doing so shall offer. Pray for us and for the state of our kingdoms, for we always loved your predecessors; and it is our earnest desire, above all things, to love you most sincerely, and to listen to you most obediently."

Such a style of reply would be likely to check any further attempt on the part of the court of Rome to claim obedience in matters that were not strictly of a spiritual nature. Thus William descended to the grave in peace, and his son Rufus succeeded to the throne of England in the year of our Lord 1087. The venerable prelate Lanfranc survived his accession little more than a year, but during this short space of time he maintained a powerful ascendancy over the fierce passions of the new king. It was indeed the power of the primate which had secured William's succession, though he was not the eldest son of the Conqueror, and he had two brothers alive of sufficient pretensions to give him alarm, and to prevent his embroiling himself with so powerful a body as the Church. On the death of Lanfranc in 1089, the unprincipled monarch broke the bonds of restraint, and suffered the see of Canterbury to remain vacant about four years, whilst he exhausted its revenues in a round of daily and most unblushing debaucheries. A serious illness reminded him of his latter end, and he endeavoured to atone for his crime by forcing Anselm, abbat of Bec, against his will, to become the successor of Lanfranc in the archbishopric. The new prelate, of a milder personal character than his predecessor, seems however to have been a less able courtier; and we may, without unfairness, ascribe to him many little peculiarities of conduct in his behaviour towards the king, which, though they would have been overlooked by a more generous sovereign, would be readily taken advantage of by so base a man as William Rufus. Anselm was a much more learned man than Lanfranc, and the most profound theologian of his day: but was not this also a circumstance likely to widen his breach with a king who so utterly despised and ridiculed every thing that savoured either of learning or theology? There was, however, another point in Anselm's character, in which he cannot be said to have surpassed his predecessor, only because it was a point in which the character of his predecessor never had been tried—his inflexible firmness in defending his order against the real, or supposed, aggressions of the state.

It is not our intention, in this place, to do more than briefly allude to the quarrels between Anselm and the two immediate successors of the Conqueror. The greater part of Anselm's episcopacy was spent in exile, partly voluntary, and partly, perhaps, arising from the injurious treatment which awaited or would have awaited him in England. During the whole reign of Rufus the archbishop set his face firmly and perseveringly against the rapacities which the king, with equal pertinacity, practised on the vacant revenues of the Church. In his refusal to do homage for his archbishopric he shewed equal determination; and though in the present times hardly a voice would be raised in favour of any ecclesiastical person who should thus withhold fealty from the first magistrate of the state, yet we should not argue rightly if we thus judged of the events of the 11th, 12th, and 13th centuries by principles which are universally acknowledged at a period so much later. Whatever may be the opinion which a longer experience may suggest of the real nature of these disputes, it cannot be denied, and the present generation will surely attach weight to the argument, that the mass of the people invariably sided with the Church, to which they looked as their natural protector from the secular power. It is also admitted, on the other hand, that the whole conduct of the barons, and of the king at their head, was marked by rapacity and extortion in peace, a ruthless and bloodthirsty spirit of vengeance in war, and injustice of the deepest dye in all the proceedings of the courts, towards the unhappy vassals whom they held in feudalage.

The reign of Stephen will furnish little subject for observation: his defective title, and the turbulence of his military reign, were favourable opportunities for the Church, and when, in the year 1154, Henry II., surnamed Plantagenet, ascended the throne of his grandfather, the venerable Theodore presided over the church of Canterbury, and by the gentleness of his character, and the unblemished conduct of his life, had won golden opinions from all classes of the people. This brief summary will enable the reader to enter with better preparation on the deadly feud which was so soon to arise, like a revived flame, out of the smouldering embers of a former struggle.

CHAPTER II.

OF THE BIRTH AND PARENTAGE OF BECKET.

From the list of authorities given in the preface, it will be evident to the reader, that there is no want of contemporary testimony to the life and actions of the great man who is the subject of our present narrative. In executing the task which I have undertaken, of reducing the accounts of all these writers into one continued history, I shall endeavour, as much as possible, to let each person speak in his own words; and it is a singular fact, which deserves mention here, that so many writers have seldom handled the same subject with so few discrepancies between them, whether in modes of expression, or in matters of fact. In commencing the life of Saint Thomas, all his biographers indulge, as was usual in such cases, somewhat in the marvellous. Let' us follow the recital of Fitz-Stephen.

"The Lord knew and predestined the blessed Thomas before his birth, and declared in a vision to his mother, what manner of man her son would be. For she saw a vision, wherein she fancied that she bore within her the whole Church of Canterbury; and immediately after the birth of the child, the midwife lifting him up in her arms exclaimed, 'I have raised from the ground a future archbishop!' Whilst he was still an infant in the cradle, his mother dreamt that she rebuked the nurse for not putting a coverlet over the baby. The nurse replied, 'Nay, my lady, he has a very good one over him.' 'Show it to me,' said her mistress. The nurse brought the coverlet and showed it to her, but when she attempted to unfold it, she found herself unable, and said to the mother, 'It is too large for me to unfold it in this bed-room.' 'Nay, then,' said the mother, 'come into the hall and unfold it there.' The nurse did so, and again attempted, but in vain, to unfold the whole of it. The mother in astonishment, said, 'Come out into the market, which at present is empty, and you will, no doubt, be able to unfold it there.' But the nurse, again, found herself unable, and exclaimed to the mother, 'It is become so big that I can see no end to it: it seems as if all England would not be large enough to contain it.'

"This, then, was the manner of St. Thomas's birth—in lawful wedlock and of creditable parents. His father was Gilbert, who also was Sheriff of London: his mother's name was Matilda. Both were citizens of the middle class, who neither made money by usury, nor practised any trade, but lived respectably on their income."

The place in which this miracle of the coverlet was exhibited, is said by others of the biographers to have been Smithfield, at that time without the walls of the city. But the latter part of the passage just quoted demands a few observations, because the expressions used by some of the other writers do not entirely coincide, and an error has recently gone abroad to the public, which, in itself, would have been of little consequence, had not some of our first living historians adduced it as an argument in support of a theory, which it rather has a tendency to impugn.

Whilst the writer, from whom the above extract has been quoted, represents Becket's father as a gentleman living on his fortune, and who had also been Sheriff of London, Herbert de Bosham describes him, as "born in the flesh of one Gilbert, and his mother's name was Matilda [1]." By William, sub-prior of Canterbury, he is called "the illustrious son of moderate parents." These, and similar expressions may, however, counteract one another, and be taken to signify that the family of Becket belonged to what are now called the middle classes, possessing a decent competency, though not abounding in all the luxuries and profusion of the rich and noble. It is of more im-

---

[1] Nescio a quo Gilberto patre et matre Matilda carnaliter procreatum.

AND PARENTAGE OF BECKET. 13

portance to notice the error above alluded to, which, from the use that has been made of it, tends to introduce a serious mistake into the real character of the struggle in which Becket was involved. It has been suggested by the French historian[2] who has written the history of the Norman Conquest, that he was the first of Saxon lineage who had been elevated to any post of honour since the Norman Conquest, which accounts for the enthusiasm with which all the common people espoused his cause. But what says the contemporary historian[3]:—

"Among the towns, cities, and villages of England, London is the largest and the principal. When the kingdom fell into the hands of the Normans, large numbers flocked thither out of Rouen and Caen, which are the principal cities of Normandy, choosing to become citizens of London, because it was larger and better stored with the merchandise in which they used to traffic. Among these was one Gilbert, surnamed Becket, born at Rouen, and distinguished among his citizens for the respectability of his birth, the energy of his character, and the easy independence of his fortune[4]. His family was creditable, but belonged

---

[2] Thierry. [3] MS. Lamb.
[4] Genere, strenuitate, facultatumque possibilitate. I think I am right in my translation of the last two words, but I am not quite sure.

to the class of citizens; he was industrious in commerce, and managed his household in a creditable manner, and suitably to his station in life; whilst among his fellow-citizens he was known for a worthy man, and without reproach. His wife was Rose, a lady of Caen, also of a respectable civic family, fair in person, and fairer still in conduct, an able mistress over her household, and, saving her duty to God, an obedient and loving wife."

This is not the only positive statement which has come down to us of the Norman lineage of Becket, for this fact is stated by Fitz-Stephen to have been a bond of connexion at a later period between him and Archbishop Theobald, who was also a Norman; but the same conclusion might be drawn from the family name, Bequet, which is undoubtedly Norman, and not Anglo-Saxon. The writer of the extract above quoted is not, however, equally to be relied on in his account of Becket's mother, whose name, as we are informed by nearly all the biographers, was Matilda, and not Rose. The following beautiful legend has come down to us, of the loves of Gilbert and Matilda, and there seems no reason to doubt the facts which it relates [a].

" When Gilbert was a young man, he took

---

[a] The first quadrilogus.

upon him our Lord's cross by way of penance, and set out for the Holy Land, accompanied by a single serving man, whose name was Richard. As these two were on their way with others to offer up their prayers at the holy places, they were surprised by an ambuscade, made prisoners, and given in chains to be the slaves of a certain Amurath, and chief of the Pagans. Here they remained some time, earning a scanty subsistence by the daily labour of their hands. A year and half passed away in this Sclavonian bondage, and Gilbert began to attract more notice and respect than the others, particularly in the eyes of Amurath, with whom he got into such favour, that he often, though still in chains, waited on him at table, and conversed with him and his guests on the customs and manners of different countries. For his sake, also, much favour was extended to his fellow captives, principally by the mediation of Amurath's only daughter, a beautiful and courtly damsel, who, as will be shown presently, was smitten with love for the captive Gilbert. One day the young lady took an opportunity of speaking to him more freely than usual, and asked him what country and city he came from, also about the doctrines and life of the Christians, what was the nature of their creed, and hope of reward in a future life. To this Gilbert replied, that he was an Englishman, and that he lived at London, to which

he added an exposition of the Christian faith, as
he was best able to give it. "And would you
dare to die," says the damsel, "for your God, and
for that faith of Christ which you profess?"
"Most willingly," replied he, "would I die in the
cause of my God." On hearing this, the girl
seemed penetrated with the words which he had
spoken, and declared, that for his sake she would
become a Christian, if he would pledge himself,
by the faith which he professed, to take her for
his wife." But he said nothing in reply, delibe-
rating within himself, and apprehensive of deceit;
and though she urged it, he not only declined to
acquiesce at once, but put her off from day to day,
and showed great reluctance to consent at all to
her proposal. The damsel was much afflicted at
his continued hesitation, and became, as is usual
with women, a prey to anxiety. Meanwhile, at
the end of a year and half from their first capture,
Gilbert and his fellow-prisoners began to form
plans of escaping. One night they broke their
chains, and issuing from their prison, arrived,
after travelling the whole night, within the Christian frontiers. In the morning, the overseer of
slaves went, as was his custom, to bring them out
to their work, and finding the prisoners gone,
pursued them at the head of a numerous band,
until he arrived at the territory of the Christians,
where in anger he was obliged to abandon the

pursuit. But Amurath's daughter, learning this intelligence, began from that moment to meditate on the best way of securing her own escape and following the fugitives. Night and day were given up to deliberation, until at length, one night, when all were buried in sleep, she arose by herself, and concealing her design from every one, she took a small quantity of provisions with her, that she might not be encumbered, and committed herself to all the dangers of such a stealthy flight, forgetful in the excitement of her anticipated escape, of all the wealth of her father, which would, after his death, have come to her. Wonderful indeed was the courage of this woman, and the depth of her love which emboldened her to execute so difficult and dangerous a deed! Noble as she was, and the heiress to a rich estate, she cast aside the parental tie, and though frail and delicate, she braved all the terrors of poverty, all the dangers of a long extent of country and of a stormy sea, alone and unaided, for the love of one man so far away from her, so utterly a stranger to her; though it was uncertain whether she ever should find him, or even if he was yet alive, still less certain whether he would marry her, even when he should be found!

"After having traversed the territories of the heathen, she embarked in safety on board a vessel with some foreigners and merchants who understood her language, and were returning to their native country. They arrived safely in England, without suffering from the numerous perils which assail voyagers, and the young female bade farewell to her companions, with no other means of making known her wishes, than by exclaiming, London! London! which was the name of the place she was seeking. At this city she speedily arrived, and wandering through the streets, looked wildly into the faces of the passers-by, to all of whom she afforded subject of derision, particularly the children, who followed her, laughing and marvelling at her foreign dress and uncouth accents. In this guise she passed in front of the house where Gilbert was living, in one of the more open and better frequented quarters of the city, where now stands the hospital erected in honour of St. Thomas. It was soon told in the house that a young crazy girl was going by, followed by boys and others who were laughing and mocking her. Gilbert's man, Richard, who has been mentioned above, ran out with others to see the sight. On approaching nearer he recognized the damsel, and returned with all speed to tell his master, that it was Amurath's daughter who had attracted so great a concourse of people. At these words Gilbert was struck with amazement, and could not believe a thing which he considered absolutely impossible: but as Richard persisted in what he said, his master's incredulity somewhat abated. In doubt what could be the cause of her coming, he nevertheless judged it wiser not to admit her into his own house; wherefore he sent Richard to conduct her to the house of a widow lady, who lived near him, who would treat her as if she were her own daughter. The damsel no sooner saw and recognized the man, than she fell down in a swoon as if dead outright. When she had recovered her senses, and risen from the ground, Richard conducted her, as he had been directed, to the widow lady's house. Meanwhile, Gilbert's mind was distracted with the event which had just happened, and in his doubt what course to take, he determined to go to St. Paul's and consult the Bishop of London. Thither he accordingly went on a certain time, when six of the bishops had met there to deliberate on some important business either of Church or State. In their presence he related the whole affair as it has been here described, when the Bishop of Chichester anticipating the others, exclaimed with prophetic voice, that it was the hand of God, and not of man, which had conducted that woman from so far a land, and that she would be the mother of a son, whose sanctity and sufferings should elevate the whole Church, to the glory of Christ the Lord! The other bishops agreed with the Bishop of Chichester in this opinion, and advised that Gilbert should marry the young woman, provided she would consent to be baptized. A day was then fixed, namely the morrow, on which she was conducted into the presence of the aforesaid bishops in the Church of St. Paul, where was a baptistery prepared in which she should be baptized. Upon her being asked before the whole congregation, according to the custom of the Church, by means of the above-named Richard, who acted as interpreter between them, if she was willing to be baptized; she replied, "It was for this purpose that I came here from so distant a land, only if Gilbert will take me for his wife." She was, therefore, at once baptized with much solemnity by the six bishops above-named, for she was a woman of a noble family, and was more ennobled still by the call which she had received; yea, the call of God himself. The bishops afterwards bestowed her upon Gilbert as his wife with all the forms of the marriage ceremony, when she had previously been instructed in the nature of the Christian faith. They returned home together, and at the very beginning of their wedlock she conceived, and bore to her husband the blessed Thomas of Canterbury, archbishop and martyr. On the morning after the marriage, Gilbert was again smitten with a strong desire of visiting the Holy Land, so that he began to be more and more uneasy, and could not dissemble the vexation which showed itself upon his countenance. But he reflected on the frail sex of his young wife, whose tender age was exposed to all kinds of temptations, besides which, her ignorance of the language of the country would be the cause of much danger to her in the absence of her husband so far from home. But his wife saw that his countenance was different from what it had been before, and was troubled with apprehension that, perchance, she might be the cause thereof. She, therefore, did not cease, day and night, to entreat him to tell her the cause of his dejection, and at length she won from him the secret. For Gilbert yielded to her importunities, and declared what he so eagerly longed for; and she, being a woman of high hopes, and already firm in the faith of Christ, not only assented to her husband's wishes, but strongly urged him to have no regard to her, but to execute with zeal and devotion whatever plans he should be led to form that might tend to give glory to his Creator. 'For me,' added she, ' I trust firmly and stedfastly in my God, who has called me to the knowledge of his name, and will not desert me when you are gone, but as he once before preserved me from every danger, when I did not know him, so will he again protect me now. Only leave Richard at home with me, because, by his knowledge of my native language, he will be better able to minister to my necessities.' Gilbert was delighted at these words, and immediately began to prepare what was necessary for his journey. When he had made every provision for his wife and family during his absence, he set out for Jerusalem, where he remained three years and half; after which he returned home, and found a son named Thomas, a beautiful boy, and high in favour with all his friends and neighbours [7]."

[7] We are told by Benedict, that Becket was murdered in the fifty-third year of his age: he was therefore born in 1117, or 1118.

CHAPTER III.

OF BECKET'S CHILDHOOD AND EARLY YEARS.

The romantic legend given in the last chapter is consistent with the whole of Becket's wild and meteor-like career, and the Oriental parentage of the child has been referred to by certain recent writers as sufficient to explain the impetuous temperament of the man. But his pagan mother faithfully and ably fulfilled the duties of a mother according to the new faith which she adopted. The lad learnt from her, as he afterwards confessed to his friend John of Salisbury, " the fear of the Lord, and the reverence which was due to Christ's mother, the holy Virgin Mary, whom, next to her divine Son, he adopted as his patroness, frequently invoking her name, and casting all his trust upon her." This description is probably more than mere verbs; for besides the respect which has in all ages been paid to the Virgin Mary, a young female converted to the Christian faith, under such circumstances as those of Matilda, would naturally cling in heart and feelings to the image of such a bright and spotless character, and adopt her for her guide and patroness.

The feelings of the mother were instilled into her child, who is described as possessing many excellent gifts of nature: "he was modest and agreeable in speech, in person tall and elegant, easily led by good example, prudent beyond his years, combining the personal beauty of youth with the gravity of a more advanced age[1]." "So great was the force of his intellect, that he could answer questions of the greatest difficulty on subjects with which he had been previously unacquainted, and his memory was so strong that what he had once learned, he seldom found it difficult to remember and to repeat. In this quality he surpassed many who were more learned than himself, and they wondered at such a facility of memory in a man whose attention was distracted by so many pursuits[2]." These qualities apply properly to a later period, and, indeed, to the whole of his life, but they no doubt showed themselves in his childhood, when he still had the advantage of a mother's instructions, without which life seldom can be happy, and those are to be pitied who never have experienced such a blessing.

The fond parent of Thomas Becket used to connect her little boy in a singular and somewhat whimsical manner with her deeds of charity to the poor. She weighed him at stated times, placing in

---

[1] Will. Cant.   [2] John of Salisbury.

the opposite scale, bread, meat, and clothing, until they equalled the weight of the child; all these were then given to the poor; and the mother, in unison with the belief of the times, commended her son to the protection of the blessed Virgin, in requital of her bounty to the needy. However this might be, it is certain that young Becket could not fail to imbibe under her teaching the first elements of that Christian virtue, which shone so brightly throughout the whole of his afterlife. But the mother of Becket died when he was twenty-one years old, and he was left to the charge of his father only[3], whose means also had been narrowed by "frequent fires[4]," and perhaps other losses. It is recorded that he "spent the years of his infancy, childhood, and youth, in the frugality of his father's house, and in frequenting the schools of the city[5]." His education might perhaps have been limited to such instructions as these schools afforded, together with the domestic teaching of his mother; but we are informed that "he was destined from his infancy to the spiritual warfare, and his pa-

[3] Roger de Pont.

[4] Will. Cant. One of the biographers tells us that the night on which young Becket was born, was attended with a signal calamity, for that a fire burst out which consumed his father's house and a large part of the city.

[5] Fitz-Stephen.

rents took measures accordingly to give him a liberal education[6]." It is not necessary to suppose that "his father had received some intimation from heaven of the future character of his son," or that this was the reason why "he was committed for some time to the charge of Prior Robert, to be educated in the religious house of the canons of Merton[7]." The reputation of that monastery as a religious seminary was a sufficient reason why a young man designed for the priesthood should be placed within its walls.

"One day the father came to see his son, and when the boy was introduced into the presence of his father and the prior, his father prostrated himself at his feet. At seeing this, the prior said in anger, "What are you about, you foolish old man; your son ought to fall down at your feet, not you at his!" But the father afterwards said to the prior in private, "I was quite aware, my lord, of the nature of what I was doing; for that boy of mine will one day or other be great in the sight of the Lord[8]."

Such anecdotes as these sound strange in the ears of the present generation, but they form a large portion of the history of past ages, and must not be cast aside as worthless or unimportant, for

[6] Anon. Lamb. MS.   [7] Fitz-Stephen.
[8] Fitz-Stephen.

even if false, their having passed for truth is a fact which will enable us to measure the credulity of our forefathers.

"When he was grown up to young man's estate, he studied at Paris; and on his return, began to take part in the affairs of the city of London, and was made clerk and accountant to the sheriffs. In this station he conducted himself praiseworthily, and acquired such a knowledge of the world, that in after-life he had no difficulty in managing the common interests of the whole Church, and the public business of the kingdom, which he conducted with the utmost splendour and magnificence, whereby he verified the words of the poet,

> " Thus the young hound, that long waged mimic strife
> On a stuffed skin, devoid of sense and life,
> At length full-grown, thirsting for flesh and blood,
> Drives his scared quarry through the leafy wood*."

But a serious accident befel Becket in the early part of his life, which had well nigh snatched him prematurely from the brilliant career and horrible termination of it, to which he seemed destined; and though, like every other event of his life, it has been invested with a supernatural character,

* Fitz-Stephen.

yet this incident at least is such, that every reader can divest it of the miraculous circumstances with which the narrative is accompanied.

There was a certain knight called Richard de Aquila, who used to lodge in the house of Gilbert Becket when he was in London. This man, being much addicted to hunting and hawking, became a great favourite with the young lad Thomas, his host's son, in whose growing talents, which already were conspicuous in various ways, he in return seems to have felt much interest. It happened during one of the half-yearly vacations, when Thomas was at home from school, he accompanied his father's guest on one of his hawking expeditions. They were both on horseback: the knight was in advance of his companion, who followed him a few paces behind. They arrived at a narrow bridge, fit only for foot-passengers, and leading across a mill-dam. The mill was at work below, and the current was running very strong in the direction of the wheel. The knight did not hesitate to spur his horse over the narrow foot-path, and reached the opposite bank in safety. Thomas hastened to follow his example, but as ill-luck would have it, his steed made a false step midway, and precipitated both himself and rider into the rapid tide beneath. The falcon, which Thomas was carrying on his wrist, seems to have shared the same fate, and Thomas, not content with saving himself, was eager to save the bird, and thus was carried imperceptibly almost under the wheel of the mill. A cry of help was raised on all sides, and his death seemed inevitable, when, to the surprise of all, the water was let off from the wheel, and the mill suddenly stopped. The miller at the same instant came out, and seeing the young lad in the water, drew him out without much difficulty, though panting for breath, and more dead than alive. The biographers have not failed to represent this escape as an especial act of Divine Providence, by whose interference the mill was suddenly stopped. But Providence, in most cases, developes its agency by the hand of man, and, by inference, the miller was allowed to hear the cry for help, which had been raised from without; on hearing which, he stopped his machinery, and ran out to rescue young Thomas from the death which seemed to be awaiting him [1].

The death of Matilda was felt deeply by her son, who now began to absent himself from his father's house, and to attach himself to those whose company pleased him, or who seemed likely to advance his prospects in life. Among these there was one Osbern, surnamed Octonumini, a rich man, and related to the family of the Beckets.

---
[1] Roger de Pontigny and E. Grim.

This man was so pleased with the manners and deportment of young Thomas, that he kept him in his house three years, and employed him in managing his accounts [a].

There are two other of his friends mentioned by his biographer, whose interest in the young man led more immediately to his advancement in life. These were Archdeacon Baldwin and Master Eustace, from Boulogne, who used to lodge in Gilbert's house, and were, moreover, acquainted with Theobald, Archbishop of Canterbury. This excellent man, like several of his predecessors, had been Abbot of Bec, and was from thence promoted to the primacy of England, in which he distinguished himself by the simplicity and kindness of his manners, as much as by the skill and moderation with which he managed all the business, whether spiritual or secular, which devolved upon him. Some of his officials, and amongst others the two who have just been mentioned, used to frequent the house of Gilbert Becket, who was of Norman extraction like themselves, and from this friendship of the father, a most important advantage resulted to the son, whose talents became so manifest to their guests, that they strongly exhorted the young man to allow them to introduce him to the notice of the arch-

---

[a] Grim. Roger.

bishop. But this step was repugnant to his feelings, and for some time he hesitated to thrust himself uninvited into the notice of the archbishop. This unwillingness was, however, at last, overcome, and Thomas Becket presented himself at the archiepiscopal court, where magnificence, equalling that of royalty, was displayed on all sides, whilst every species of learning and development of the human intellect found there that protection which they might seek in vain at the court of the king himself. Among the men of that household the youthful Becket was introduced, and speedily found such favour in the eyes of Theobald, that careful observers already began to foresee that his talents would infallibly elevate him high above that station in which his birth had placed him[3].

[3] Fitz-Stephen.

CHAPTER IV.

OF BECKET'S ADVANCEMENT AT THE COURT OF ARCHBISHOP THEOBALD.

THE household of the archbishops of Canterbury, from the earliest period, had been maintained on a scale suited to the rank of the second person in the state, and the Norman conquest, which was fatal to almost every other ancient dignity, not only left the see of Canterbury untouched, but invested it with fresh power and privileges. The first archbishops after the conquest were men of superior character; none of whom, for personal merits, surpassed him who ushered Thomas Becket into public life. The venerable Theobald presided over the metropolitan see of Canterbury during the long period of two and twenty years [1], and his court was frequented by a large number of able and learned men, who there acquired or developed those qualifications which fitted them for the several ecclesiastical stations in the kingdom, to which they were successively appointed. On this point, as on almost every other, there was

[1] From A.D. 1141 to 1163.

a strong resemblance between the castle of the baron, and the palace of the bishop, both of which were a sort of school, in which junior members pursued those studies that were calculated to advance them in the profession of arms, or of religion. Among others who at this time resided at the archiepiscopal palace was Roger, surnamed Dupont[2], afterwards successively archdeacon of Canterbury and archbishop of York, who seems to have conceived an aversion to Thomas Becket almost at first sight. The archbishop had indeed declared publicly that he had never seen greater zeal and fidelity than that which his new follower displayed in his service; and this excited the jealousy of Roger, who was not yet sufficiently elevated in the church to render it impossible that he might be eclipsed by this new candidate for promotion. He vented his spleen against him, whom he looked upon as a rival, by nicknaming him Baille-hache[3], after the name of the man in whose company he had first appeared at court. The allusion to an axe, which this

---

[2] The Latin name is "de ponte episcopi," but I use the name Dupont, because it is most probably the modern form of all such Latin surnames, whatever may have been the word following " de ponte." We have another such name in the case of Guarinus de ponte Maxentii, author of a poetical life of Becket in Norman French.

[3] Roger de Pontigny.

epithet conveyed, has given occasion to one of the biographers[4] to moralize as follows:—

"In good truth, Thomas did, at a later period, and at a fitting opportunity, take the axe in hand; yea, rather the sword of Saint Peter himself, wherewith he hewed away Roger and his accomplices from the communion of the faithful, so that, as they also complained to the king, he left them not so much as the power to make the sign of the cross to bless their victuals."

The clerks of the palace were superior to Becket in learning: this may be ascribed to his desultory and somewhat superficial education; but in all other respects they were behind him. He was more active in discharging the duties which were imposed on him; and by the gentleness and modesty of his manners, secured the good will of all those who saw no impediment arising from his virtues to their own aggrandizement. Many of the clerks who filled the court of Theobald were eminent for their superior attainments; and Becket at first felt the want of a more regular and extended education; but his natural prudence soon suggested to him the propriety of applying steadily to his studies, in order to remedy a defect which might seriously interfere with his promotion. This determination was immediately

---

[4] Ed. Grim.

acted upon, and in a very short time, whilst he still retained the superiority of manner, which he at first manifested, he came to be not a whit behind his fellows in learning also, and at a later period, says Fitz-Stephen, his biographer, his acquirements were of the very first order. He gave his attention principally to the canon and civil law, and so qualified himself for transacting such business as was at that time, much more than at present, brought into the ecclesiastical courts [5]. The enmity of Roger Dupont caused him twice to be removed from the palace; but on both these occasions he took refuge with Walter, the archdeacon of Canterbury, brother of the archbishop. By his intercession Becket was replaced in the palace, and restored to favour. When Walter was removed to the see of Rochester, the hostile Roger succeeded in the archdeaconry of Canterbury [6].

This would probably have been attended with serious consequences to one whom the new archdeacon hated so violently, but a fresh position of things was brought about soon after by the death of William, the venerable Archbishop of York: the enemy of Becket, recommended by the powerful influence of Theobald, succeeded to the vacant dignity; and Becket himself was appointed by

---

[5] Roger de Pontigny.   [6] Fitz-Stephen.

his patron to fill the station which Roger had quitted.

An occasion had already offered for the zeal and ability of the young man to be tried in a matter of considerable importance. A mission to Rome was necessary; and the archbishop chose Becket to transact the negotiation with the sovereign pontiff. In this business he was eminently successful; for he not only accomplished the object for which he had been sent, but secured for himself the good will and friendship of the pope and the whole Roman court [7]. For this service he was rewarded by the archbishop with the presentation to the church of Otford; but he had already before this received preferment, having been presented by John, Bishop of Winchester, with the living of St. Mary, Littory [8]. At a later period he received a prebend in St. Paul's, besides a second in the diocese of Lincoln. It is by no means certain that he had taken deacon's orders before he obtained such extensive preferment, for the biographer [9], who gives this list of benefices, continues the narrative as follows:—" After this he procured from the archbishop leave to travel, and studied civil law for the space of one year at

[7] Fitz-Stephen. Roger de Pontigny states that Theobald himself went to Rome, taking a noble retinue, in which was Thomas Becket, along with him.
[8] Roger. Grim. Fitz-Stephen.   [9] Fitz-Stephen.

Bologna and Auxerre. In process of time the archbishop *ordained him deacon*, and made him archdeacon of Canterbury, which is the highest ecclesiastical dignity in the kingdom, next to the bishop and abbats; it brought him in annually one hundred marks!"

As the archdeaconry of Canterbury, to which he was promoted, fell vacant in consequence of the elevation of Roger, his old enemy, to the archbishopric of York; so it is not improbable that he at the same time received the priory of Beverley, which had also been held by Roger, together with the prebend of Hastings, and which were now also added to the long list of benefices, which marks the rapid promotion of this extraordinary man[1].

So large a number of benefices, held by the same individual, has in no period of the church's history been regarded with satisfaction, nor is it possible for any individual, whatever may be his talents, to discharge the duties of appointments differing so much in their nature, and lying so far apart: but if it should seem surprising that the subject of our memoir held some of these appointments even before he was in deacon's orders, it must be remembered that the deacon was not the lowest ordained person in the church at that period. The distinction between

---

[1] E. Grim. Roger de Pont.

clerics and laics was such, that the subordinate ranks of the clergy were fully competent to fulfil all the duties of instructing the ignorant people committed to their charge. However this may be, it is certain that Thomas Becket owed to no other influence than to his own rare and numerous talents all the honours and emoluments that were showered upon him; and it is the unanimous eulogy of all those who, from their own personal knowledge, compiled the history of his life, that he did not cease to practise still the virtues which led to his promotion. Among these have been particularly noticed, his condescension to all below him, and his charity to the poor. It is perhaps not a high virtue to practise abstinence or moderation in such enjoyments as would, if indulged in, materially interfere with a man's success, because he would, by indulgence, defeat his own object; but it is recorded of Thomas Becket, that he was singularly exempt from such sinful indulgence of his passions, and this was also the case at a later period, when he was at the court of a king, not remarkable for correctness of conduct, and surrounded by temptations which might have been an excuse for greater laxity of morals. He was, however, proof against such temptations; and possesses a higher claim on our admiration from the fact, that he never forgot his first origin; never identified himself with the nobility of the land, to whose level, nay above whose level, he had risen. On the contrary, he ever bore in mind, and as we shall see hereafter, he acknowledged in his letters to his public enemies, that he gloried rather to be "one in whom nobility of mind constituted his birth-right, than one in whom nobility of birth had degenerated!" In the whole course of his life, whilst his energies were directed forwards to the attainment of every honour, to which his high talents entitled him, he never forgot that he was one of the people; and the enthusiasm which the great mass of the English showed in his cause up to the moment of his tragical death, together with the honours (however superstitious) which they bestowed upon his memory, are sufficient to show that he is entitled to the name of a good as well as of a great man.

CHAPTER V.

OF HIS INTRODUCTION TO THE KING'S COURT, AND APPOINTMENT TO BE CHANCELLOR.

In the year of the Lord 1154, the death of Stephen led to the peaceful accession of Henry the Second, son of the empress Matilda, to the throne of his grandfather. The wars which had so long exhausted the strength of the kingdom during the reign of Stephen, had been ably settled by the united consent of all men, that Stephen should adopt his young rival, who should thus unite in his person the claims of both the parties to the throne. Eustace, Stephen's son, protested against this arrangement, but his protest was unheeded, and his death, which happened soon after, left the way open to the establishment of things upon a secure and lasting basis.

But though the public wars for the succession had ceased, the kingdom was by no means in the enjoyment of undisturbed tranquillity: the necessities of both the contending parties had led them to engage hired soldiers in their cause; moreover, the chances of war had thrown many of the nobles, together with their retainers, out of the possession of their estates, and these had formed themselves into bands, which maintained themselves by pillaging both parties alike. Large numbers of Flemings had been introduced into the country, who, as the party for which they contended became victorious, dispossessed the natives of their estates, which they themselves occupied; and in this way the whole of Kent in particular groaned under the domination of foreign soldiers. Every third town or village was a military camp, and this state of things, having lasted ten years, seemed so difficult to be changed, that the older counsellors of the kingdom were filled with apprehension for the future, when they considered the youthful age of their new sovereign.

Henry, Bishop of Winchester, was the brother of Stephen, the late king, and during a long period had acted with that prudence which is often shewn by able politicians, who have to steer their course between conflicting parties when success is doubtful. There are conjunctures when an enthusiastic attachment to a falling cause becomes detrimental both to the public and to the individual. If Henry of Winchester was a timeserver, it was decidedly for the good of his country, and his exertions to restore tranquillity were ultimately successful, though in the interim it might be difficult to discover on which side his sympathies really were enlisted. The critical state of affairs at the accession of Henry II.

did not escape the notice of this able man, and he strongly urged Archbishop Theobald, over whom he possessed almost unlimited control, to provide some person who might be introduced to the notice of the king, calculated by his agreeable manners to secure his affections, and by his talents to support the cause of the Church, against the secular nobility.

The heads of the Church were keenly sensible to the possibility of the young king combining with the nobles against the spiritual orders: and they no doubt feared that the augmentation of their privileges, which had been favoured by the necessities or fears of Stephen, might experience a check from the union of the king with their natural rivals, the barons. The same apprehension no doubt served to strengthen the alliance between the Church and the commons, who on all occasions looked on the ecclesiastics as their advocates and protectors. The house of commons was not then in existence, but its duties were not less ably performed by a class of men, better qualified by intellect and education, and not more liable to bias or corruption than those who in later times have charged themselves with the defence of English liberty.

. It was notorious at the court of Henry II., that many collateral branches of their young king's family entertained views sinister to the privileges and independence of the Church; and we shall find by the sequel that these same parties goaded on the king to the contest which took place between him and the clergy[2]. The Archbishop followed the advice of the Bishop of Winchester, but previously took into his counsels, Philip, Bishop of Bayeux, and Arnulf, of Lisieux. This last was a politician, whose acuteness was equal to any contingency. He will again appear, from time to time, in the course of this eventful history; and though we are not informed what view he entertained of the apprehensions, which, in the mind of the Archbishop and Henry of Winchester, formed the existing emergency, he seems to have approved of the advice which Henry gave, and with his consent and that of the Bishop of Bayeux, Thomas Becket was introduced to the new monarch, to fill the office of chancellor, and in the execution of the duties which thus devolved upon him, to be the companion of the king in his sports and amusements, as well as his agent in transacting the more serious business of the realm. In this situation, it was thought, he might be of use to themselves in keeping a watchful eye over the movements which the enemies of the Church might make to deprive her of her liberties, and so impede, if not defeat, the

[2] Rog. de Pont.

exertions which they might make to her detriment[3].

"The dignity of the Chancellor," says the contemporary[4] writer, "makes him the second person in the kingdom after the king: he keeps the royal seal, and uses one side of it to seal his own ordinances: the king's chapel is under his care and superintendence; he also takes into his keeping all vacant archbishoprics, bishoprics, abbacies, and baronies, when they fall into the king's hands: he attends all the king's councils, even without being summoned; the king's seal is placed by the hand of his clerk on all papers that require it; and nothing is done without his counsel, so that if, by God's mercy, his own merits should not be wanting, the king's chancellor always dies an archbishop or bishop, if he pleases. And for these reasons," says the writer, "the chancellorship is never sold for money!"

This was the office which was now bestowed on Thomas Becket, in the year of our Lord 1155, and consequently, when he was about thirty-eight years of age. He was in deacon's orders, and therefore not a layman, but this was not a solitary instance of high offices of state being placed in the hands of churchmen; for the laity at that period, even including the nobility, were generally

[3] Rog. Pont and W. Fitz-Stephen.   [4] Fitz-Stephen.

too uneducated to fill stations which furnished occupation principally for the mind: indeed, large numbers of them, even to a much later period, were unable to read and write. But the progress of civilization was beginning already to lead to a separation of spiritual and temporal duties, and one of our contemporary biographers[5] tells us, that "Thomas, now as it were laid aside the deacon, and took upon him the duties of the chancellor, which he discharged with zeal and ability." Another[6] writer tells us, that "it is difficult for him to describe the way in which he filled both characters, that of the clerk and of the courtier,- for in the very outset he was so assailed by the jealousy of his rivals and the tales of scandal which were unblushingly circulated about him, that he complained of them to the archbishop as well as to his private friends; and assured them that if he could do so without reproach, he was inclined to withdraw himself altogether from the court." But this may have been a hasty thought; for no further mention is made of it, and it may have died away almost as soon as it was conceived; for the new life, to which he was now introduced, had much to recommend it to the notice of one who was not destitute of ambition. The king seemed to delight in his company, and

[5] Herbert de Bosham. [6] Rog. Pont.

gave up all matters of state to his direction and guidance. Thus whilst Henry occupied his time in all kinds of youthful sports and exercises, Thomas was discharging all the royal duties for him with the greatest activity and power: at one time he was marching, in complete armour, at the head of the chivalry of the kingdom, at another time, when there was no military expedition on foot, he administered justice to the people. It was only in name that he differed from the king himself, for everything was at his disposal: the nobles and magistrates were all under his orders; and it was manifest to all men, that in order to obtain a point with the king, it was absolutely necessary first to secure the approbation of the chancellor[7]. Meantime, those about the king found no opportunity of instigating him to make any attack upon the ecclesiastical liberties; and things went on peaceably between the Church and State by the secret agency of the chancellor, who contrived, though cautiously and indirectly, that he might afford no suspicion, to frustrate all the private machinations of the enemy[8].

Circumstances thus placed Becket in a position which enabled him to perform most essential services to his country, but the result shows how unhappy was the error into which the king was led.

[7] Rog. Pont.   [8] Rog. Pont.

Such was the attachment which he conceived for his chancellor, that he blindly fancied him devoted to his service in every particular: he did not recollect that Thomas Becket had already sworn fidelity to another master, whose servant he more especially was; the stamp of the Church had been set upon him, which no civil honours could efface. Though he might "lay aside the deacon and assume the chancellor for a while," yet nothing could divest him of the tendency of his early education. He had been destined for the Church, and had followed his bent, until a period of life which was too advanced to allow him to forget his first calling; and when King Henry fancied he saw in the chancellor an able tool wherewith to cast down his supposed rival the Church, he found out, when it was too late, the fatal error which he had committed. The man whom he elevated to be the head of the English Church, expressly to betray her cause, was found to be her firmest defender; and when deserted by all around him, restored her to higher rights and privileges than she had before enjoyed, by dying a martyr in her cause.

CHAPTER VI.

OF THE REFORMATION EFFECTED IN THE GOVERNMENT BY BECKET'S INFLUENCE—ANECDOTES OF HIS CHANCELLORSHIP.

When Henry the Second succeeded to the throne, he found his kingdom exhausted by bloody wars, and groaning under foreign usurpers. It is supposed, and apparently with reason, that the reformation which he speedily effected in the state of things was brought about, in a great measure, by Becket's prudent counsels. Though he was not created chancellor immediately on Henry's accession, yet he was apparently introduced at court without delay after the coronation. Certain it is, that within three months, a decided improvement began to appear in the state of the country. The foreign adventurers, who had received lands for their warlike services, found themselves unable to retain their possessions, and left the country in despair. Among them was William of Ypres, the Fleming, who was compelled, though with bitter regret, to give up his lands in Kent, and to return to Flanders. Among other important reforms, most of the castles and fortresses, which the barons had built during the late wars, were razed to the ground, and the crown recovered its integrity by the revocation of rights and privileges that had been extorted from it during the unsteady reign that preceded: numerous families that had been dispossessed recovered their rightful inheritance; those who had taken refuge in the woods, abandoned the life of plunder, to which necessity and not choice had driven them, and shewing themselves in the towns, rejoiced in the prospect of a firm and lasting peace; many an unfortunate man was saved from the gallows, to which his unvoluntary crimes would speedily have led him; and agriculture and the mechanical arts began to flourish on all sides[9]. We might ascribe these reforms to the genius of the new king, if we were not assured by all the contemporary historians that his chancellor had a considerable hand in them. All parties, indeed, commons and nobles, both spiritual and temporal, combined to promote the prosperity which was dawning upon England after its late troubles; so that "it seemed (in the words of Fitz-Stephen) to enjoy a second spring: the Holy Church was honoured and respected: every vacant bishopric or abbacy was given to some deserving person without simony: the king, by the favour of Him who is the King of kings, succeeded in all he undertook: the

---

[9] Fitz-Stephen.

realm of England became richer and richer, and copious blessings flowed from plenty's horn. The hills were cultivated, the valleys teemed with corn, the fields with cattle, and the folds with sheep."

The whole course of English history presents us with no similar instance of an attachment between a king and his subject;—alas! that it should present us with such an awful instance of the closest friendship turned into deadly hate; and that so fatal a result should have flowed from a quarrel of which religion was the cause! The chancellor possessed almost every virtue both of mind and body, which could earn the affection of a young enthusiastic king, who had succeeded in all his undertakings, and seemed born to promote the happiness of all his subjects, as well as his own. "The countenance of Thomas was mild and beautiful: he was tall of stature[1], with

---

[1] Many relics of Thomas Becket are preserved in France: his rochet still exists in the possession of the Cardinal-bishop of Arras: a chalice, said to have been used by him, is preserved at a small village near Dieppe. I have heard a tradition still existing among the clergy of French Flanders, that he was six feet two inches high; and the report is confirmed by the extreme length of the sacerdotal garments, which are still preserved. I have had no opportunity of seeing them myself. Among other memorials of this great genius which remain to our own times, is said to be the species of fig-tree which grows so

a nose elevated and slightly aquiline: in his senses and physical perceptions he was most acute; his language was refined and eloquent, his intellect subtle, and his mind cast in a noble mould. His aspirations after virtue were of a lofty kind, whilst his conduct, amiable towards all men, exhibited singular sympathy towards the poor and the oppressed: whilst to the proud he was hostile and unbending. Ever ready to promote the advancement of his friends, he was liberal to all men, of a lively and witty disposition, cautious alike of being deceived or of deceiving others. He distinguished himself for his prudence at an early age, even whilst he was a child of this world—he who was afterwards to become a child of light!"

Of Becket's chancellorship, which lasted seven years, many anecdotes have been preserved, principally by his secretary, Fitz-Stephen. We shall give them here, at full-length, in the words of the original writer, as near as the idiom of a translation will allow.

"Chancellor Thomas caused the palace of

---

plentifully in Sussex. At West Tarring, in that county, is an ancient house, now the rectory, where he is said to have resided occasionally, and to have planted the original fig-tree which he brought from Italy, and from which the other trees of that species derive their origin.

London, which is the seat of the monarchy, and was become almost a ruin, to be put into repair; and proceeded with such marvellous rapidity that this great work was completed between Easter and Whitsuntide; so many carpenters and other workmen were labouring together, and made such a din in their haste to finish their labours, that even those who were standing close together could hardly hear one another speak.

"The popularity of the chancellor was excessive, whether among the clergy, soldiers, or people. He might have had all the parochial churches that were vacant, both in the towns and castles, for no one would deny him, if he would only ask: but he shewed such greatness of mind in repressing all views of interest, that he disdained to forestall the poor priests or clerks, or take from them the opportunity of gaining those churches for themselves. His great mind rather aimed at great objects, such as the Priorship of Beverly, and the presentation to the prebends of Hastings, which he got from the Earl of Augy, the tower of London, with the service of the soldiers belonging to it, the Chatelainship of Eye, with its honour of two hundred and forty soldiers, and the castle of Berchamstead.

"He generally amused himself, not in a set manner, but accidentally, and as it might happen with hawks and falcons, or dogs of the chase, and in the game of chess,

> 'Where front to front the mimic warriors close,
> To check the progress of their mimic foes.'

"The house and table of the Chancellor were common to all of every rank who came to the king's court, and needed hospitality: whether they were honourable men in reality, or at least appeared to be such. He never dined without the company of earls and barons, whom he had invited. He ordered his hall to be strewed every day with fresh straw and hay in winter, and with green branches in summer, that the numerous knights for whom the benches were insufficient, might find the area clean and neat for their reception, and that their valuable clothes and beautiful shirts might not contract injury from its being dirty. His board shone with vessels of gold and silver, and abounded with rich dishes and precious liquors, so that whatever objects of consumption, either for eating or drinking, were recommended by their rarity, no price was great enough to deter his agents from purchasing them. But amid all these, he was himself singularly frugal, so that his rich table provided rich alms for those who partook thereof: and I have heard from his confessor, Robert, the venerable canon of Merton, that from the time of his becoming Chancellor, he never gave way to licentious habits. This too was a subject on which the king was continually tempting him night and day; but as a man of prudence, and ordained of God, he was ever sober in the flesh, and had his loins girded up about him. As a wise man, he was bent on administering the government of the kingdom, and whilst busied in so many matters, both public and private, he rarely yielded to such temptations. For what says the poet,—

' For he that hath no leisure, hath no time
To shoot shafts from the bow of strong desire.'

A modest man, indeed, was the Chancellor,—a foe to depravity and uncleanness; and when a clerk of his, of high birth, Richard of Ambly, had carried off the wife of a friend, who had been long absent beyond the sea, and persuaded her that her husband was dead, he removed him from his house and his friendship, and caused him to be kept prisoner in the tower of London, where he was detained for some time loaded with irons [2]."

Another anecdote, similar to this, has been

[2] Fitz-Stephen.

preserved by William of Canterbury. It is said that the chancellor was one day with the king at Stafford: the citizen in whose house he lodged, suspected him of being on terms of improper intimacy with a distinguished lady of the court; and had the curiosity one night to enter his bed-room in order to ascertain whether he slept there. The appearance of the bed was such that he had evidently not occupied it that night. The host was retracing his steps, satisfied with the correctness of his suspicions, when, to his astonishment, he saw the chancellor asleep on the floor, stretched at length on the bare boards, and only partially covered. This anecdote leads us to the inference that Thomas Becket was not like most royal chancellors, or even like courtiers in general, who are supposed for the most part to study rather to gratify the desires of the flesh than thus to mortify them.

"The nobles of England and of the neighbouring kingdoms, sent their sons to serve in the chancellor's house. When they had received from him the proper nurture and instruction, he bestowed on them the belt of knighthood, and sent them home with honour to their parents and relations, whilst he retained some of them in his service. The king himself, his master, committed his son and heir to his charge, and the chancellor placed the young prince in the midst of the sons of the nobility, who were of the same age, where he received due attention from all of them, and had masters and proper servants as his rank required.

"But amid all this pomp of worldly honours, he often bared his back in private to the scourge, and received the lash of discipline, from Ralph, Prior of the Holy Trinity, when he was in the neighbourhood of London, and at Canterbury from Thomas, a priest of St. Martin's. He was humble to the humble, but to the proud he was stern and haughty, as if it were his innate disposition

' To spare the prostrate, but to quell the proud.'

"Numbers of noblemen and knights did homage to the chancellor, and all of them were readily received by him, always saving their allegiance to the king, and as being now his vassals, were promoted under his patronage.

"Sometimes when he was preparing to cross the sea, he had six or even more vessels in his train; he never suffered any one who intended to cross, to remain behind, but when he came to land, he rewarded his masters and seamen to their satisfaction. There never passed a day, on which he did not make large presents of horses, birds, clothes, gold and silver plate, or money. For so it is written: Some are lavish of their own, and always abound: some are greedy of what belongs to others.

'And their scant substance ever needs increase.'

But the chancellor gave his gifts with such a grace, that all the Latin world loved him, and delighted in him[3].

"The poor and the oppressed found ready access to him: the cause of the widow did not come before him in vain: he gave justice and protection to the weak and the needy. He was followed by so large a retinue of soldiers and persons of all ranks, that the royal palace seemed empty in comparison[4]; the king himself was left almost alone, and sometimes complained to the chancellor that his court was drained[5]."

By Divine instigation, seconded by the chancellor's advice, our lord the king was led to fill up without delay the vacant bishoprics and abbacies, so that the patrimony of our crucified Saviour might no longer be paid into his own treasury; (as was afterwards done, and God forbid that he should do it again;) nay, he bestowed them readily on deserving persons, and in a manner calculated to please God.

[3] Fitz-Stephen. [4] Rog. Pont. [5] E. Grim.

Furthermore, by the advice of the chancellor, our lord the king took into his favour and protection the religious house of the canons of Merton, and at his own expense completed the edifice, which had been commenced by the priests, and endowed it with a perpetual revenue. Here he occasionally kept watch by way of penance, for three days before Easter, in company with the religious fraternity. After the nocturnal devotion, which is said to be done whilst it is dark, but really in the light, on the day of preparation, until the ninth hour takes place, he used to go round to the small churches of the neighbouring villages, to pray, walking on foot, wrapped up in his cloak, and accompanied by only one attendant to show him the way.

It was at the suggestion of Chancellor Thomas, that the king recalled home those poor people of English birth residing in France, if they were of a good character, either as monks for their religion, or as teachers in learning: these persons he settled in his own dominions. Among them was Master Robert of Melun, who was appointed to the cathedral church of Hereford, and William de Campis, a monk of St. Martin's, whom he placed in the abbey of Ramsey.

Thus, by his innate merit, his greatness of mind, and the excellent qualities which developed themselves in him, the chancellor was in great favour with the king, the clergy, the soldiery, and the people. When business was over, the king and he used to play together, like boys of the same age, in the hall, the church, and whilst they were sitting or riding together. One day they were riding through a street in London, when every thing was thrown out of its natural course by the severity of the winter. The king saw at some distance an old man coming towards him, very poor, and dressed in a thin and ragged coat. "Do you see that old man?" said he to the chancellor. "Yes," replied the chancellor. "How poor and infirm he is," said the king, "and he is almost naked. Would it not be a great charity to give him a thick, warm cloak?" "It would indeed be a great charity," rejoined the chancellor, "and you as king ought to keep this matter in your eye." Meanwhile the poor man came up, and the king and chancellor stopped. The king accosted the poor man in a mild tone, and asked him if he would like to have a nice cloak. The poor man, not knowing who they were, thought they were only joking, and meant nothing serious. Said the king to the chancellor, "You shall have the credit of doing this great act of charity," and laying hands upon his cloak, endeavoured to pull off the new cape of scarlet and grey which he had on, whilst the chancellor struggled to retain it. A grand disturbance arose, and the nobles and knights who were following them, hastened up in astonishment to know what was the cause of this sudden struggle betwixt them. But nobody could tell them: each of the two had his hands fully occupied, and they more than once seemed likely to fall off their horses. The chancellor, after some resistance, gave way to the king, who pulled the cape from him, and gave it to the poor man. He then told the story to his attendants, who all burst out into a laugh, and some of them offered their capes and cloaks to the chancellor. Meanwhile the poor man walked off with the chancellor's cape, having got an unexpected prize, for which he thanked God, and was much pleased.

Occasionally the king came to the chancellor's house to dinner, sometimes for the pleasure only, at other times from curiosity, to see whether what fame said of his table and establishment was true. The king sometimes rode on horseback into the hall where the chancellor was sitting at table, with an arrow in his hand, as on his return from hunting, or on his way to the forest: sometimes he would drink a cup of wine, and, when he had seen the chancellor, take his departure; at other times he would jump over the table, sit down and eat with him. Never were there two men more friendly, or on better terms with one another, since Christianity first began.

Once upon a time the chancellor was seriously ill at St. Gervais at Rouen, and the king of France came, in company with the king of England, to see him. At length he showed symptoms of getting better, and becoming convalescent, he sat up one day to play a game of chess, dressed in a cape with sleeves. The prior of Leicester, Aschetinus, came in to see him on his way from the king's court, who was then in Gascony. Having saluted the chancellor in a free and blunt manner, he exclaimed, in the spirit of familiarity, "How is this, that you make use of a cape with sleeves? That dress is rather adapted for those who carry hawks: but you are an ecclesiastic; and though only one person, yet you have to support the dignity of several, being Archdeacon of Canterbury, Dean of Hastings, Prior of Beverly, canon of this place, and canon of that place, proctor to the archbishopric, and as it is extensively rumoured in the court, likely to become archbishop yourself." The chancellor in reply, amongst other points, alluded to this last sentence. "I know," said he, " three poor priests in England, either one of whom I would rather see advanced to be archbishop than myself; for if I were promoted by any chance to that rank, so well do I know my lord the king, I should be obliged either to lose his favour, or, which God forbid, to set aside my duty to my God, to please him." And so indeed it afterwards happened.

The king of England has his own ship when he crosses the sea. Now the chancellor caused three new ships to be made for him, the best that could be built, and furnished with every thing that was necessary, and he made a present of them to the king, his master.

There once came into England some ambassadors from the king of Norway, and the chancellor, hearing of it, sent messengers to meet them, and escort them to the king's court: meanwhile their charges were defrayed in the chancellor's name.

Nicolas, Archdeacon of London, once incurred the king's anger, the consequence of which was that his family was expelled from their residence, and the house locked up by the king's orders, and put up for sale by auction. But the good chancellor did not rest, until in the same day he had reconciled the archdeacon to the king, and procured the restoration of his property.

In the same way he once rendered a service to the Bishop of Le Man, and to Gilo, Archdeacon of Rouen: for in the schism of the Roman Church, Octavian and his supporter, the emperor Frederic, on the one hand, and the Catholic Pope Alexander, by the advice of his cardinals, on the other hand, sent ambassadors to the king of France, and also to the king of England, who then happened to be in his foreign dominions. They immediately summoned most of the bishops and nobles of their kingdoms at Nieumarkt to hear the arguments of both parties, and to choose which had the best claim on their obedience. At length the election of Alexander seemed (and rightly too) to be the most just and regular: because Hugh, the Archbishop of Rouen, supported it, and gave orders to his suffragan bishops, through Gilo, his grandson and archdeacon, to recognize him as pope. King Henry was very angry, and ordered the houses of the archdeacon to be destroyed; for the king did not dare openly to vent his wrath on the aged archbishop, who was a worthy man. The chancellor then said in a submissive manner to the king, "My lord king, the house which you are ordering to be destroyed, belongs indeed to Archdeacon Gilo; but it is the house in which I am residing." This was an argument well calculated to produce persuasion, and the king in consequence became mollified, and not only pardoned the archdeacon, but restored to him his house. The next day information was brought that the Bishop of Le Man had followed the example of the Archbishop of Rouen, by recognizing Alexander, and promised his messengers that he would yield obedience to him as pope. The king was angry that he should have done this without waiting for his command or license, or even his opinion, and his mareschals, perceiving his anger, or perhaps by his commands, went to the residence of the bishop, turned out the horses, carried the bishop's baggage out into the streets, and expelled him from his lodgings: thus the bishop was compelled to leave the court in disgrace. The king ordered a warrant to be prepared for the destruction of his house at Le Man, and when it was got ready, he held it up in his hand, and said to the by-standers, "I'll warrant the townsmen of Le Man will hear something about their bishop." All the clergy who were present at the court of the two kings were grieved, especially the chancellor; but when he perceived how impossible it was to speak to the king, or attempt to appease him, whilst he was so angry; he told the king's messengers, who carried the letters, not to make much haste on their journey, but to take four days to accomplish it, though it might be done in two. To this they consented, and the next day the chancellor made the bishop go and entreat the king to forgive the Bishop of Le Man. Some of them went, but found the king inexorable. Again, others of them went at the suggestion of the chancellor, but they also were repulsed. At length the chancellor went himself, and begged the king to pardon the bishop, and he did so again the next day. This perseverance on his part succeeded, and the king gave his consent; but he now had no doubt in his mind that the bishop's house was either wholly or in great part destroyed. The chancellor immediately sent the bishop's letters of pardon to the préfet of Le Mans, by a special messenger, whom he enjoined, as he valued his friendship, to rest neither night nor day till he reached his journey's end. The messenger arrived at his destination on the same day as the former messengers of the king, and found that the bishop's house was not yet touched, though the king's warrant for destroying it had already been delivered. The king afterwards was glad that he had been deceived by this commendable stratagem.

The chancellor had fifty-two clerks in his employ, most of whom were in attendance on himself, and took care of the vacant bishoprics and abbacies as well as his own ecclesiastical preferments[6].

[6] Fitz-Stephen.

CHAPTER VII.

OF HIS MILITARY ABILITIES AT TOULOUSE, AND IN THE WAR WITH FRANCE.

AMONG the nobles who accompanied the Conqueror to England were many ecclesiastics, who thought it no disgrace to appear in arms on the field of battle. The warlike Bishop of Beauvais, we are told, bore a mace, in order, as he said, to observe the canon, which forbids a priest to shed blood; but the injunction must have sat very light on the conscience of one who could hope to avoid it by such a facetious quibble. In the time of Becket, a broader line was drawn between the military and the clerical professions, and though the necessary defence of the land has led ecclesiastics in our own time to put on the character of soldiers, no less urgent reason has ever been accepted as an excuse for such an incongruity.

But even in the latter part of the twelfth century, a vast interval was supposed to lie between the deacon's and the priest's offices, so wide, indeed, that the former was at liberty to act, in almost every respect, as a layman. It is not necessary, therefore, to defend the character of Becket from censure, founded on the fact. that though in deacon's orders, he took arms and acted for the king's service on the field of battle. If it even were considered as a defect in his character, it has been well observed by a modern writer [1], that it should not be allowed to " efface the very rare and noble assemblage of qualities of which it is the solitary blemish."

We shall see in the course of this narrative, that Becket rose to eminence in every thing which he took in hand. As the principal law officer in the kingdom, he contributed in a great measure to re-establish order and good government in a country that had for so many years been harassed by war, and every evil which a state of anarchy produces. "As a diplomatist, he acquired such an influence over the king and nobility of France, that notwithstanding the losses he had occasioned them in the field, and the concessions he had extorted from them by negotiation, he was received in that country with open arms, and provided with an asylum, principally at the king's expense, during the six years of his proscription .... In short, there seems to have been a sort of fascination about him, which triumphed alike over the interests and prejudices of all he came in contact with [2]."

We are now to consider him as a military commander; and at a time when one sprung, like him,

---

[1] Froude's Remains, II. p. 9. [2] Ibid.

from the middle classes, might be likely to find many impediments to his advancement. He lived at a time, when nobility of birth was considered as a first and most essential element of success: without which, it might seem hopeless for an adventurer to carve his way to fame and fortune. But in this department also Becket's success was as signal and complete as in every other position of life which he had filled. Of this we have ample evidence in what happened to the English army before Toulouse. The origin of the war was as follows:—

Henry II., of England, married the divorced wife of the king of France, and in her right urged a claim on the dominion of the count of St. Giles, otherwise called the count of Toulouse. An English army lay siege to the city of Toulouse, "where were assembled the chivalry of all England, Normandy, Aquitaine, Anjou, Bretagne, and Scotland, in the cause of the king of England. The chancellor was there with a chosen band of seven hundred knights of his own household. And indeed, if his advice had been listened to, they would have taken, not only the town, but the king of France, who, for the sake of his sister, the countess Constance, had introduced himself into it most incautiously without sufficient troops; so numerous was the king of England's army. But the king listened to the counsel of others, and from foolish superstition and respect towards the king of France, who was his superior lord, hesitated to attack the town: though the chancellor asserted, on the other side, that the king of France had laid aside the character of his superior lord, by appearing as his enemy in defiance of existing treaties. Not long after, the troops that had been summoned by the king of France entered the city; and the king of England, with the Scottish king, and all his army, retired without having accomplished their purpose. However, they took the town of Cahors, and several castles in the neighbourhood of Toulouse, which either belonged to the count of Toulouse and his vassals, or had previously been taken by him from the partizans of the king of England. But all the other barons refused to take charge of them after the king's departure, so that the chancellor with his retainers, and Henry of Essex, alone remained. He afterwards put himself in full armour at the head of a stout band of his men, and took three other castles, which were strongly fortified and looked upon as impregnable. He then passed the Garonne with his troops in pursuit of the enemy, and having confirmed the whole province in their allegiance to the king, he returned in high favour, and crowned with honour.

"Afterwards, in the war between the French king and his own master, the king of England, when the armies were assembled in March, at the common boundaries of their territories, between Gisors, Trie, and Courcelles, the chancellor, besides the seven hundred knights of his own household, maintained twelve hundred other stipendiary knights, and four thousand serving-men, for the space of forty days. To every knight were assigned three shillings per day of the chancellor's money towards their horses and esquires, and the knights themselves all dined at the chancellor's table. One day, though he was a clerk, he charged with lance in rest and horse at full speed against Engelram of Trie, a valiant French knight, who was advancing towards him, and having unhorsed the rider, carried off his horse in triumph. Indeed, the chancellor's knights were everywhere foremost in the whole English army, doing more valiant deeds than any of the others, and every where distinguishing themselves; for he himself was always at their head, encouraging them and pointing out the path to glory: he gave the signal for his men to advance or retreat, on one of those slender trumpets which were peculiar to his band, but which were well known to all the rest of the army around. Wherefore, though he was the enemy of the French king, whose territories he laid waste with fire and sword, he was nevertheless in high repute with him, and with all the French nobles, his high character for unimpeachable faith and nobleness of character spoke in his favour, and at a later period the king had an opportunity of showing this good-will, when it was of much service. Thus is virtue honoured even in an enemy."

Thus in the field, as well as in the cabinet, did Henry derive benefit from the superior abilities of his chancellor. But the king was still apprehensive amid all his triumphs, that his large dominions might be snatched from his descendants as lightly as they had passed from those who had gone before him. Wherefore, when his own Henry was placed for training in the chancellor's hands, he was commanded by the king to exact an oath of homage towards the young prince from all the nobles of the realm. This service was performed with the same success which attended all the chancellor's undertakings: no one hesitated to obey the summons, and all wondered that so difficult and delicate a business had been so cleverly effected during the king's absence [3]. It is not unlikely that the military abilities of the chancellor being already known when this service was required of him, the barons were impelled as much by fear as by duty, to bind themselves by an obligation which the lax morality of the period shows to have been as frail as it was sacred.

[3] Rog. de Pont.

CHAPTER VIII.

OF THE CHANCELLOR'S EMBASSY TO THE FRENCH KING.

An occasion now arose for Becket's abilities to be called into action on a matter of much importance to his royal master. It was judged expedient by the king and his councillors to strengthen the throne by an alliance between prince Henry and the princess Margaret, daughter of the French king. To convey an intimation of this wish, and to demand the young princess in marriage, was reserved for the chancellor himself; who consented to the task required of him, and immediately began to make preparations on a large scale, to discharge with suitable magnificence so important an embassy. The reader will smile at the description which Fitz-Stephen gives us of the style in which the chancellor travelled through Normandy, till he arrived at the French court; it is as follows.—" Every thing had been prepared that might display English luxury to the greatest advantage; that the person who sent him might be honoured in him by all and before all, and that his own person might be honoured in himself. He had with him two hundred men on horseback of his own family, soldiers, clerks, butlers, serving-men, knights, and sons of the nobility, who were performing military service to him, and all equipped with arms. They and their whole train shone in new holiday clothes, each according to his rank. He had also four and twenty changes of garments, almost all of which were to be given away and left in foreign parts, elegant tartans, grieze and foreign skins, cloaks and carpets, such as those with which the bed and chamber of a bishop are adorned. He had with him dogs and birds of all kinds, such as kings and rich men keep. There were in his train eight *bigæ* or carriages, each drawn by five horses, in size and strength equal to chargers. Each horse had his appointed groom in a new vest, walking by the side of the carriage; and the carriage had its driver and guard. Two carriages were filled with beer, made by a decoction of water from the strength of corn, in iron-bound casks, to be given to the French, who admire that sort of liquor, for it is a wholesome drink, bright and clear, of a vinous colour and superior taste. One carriage was used for the chancellor's chapel, one for his chamber, and another his kitchen. Others carried different sorts of meat and drink; some cushions, bags containing night-clothes, bundles

74 THE CHANCELLOR'S EMBASSY [A.D.

and baggage. He had twelve sumpter-horses; and eight coffers to carry his plate of gold and silver cups, pitchers, basins, salts, spoons, knives, and other utensils. There were coffers and chests to contain the chancellor's money, enough to pay for his daily expenses and his presents; together with his clothes, a few books, and such like articles. One sumpter-horse, that went before the others, contained the sacred vessels of the chapel, the books, and ornaments of the altar. Each of the sumpter-horses was attended by a suitable groom, trained to his duties. Moreover, each carriage had a large dog tied to it, either above or below, fierce and terrible, and capable, one might suppose, of conquering a lion. There was also a long-tailed ape on the back of each sumpter-horse,

'An ape, that aper of the human race.'

In his entry into the French villages and castles, first went the footmen, about two hundred and fifty in number, going six or ten together, and sometimes more, singing some song or other after the fashion of their country. At some interval followed the dogs in couples, and harriers fastened by thongs, with their keepers and attendants. At a little distance followed the sumpter-horses, with their grooms riding on them, with their knees placed on the haunches of the horses. Some of the French came out of their houses at the noise, as they passed, and asked who it was? whose family was it that was passing? They received for reply that it was the chancellor of the king of England, going on an embassy to their lord, the king of France. The French said, 'What a remarkable man the king of England must be, if such a great man as this is his chancellor!' After these came the squires, carrying the shields of the knights, and leading their chargers: then came other squires, then young men, then the falconers with the birds on their wrists, and after them the butlers, the masters and attendants of the chancellor's house, then the knights and clerks, all riding two and two together: lastly came the chancellor, and about him some of his particular friends."

Such was the style in which Thomas Becket traversed the northern parts of France! Immediately on landing, he had dispatched a messenger to inform the French king of his coming, and to request that he might be informed where it was his majesty's pleasure to receive him. King Louis sent back for answer, without delay, that he would receive the chancellor at Paris, naming the day.

In the foregoing account of the retinue which followed Becket to Paris, we may discover some traits of that love of pomp and ceremony, which, to a certain extent, has always belonged to the English character [1]. In the style of his reception at the French court, we may also recognize the chivalrous and lavish munificence which has always distinguished them in their behaviour towards foreigners of distinction. "It is a custom," says the biographer [2], "and point of honour with the French king, to suffer no stranger who comes to his court to live at his own charge, but the king provides for him as long as he remains." In order to maintain this custom in the case of so distinguished a guest as the chancellor of the king of England, a proclamation was issued at Paris, that no one should sell anything to either the chancellor or his agents. But this precaution on the part of the royal host was frustrated by the determination of his guest not to be out-done in magnificence. Intimation of the French king's intentions was conveyed to the chancellor, who dispatched messengers to the neighbouring mar-

---

[1] Another peculiarity of the English, noticed in one of the contemporary writings of this period, is their disposition to fill their houses most profusely with furniture, and every kind of necessary. Seven hundred years have produced much less change, both in our manners and language, than is generally believed; for those who have travelled much abroad may still remark this striking difference between the English and other nations.

[2] Fitz-Stephen.

kets of Lamaci, Corbeil, Pontoise, and Saint Denis. Whilst these were performing their commission, the embassy entered Paris, and proceeded to take up their quarters in the Temple, which was assigned for their residence. Here the emissaries, who had been sent to buy provisions, met them, and reported what they had done. In order to baffle the agents of the French king, who might interfere to prevent them, they had changed their dress, and assumed false names. By this device they had succeeded in purchasing plenty of provisions, and they told their master as he was entering his hotel, that he would find it stored for a stay of three days, and enough for a thousand men each day. Such house-keeping as this was certainly formed on a gigantic scale; and there was equal magnificence in its minute details; for we are told that a dish of eels was one day purchased for the chancellor's table at the high price of a hundred shillings. From this single fact it may be inferred, without doubt, that the chancellor's table was equally sumptuous in other respects, and when this instance of his prodigality was known at home at England, it became a proverb in the mouths of men for a very long time. We meet with other intimations in the contemporary biographers, which leave no room to doubt that Becket's table was rich, and even luxurious, not only whilst he was chancellor, but even after his promotion to the archbishopric of Canterbury; but it is also admitted by all, that he partook but frugally of what was set before him, and even if this was not the fact, we should not infer that he was addicted to the pleasures of the table from the anecdote above-mentioned, which merely tends to show that he was anxious to display his magnificence and riches in the eyes of the French people.

If this was his object, and it certainly was not ill-calculated to promote the negotiation on which the king had sent him, he seems to have spared no expense to gain the favour of all classes of the Parisian citizens: for he was most prodigal of his gifts, making large presents not only to the king's servants, but to the nobles, barons, and knights. He gave away all his gold and silver plate—all the bundles of rich and costly clothing, which figured in the description of his progress through the country, were most lavishly bestowed on those who flocked to see him—to one he gave a cloak, to another a horse, to a third a war-charger; and amongst others, he bestowed substantial marks, both of his politeness and his bounty, on the French scholars, and masters of schools. The king and his nobles were not backward in this rivalry of courtesy and politeness: they treated their distinguished guest with every mark of honour and respect: and in a short time nothing could exceed the enthusiastic good-will which existed between the parties. As the necessary result of all this, he discharged his embassy with success, and left the French court, having obtained the object for which he had been sent.

On his return homeward, he performed another signal service to his master, by capturing his enemy, Guy de la Val, who infested the highways and plundered the whole country.

CHAPTER IX.

LETTERS TO BECKET AS CHANCELLOR—FURTHER REMARKS ON HIS CHARACTER—CHARGES BROUGHT AGAINST HIM REFUTED.

THE accounts of Becket's chancellorship are, as we have seen, written in rich and glowing terms, not more so, probably, than the subject required, or than his rapid career of honours justified. We should, however, have been glad, if among the mass of letters which have come down to us connected with his history, a larger portion had borne reference to the period when he was chancellor. We might have hoped to find in them valuable observations on the many scenes in which Becket took an active part, and more particularly of his own personal character, which could not fail to attract the notice of all who were capable of noticing what was passing around them. Of such writings, however, few are still extant: we shall quote three of them, to which the reader will, no doubt, attach much value, as presenting him with information concerning a period of Becket's life, of which so few private notices remain. The first we shall give, is from that elegant scholar, and experienced politician, Arnulf, bishop of Lisieux, who has already appeared on the stage, as having advised Theobald to introduce Becket to the king.

LETTER IV.

"TO HIS RESPECTED AND DEAR FRIEND THOMAS, ILLUSTRIOUS CHANCELLOR TO THE KING OF THE ENGLISH, ARNULF, HUMBLE MINISTER OF THE CHURCH OF LISIEUX, HEALTH AND HIS BEST LOVE."

"I HAVE received your highness's letters, every word of which seemed to me to drop honey, and to be redolent with the sweetness of affection. I was delighted to find that I had not lost the privilege of our early intimacy, either by the wide distance which separates us, or by the multitude of affairs in which you are involved. I was delighted, I say, because the matter is put beyond all doubt, by the receipt of your letter, which it would be unworthy of me to suspect either of flattery or of falsehood. The same interest in you exists also in my bosom, which though it has seldom an opportunity of exemplifying itself by deed, yet still lives in the devoted yearnings of the will. For in friendship, it is the will alone which is concerned, and there is no room for questions of bartering, lest our affection be thought to be prostituted or mercenary. Friendship is complete in the purity of its own existence, and gains but slight addition from being demonstrated in deed;

it is but little exposed to the caprices of fortune, and derives its own dignity from itself. So true is this, that it is seldom found among the rich, for it hates riches, and seems to attach itself to the single-minded, and to the poor. It is, indeed, a rare virtue, and therefore the more precious; but no where is it more rarely found than between those who are invited to administer counsel to kings, and to transact the business of kingdoms. For, to say nothing of other points, ambition sits with anxious weight upon their minds, and whilst each fears to be outstripped by the vigilance of the other, envy springs up between them, which, ere long, fails not to become open hatred. For it is an old feature in the character of the envious, that they look upon others' success as their own ruin, and whatever others gain, they think has been subtracted from themselves. Envy ever suffers torment, and dissembles its hidden pains under a smiling look, and thus a deceitful exterior cloaks secret treachery. Moreover, if the favour of the prince is changed, and he begins to look on a man with a clouded brow, all the support of his companions fails him, the applause and obsequiousness with which they crowded round him die away; those from whom he expected consolation, insult him; and when occasion offers, remind him of the wrongs he had once done them: nay, his very benefits are designated as acts of injury.

Such is the sea on which you are sailing; such the turmoil amid which your life is cast, wherein you will have to guard against the siren smiles of those who applaud you, and the venomed strains of flatterers. From all these you have but one way to escape—sincere faith accompanied with uprightness in well-doing; seek rather, with the Apostle, to obtain glory to yourself from the testimony of a good conscience, than the uncertain honours of public report, and of slippery and popular applause. Popularity departs from a man more rapidly than it came; whereas those other virtues, though they may be unpalatable in acquiring, yet lead to a happy sequel. I write to you thus plainly, not because I would, according to the proverb, teach Minerva letters: but in speaking to a friend, I could not restrain the current of my thoughts, particularly when urged by the impulse of my mind to offer you my congratulations.

"I beg to commend to your care my lord Serlo, a faithful friend of mine, together with the little matters of business which he has in hand. I will only further add my request, that you use all diligence in preserving for me the favour of our prince, which I formerly earned by my services, but which may flag during my absence; for the favour of princes, particularly the young, often fails and dies outright for want of some one to remind them of it. Fare you well for ever!"

This letter was probably sent to the chancellor soon after his promotion; and its writer at a later period experienced in his own person the dangers which he here points out to his friend. The fickleness of kings, and the risk of placing confidence in princes, have been favourite themes with many,—with none more so than with those who have done their best to obtain that which they appear to despise. This was the case with Arnulf, who after having played a part in every intrigue, and been engaged in almost every public transaction of that stirring period, fell into disfavour with Henry II., and died at Paris in the Monastery of St. Victor's.

Another of Becket's correspondents, and of rather more steady character than the preceding, was Peter of Celles, afterwards abbat of St. Remy, whose letter addressed to the Chancellor about this time, is creditable both to the writer and to his correspondent.

LETTER V.

" TO HIS DEAR LORD AND FRIEND THOMAS, THE CHANCELLOR OF THE KING OF ENGLAND, HIS BROTHER PETER, SERVANT OF THE SERVANTS OF GOD, HIMSELF AND ALL THAT IS HIS [1]!"

"THE man who is not puffed up by prosperous fortune, is to be admired more for his humility than

---

[1] The inscriptions prefixed to the letters of this period, are of the most varied and quaint description.

for his promotion. In you, as I have heard from those who have seen you, glory struggles with good fortune, and the struggle is one rather of ambition than of strife: defeat brings with it no confusion, and victory no triumph. Each seems in turn victorious, but it is glory and not pride; it is good fortune, but without excess. From this cause it is, that from the height of your exaltation, not being able to come yourself, you have addressed a letter to my insignificance. You ask of me familiarity and friendship, which, if I asked you, and you granted me, would, indeed, be a cause for admiration, from the unequal rank of the two parties. For what relation can exist between the abbat of Celles and the Chancellor of the king of England? Who does not know that you are the greatest man of four kingdoms, next to the king himself? I will speak briefly: for the more highly I think of you, the more lowly do I think and feel of myself. In no wise then will I hold out my hand to accept this friendship; but if you will place me among the herd of your chance friends, I shall think that your highness has dealt handsomely with me. I do not wish to change the first state of things, for I am anxious to do a greater favour.

"I have not by me master G.'s sermons, but I am inquiring for them, and will with all speed set the copyist about this work for your use. Farewell."

In this brief epistle we meet with less rhetorical flourish and parade of words, than in that of the supple and courtly Arnulf; but more of that blunt honesty which ennobles a man, and of that modest diffidence which beseems an ecclesiastic. Nor does it give us an unfavourable view of the character of the chancellor himself, who turns aside from his course of greatness to ask the friendship of an abbat, from whom he apparently could derive little profit or advantage. But this was another trait in his noble character, which exemplified itself to the end of his life, that amid all his pomp and splendour, he sought out the most eminent and learned men to be of his acquaintance, and to form his court, not only after his election to the see of Canterbury had made it to a certain extent necessary for him to do so, but even whilst, as chancellor, he lay under no such obligation.

At a later period, when in exile, he employed his scribes to copy for him the most valuable books which were contained in the libraries of France, and in this respect also, the tastes of the chancellor were the same as those of the archbishop, as is sufficiently proved by the concluding sentence of the letter which has just been quoted.

This union of a taste for magnificence and for literature, is still more apparent in a third letter, from which we shall extract only that portion which has reference to the subject. The writer is Peter Trecensis.

LETTER VI.

"Do not suppose, my dearest lord and friend, that I wish to make an invective against your nobleness and magnanimity, which throws into the shade, not only your inferiors and equals, but even, I may say, your superiors. For beyond all doubt, the report of your expenditure and of your bounty has reached even to our humble roof. I only wish to communicate to you, that I have done my best to execute your commands about copying out the sermons, and transmitting them to the archdeacon. So modest is your request, that it cannot be called a service on my part; so eager am I to serve you, that it deserves not the name of a kindness. Services are weighed by their fruits, kindnesses by the willingness of the doer. But enough of this. That Stephen you speak of is the earl's clerk."

These are, perhaps, the most important letters in existence which were addressed to Becket during his chancellorship. As so many writers have concurred in throwing odium on a character, perhaps the most splendid during a thousand years of our national history, we may be allowed to pause awhile, to weigh the testimony which these letters furnish.

The imputation which has hitherto so lightly been made against him is, that as chancellor he was indifferent to all those duties which as archbishop he held so sacred: according to his calumniators, religion was a veil under which he concealed his ambition and other worldly views. But is such the result of our inquiry into his previous life? Do we observe any traces of that laxity from which he so suddenly changed to the ascetic and the devotee? It is admitted that he attained the highest point of excellence as a diplomatist, as a statesman, and as a warrior. He aided his sovereign in restoring to tranquillity a country which had been afflicted twenty years; he secured singular advantages for the king, his master, by negotiating with foreign states; and when the king's disputes with his enemies were referred to the arbitrement of the sword, the ancient barons of the realm, whose minds and bodies were almost as hard as the iron mail in which they were sheathed, blushed not to be led to the battle by a young man, whose previous life had been passed in the cloister, and whose hands had been used rather to the missal or the breviary than the sword. Such was no doubt the necessary result of the high and splendid talents with which God had endowed him, and it is not to be doubted that Becket enjoyed the prosperity which he had earned. But what is more to the point, he used it for a good purpose: in all the contemporary accounts which have come down to us, there is nothing that was set up to his disparagement, until the moment of his election to the archbishopric. That alone was wanting to complete his worldly career; and when that point also was gained, a host of enemies rose up on every side, all his former actions were misrepresented, and a load of obloquy thrown upon his name, which has continued almost to the present day. Yet there is little doubt that if we make allowance for certain ceremonies and duties, which as archbishop of Canterbury he was obliged to adopt, he exhibited himself in much the same light in his former capacity of chancellor—" as one who had a strong, though not very consistent, sense of religion, and whose ambition was curiously tinctured with austerity[2]." This seems to be the natural inference from some of the anecdotes of what happened during his chancellorship: and that he had a strong bias towards learning, is conclusive from the passages in the letters which we have quoted.

There are, however, two detailed charges brought against him respecting this period of his life, which may be considered to require a particular answer;

[2] Froude's Remains, vol. ii. p. 572.

and as these charges have been minutely examined, and met by a recent writer[3], we shall give the account of the whole matter in his own words:—

I. "There exists, among the records of Battle Abbey, a very minute account of a transaction in which Becket is said to have been implicated, and which, if it can be trusted for correctness in its report of conversations, does certainly amount to a proof that, in the year 1157, Becket allowed a claim to be asserted by the king in a single instance, which claim, in the year 1163, he would not allow to be formally embodied in writing, and recognized as the permanent law of the land.

"According to the record of Battle Abbey, a claim had for some time been put forward by Hilary, Bishop of Chichester, interfering with the chartered liberties of that convent. This claim was supported by Theobald, Archbishop of Canterbury, and through his influence was for some time recognized by Henry II. But when the question was at last to be definitely settled, and for that purpose a great number of the chief nobility, lay as well as clerical, were assembled, it so chanced that Hilary gave great offence, by resting his claim on the assumed superiority of a pope's mandate to a king's chartered grant; and after receiving a

[3] Froude's Remains, vol. ii. p. 574.

severe rebuke from the king for comparing the pope's authority "*granted by a man,*" with his own "divine right," was reminded by the Chancellor, that the ground which he took was scarcely consistent with the oath of allegiance.

"Such is the substance of the report, as far as it affects the question before us. And it must be owned that there is no reason to suspect such a document of any intentional misrepresentation to Becket's prejudice. But even if we admit the exact faithfulness of the whole report, still the inconsistency which it proves is hardly such as to imply dishonesty. In the first place, there is a sufficient interval between 1157 and 1163 to make room for some real change of opinion. Next, even supposing that Becket's opinion was the same at both times, still in the first instance he had no power to resist, in the second he was able to resist effectually; and lastly, the difference, at that time acknowledged, between the demand to which he assented in 1157, and which he refused in 1163, is much greater than may be supposed by a modern reader. An occasional act of usurpation was not in those days so easily, as at present, construed into a precedent; and we know, as a fact, that the very claims, of which the formal assertion was so warmly resisted at Clarendon, were cheerfully submitted to, even by Becket himself, while they were acknowledged to be tyrannical. But the clearest proof of the distinction drawn at the time between an occasional concession and a written acknowledgment, is furnished us by Nicholas of Rouen. The account he gives of his interview with the Empress Matilda contains her comments on the famous constitutions of Clarendon. He tells us :—' With far the greater number she found fault; and *what offended her above all, was their being reduced to writing*, as well as the attempt to exact from the Bishops a *promise of their observance;* ' for this,' she said, ' was without precedent.' In conclusion, when I pressed her earnestly to mention some expedient for bringing about peace, we suggested this to her, and she assented. If the king applies to her for advice, she will recommend a compromise on these conditions,—that *the ancient customs of the kingdom shall still be observed, but without being reduced to writing, or enforced by a promise;* and that neither the Bishops should *abuse* the liberty of the Church, nor the civil judges *overturn* it.'

"Becket then was willing to concede as much himself, as he had allowed Henry to claim in the transaction which has been brought up against him, and therefore, supposing it real, it is not very important.

"But, in the next place, we see great reason to

suspect the truth of the whole story; not, indeed, that we suppose it misrepresented with a view to malign Becket—that is out of the question,—but because I suspect that the transaction, as it really took place, was much less creditable to the convent than the record admits; and that if it is incorrectly stated in these points, it may be in all.

"In the summer of 1168, when Becket's affairs wore the most unpromising aspect, and when the pope seemed to abandon him to the mercy of his enemies, he wrote a very earnest letter of remonstrance, enumerating the grievances which the Church had suffered, and exonerating himself from the charge of having been accessory to them. After mentioning many acts of oppression to which the Church had been subjected before he had any thing to do with its administration, he proceeds:—

"'And what success had the Bishop of Chichester against the Abbot of Battle; when on his daring to speak before the court of Apostolic privileges, and to denounce the Abbot excommunicate, he was forthwith compelled to communicate with him in the face of all present, without even the form of absolution, and to receive him to the kiss of peace? For such was the king's pleasure, and that of the court, which dared not to oppose his will in any thing. And this, most holy Father, happened in the time of my predecessor, and your Holiness.'

"The whole transaction, as here described, seems to have been a most disgraceful one, and to have been intentionally disguised in the Abbey record. And, moreover, it appears that Becket's conscience was quite easy upon the subject. For as the circumstances were generally known, and as the part Becket had himself taken in it (if indeed he took any) must still have been fresh in the minds of many, it is scarce credible that he should have so gratuitously appealed to it, and on such an occasion, if it could have a turn given to it unfavourable to himself. So much for the affair of Battle Abbey.

II. "The remaining charge, viz. that in order to prosecute the war of Toulouse he levied heavy contributions on the Church, seems to be much better founded. For though we attach no great weight to Lord Lyttleton's author, Gilbert Foliot, and though we think that the 49th letter in the collection [4] was addressed to Becket himself, not to the king, as Lord Lyttleton supposes, yet we are furnished with evidence which can hardly be disputed, in a letter from

[4] Ep. Joan. Saresb.

1159.]   IMPOSTS ON THE CLERGY.   95

John of Salisbury to Bartholomew, Bishop of Exeter, written in the summer of 1166[5].

"After an allusion to the above-mentioned exactions, John of Salisbury goes on to say:—

"'But perhaps it will be said that the imposition of the tax, and the whole in short of this disturbance, is to be attributed to the Archbishop, who then had complete influence over the king, and made this suggestion to him. Now I know that this was not the case: for he only allowed the measure to pass, he did not sanction it. Inasmuch, however, as he was the instrument of injustice, it is a suitable punishment to him, that he should be persecuted now by the very person whom he then preferred to his Supreme Benefactor.'

"This is an acknowledgment against which we have nothing to advance. It is clear that Becket was on this occasion accessory to heavy, and even iniquitous exactions, and we know of no palliation for his conduct, except the fact that he seems never to have forfeited the friendship of Theobald, who to the last regarded him with the affection of a father, and spoke of him as 'our Archdeacon, our intimate friend and counsellor[6].'

"To this charge, then, we are constrained to plead guilty; but still we do not think it warrants the

[5] Ep. Joan. Saresb. 159.   [6] Ep. J. S. 70.

inference which has been drawn from it. 'After such testimonies,' says Lord Lyttleton, 'of Becket's zeal to maintain the royal prerogative against the exorbitant claims of Rome and the Church, it was no wonder that Henry should believe him no bigot. And that opinion was unquestionably the cause of this unhappy choice, which proved a source of great disquiet to that monarch and his kingdom.' Now, I do not believe that Becket's zeal in exacting the above mentioned sums of money arose from, or, what is more to the purpose, seemed to arise from 'a zeal to maintain the royal prerogatives against the Church.' Becket's own eager character leaves me at no loss to account for his zeal in prosecuting a war which he had begun with success, and through which he saw his way clearly. Nor is there any need for supposing, that when, on his resources failing him, he applied for contributions to the Church, he was actuated by any deeper motive than a belief that through his intimacy with Theobald, he might thus supply his wants most readily. The notion prevalent at the time seems to have been, not that on such occasions he lent himself to the king's wishes, but that the king was governed by his. In the year 1161, John of Salisbury wrote to him respecting the war in Normandy.

" ' Those who have returned say, and I would

it were true, that the king and court are entirely governed by your advice; and that the peace depends upon your advocating it⁷.'

"And so conscious was the king of the influence Becket had exerted over him, that after the misunderstanding had arisen between them, he could not bear to be reminded of it. In the winter of 1165, the Bishop of Lisieux informed Becket, that, among other means resorted to by those who wished to foment irritation, 'They added that you had said among your friends, that the prince's youthful and undisciplined passions ought to meet with no encouragement, but rather steady opposition; that you were acquainted with all the movements of the king's mind, its levity, and the good points it aspired to: and that he in return acknowledged the vast superiority of your understanding, which had shown itself so clearly on many occasions, in surmounting difficulties, and turning opportunities to the best account. These words, they said, had been reported by some malignant person to the king, and had enraged him to an implacable degree.'"

"If the footing on which Becket stood with the king was such as these passages would lead us to infer, it was not very likely that on his appointment to the Archbishopric he should sink into the tool of his *quondam* pupil.

⁷ Ep. J. S. 77.

"As to the 'important reformation' which Lord Lyttleton *assumes* that the king intended to undertake, we very much doubt whether such a scheme ever entered his head till more than a year after Becket's consecration; and on this account we cannot feel it to be 'incredible that he should not have revealed his intentions concerning that affair, to a minister whom he was accustomed to trust in his most secret councils.'

"Upon the whole, we do not think that any charge which has been brought forward against Becket, when chancellor, implies more than what his whole subsequent history confirms— that he was a man of very keen feelings, who followed up with vigour whatever he took in hand, and was, perhaps, ambitiously eager about the success of his projects, and who, moreover, if we are to believe what we are told of his self-denying habits, was the very person to devote himself to a cause which afforded scope at once to his most chivalrous and most ascetic feelings[a].

---

[a] "The light in which this singular man was regarded while chancellor, by his clerical friends, may, we think, be not unfairly collected from some lines in which John of Salisbury dedicates his book, "De nugis Curialium," which appeared in 1160. The writer addresses himself to his own book, in the style of Horace, and warning it of the dangers which attended courtiers, points out whom to seek as men of worth at the

English court, and whom to avoid. Among the former class he designates the chancellor in these words:—

" Jure patronatus illum cole, qui velit esse
　　Et sciat, et possit, tutor ubique tuus.
　Ergo quæratur *lux cleri*, gloria gentis
　　Anglorum, Regis dextera forma boni.
Quæsitus Regni tibi cancellarius Angli,
　　Primus solicita mente petendus erit.
Hic est qui Regni leges cancellat iniquas,
　　Et mandata pii Principis æqua facit.
Si quid obest populo, vel moribus est inimicum,
　　Quicquid id est, per eum desinit esse nocens.
Publica privatis qui præfert commoda semper,
　　Quodque dat in plures ducit in ære suo.
Quod dat habet, quod habet dignis donat vice versa,
　　Spargit, sed sparsæ multiplicantur opes.
Utque virum virtus animi, sic gratia formæ
　　Undique mirandum gentibus esse facit.
　　　＊　　＊　　＊　　＊
Hujus nosse domum non res est ardua; cuivis
　　Non duce quæsito semita trita patet.
Nota domus cunctis, vitio non cognita soli,
　　Lucet; ab hac lucem dives, egenus, habent."

CHAPTER X.

THEOBALD'S DEATH—OF THE EVENTS WHICH FOLLOWED IT, AND OF BECKET'S ELECTION TO THE ARCHBISHOPRIC OF CANTERBURY.

Thus far had Thomas Becket risen by his talents alone to the highest civil station in the kingdom: an event now occurred which placed him at the head of the ecclesiastical affairs also; for on the 18th of April 1161, the aged archbishop Theobald was laid in the grave, after having presided twenty-two years over the Church of Canterbury. The remainder of that and half the next year would seem to have been occupied in such intrigues and negotiations as usually followed when an office fell vacant, conferring so much wealth and dignity. If it had been Henry's wish to intrude the chancellor into the see of Canterbury by every means in his power, however hasty or imprudent, he would not have suffered more than a year to elapse before the election took place: nor on the other hand, if he had wished to convert the archiepiscopal revenues to his own use, would he have limited his usurpation within so brief a period. It is more probable that the king passed the intervening months in pondering more fully on the propriety of electing the chancellor, which, perhaps, before the vacancy had actually occurred, though often lightly mentioned to his courtiers, had not yet become the settled purpose of his mind. The court was at this time in Normandy, and in the beginning of the year 1162, the chancellor was sent over to England on several matters of public business, one of which was to make preparations for crowning the young prince Henry as his father's successor, and to obtain an oath of allegiance to him from the barons, "but principally," says Gervase of Canterbury, "with the intention of getting him elected to the archbishopric of Canterbury. A short time after, namely, in the month of May, a deputation arrived at Canterbury from the king, consisting of [Hilary] Bishop of Chichester, [Bartholomew] of Exeter, [Walter] of Rochester, the abbat of Battle, and his brother, Richard de Lucy [1]," grand justiciary of the realm, "bringing the king's command under his seal, to the convent, for the prior with the other monks to meet the bishops and clergy of England at London, and proceed to the election of an archbishop and primate."

The account of what took place on the arrival of these commissioners is given as follows by the

[1] Gervas. Cantuar.

monk of Pontigny[2], somewhat more fully than by the other biographers, though in substance it is identical. "The bishops entered the chapter-house of Canterbury, and having first spoken at much length of the kindness and condescension of the king, they deputed Richard de Lucy to communicate their message to the monks: whereupon Richard de Lucy addressed them thus: 'Since my lords the bishops have determined that I shall declare to you the king's pleasure, be it known to all for a certainty, that our lord the king, as you have already heard from their lordships, is most zealous in everything which concerns the Lord God, and is devoutly attached to the service of our holy Church: and especially to this Church of Canterbury here present, to which he is bound by filial affection, as he regards her as his own especial mother in the Lord. Wherefore, that she may not be disturbed or injured by the protracted want of a pastor, be it known to you all that the election of an archbishop is left to your free choice; yet so that you elect a person worthy of such an honour, and equal to the burden of it. For you cannot be ignorant that our lord the king has never in such matters attempted to do anything, save what he has considered pleasing to God and of advantage to His

[2] Roger de Pontig.

Church. For the rest, therefore, it is your especial province and duty to elect one, under whose protection you may rejoice both before God and before men. For if the king and the archbishop shall be united together in the strong bonds of affection, and shall mutually and amicably support one another, there is no doubt that happiness will await our times, and the state of the Church continue in peace and tranquillity. But if, which God forbid, things should turn out otherwise, the dangers which may result, the troubles, the difficulties, and the tumults which may arise, together with the loss of our worldly goods, and the danger to our souls, I do not think your holinesses can have lost sight of.'"

With these words Richard concluded, and the bishops expressed their approbation of what he had said: whereupon the prior [Wibert[3],] having first given thanks to God, next with due reverence expressed his gratitude to the king for all his majesty's kindness and solicitude about them, and then on a sign from the bishops, he called to him some of the oldest of the brethren present, and left the room in their company. But when they had sat together for some time, and talked of what they had just heard, they came to the conclusion that no election could

[3] Gerv. Cantuar.

be made without the advice of Richard de Lucy and the bishops, who knew the king's wishes, on which the whole election depended. They, therefore, called in the king's commissioners, namely, Bartholomew, bishop of Exeter and Hilary of Chichester, [Walter of Rochester[4],] and Richard; and when they had entered, and discussed for some time the matter in hand, they all, both monks and bishops, united in choosing the chancellor to be the shepherd and bishop of their souls. The monks, indeed, hesitated for some time to give their consent, not because they did not know Thomas to be a virtuous man, but because he did not wear the dress of the religious order; for up to that time the Church of Canterbury had always had pontiffs who, in their dress and way of life, followed the monastic rule. For St. Augustine, the monk, who was sent here by the apostolic pope Gregory to preach the faith of Christ to the English nation, established the Church of Canterbury and others in these parts, under regular monastic discipline, and this ordinance had been hitherto more scrupulously observed here than in any other place. But when the monks considered the other virtues and graces which shone so brightly in his character, they overlooked the only point which

---

[4] Roger of Pontigny mentions only two bishops.

offended them, namely, his irregular exterior, and with willing hearts and one consent elected him archbishop. The bishops, therefore, whom the king had sent for this very purpose, appointed a day for the prior and monks of Canterbury to meet them in council at London; that whatever remained which was requisite to complete the solemnity of the election might there be done before all the bishops and abbats of the realm, and in presence of the young king his son. For the king, his father, had now given over the kingdom to him, and had procured for him, by means of the chancellor, the homage and oath of allegiance of the barons. He had, moreover, written to him about the election to the archbishopric of Canterbury, signifying that whatever should be done in that matter in his son's presence, should meet with his own approbation and consent.

In consequence of these proceedings, the bishops aforesaid, in the king's name, convoked all the other prelates and abbats of the kingdom, together with the priors of the conventual churches, the earls and nobles, and all the king's officials on a fixed day in the city of London. When they were all assembled on the appointed day, the prior of Canterbury reverently proclaimed before all the bishops then present, the election which had taken place at Canterbury, with the king's consent and by his mandate, before the three bishops whom he had sent for that purpose: stating that, by the inspiration of God's Holy Spirit, they had unanimously and according to the canons elected Thomas, chancellor of the kingdom, to be their archbishop. Whereupon the bishops, who had been sent by the king, and had witnessed the proceedings at Canterbury, having spoken in favour of the form of election, and of him on whom it had fallen, all present gave their consent, and with one accord raised their voices in thanksgiving to Almighty God.

One, however, there was, Gilbert Foliot, bishop of London[5], who opposed and murmured at the election; but when he saw the unanimity of the others, and that his own solitary malice would effect nothing, he gave his consent also. He was a man advanced in years, of much learning, and of the monastic profession; it was also the generally received opinion that he had himself long aimed at being made archbishop. After the election all the bishops approached the young king, asking his assent, favour, and approbation to what they had done: to all of which the young king, with much pleasure, gave his approbation accordingly. Moreover, the great officers

[5] Or rather bishop of Hereford; but there are great chronological difficulties attending the translation of Gilbert Foliot to the see of London.

of state, to whom the king had also addressed letters on the subject, hailed the election with joy, and devoutly gave their confirmation of it. But Henry of Winchester, no less famous for his high birth than for his prudence and piety, said to the young king, " My lord, the chancellor, our archbishop elect, has for a long time possessed the highest place in the house of the king, your father, and in the whole kingdom, which he has had entirely under his government; nor has any thing been done during your father's whole reign without his advice and pleasure. We demand, therefore, that he shall be delivered over to us, and to the Church of God, free from all civil obligation or service of the court, from all suit or accusation or any other matter whatsoever, that from this very hour and ever after he may be at liberty and at leisure to act freely in God's service. For we know that the king, your father, has delegated to you his authority in this matter, and will gladly confirm whatever you shall do therein." The young king listened with pleasure to his request, and delivered Thomas over to the Church according to the words of Henry of Winchester, free absolutely from all civil obligations. But Thomas himself, from the first moment that his own promotion was talked of, opposed it by every means in his power: knowing full well that it was impossible for him to serve two masters at once, whose wills were so much at variance; and that whoever should be made archbishop of Canterbury, would be sure either to offend God or the king. But God had ordained otherwise, and Henry of Pisa, priest and cardinal and legate of the apostolic see, and also a monk of the Cistercian order, urged him, by all means, to undertake the office; and so his election was made and brought to completion in the way that we have just described.

The most important part of Becket's elevation to the see of Canterbury was now over, for the unanimity with which all parties concurred in the choice, is certified by all the contemporary writers[e]; but there were still many minor ceremonies to be performed.

On the Thursday before Whit-Sunday, the writ of election was read by Henry bishop of Winchester, in the refectory of the abbey of Westminster, without opposition: on the following Whit-Sunday the new archbishop received priest's orders (for he was yet only deacon) in the church of Canterbury, from the hands of Walter, bishop of Rochester, who also claimed the right of performing the consecration in place

---

[e] Ralph de Diceto, archdeacon of London, and during part of the subsequent troubles secretary to king Henry, says that " Thomas, archdeacon and chancellor, was formally elected to

of the bishop of London, for the see of London had not yet been filled since the death of Richard. This claim, however, was not allowed.

"On the day fixed for the consecration, the bishops assembled at Canterbury, and with them a large number of abbats and religious men of all ranks, eager to be present at the consecration of so great an archbishop, and to participate in the prayers and blessings that would then be bestowed. Thomas also came on the appointed day, attended by a large number of the clergy and other persons of dignity: the bishops went out to meet him with the monks and clergy, and an immense multitude of the common people, receiving him with every kind of honour, and

the archbishopric, *no one objecting*:" and John of Salisbury, in a letter written to the archbishop, in 1166, comments upon one of the hostile communications which Becket had just received from Gilbert, bishop of London, in the following terms:—

"As to the falsehoods which he has dared to assert respecting your lordship's elevation, I care little for them. I was myself present at it, and saw it all. He was the solitary individual who did not express pleasure at your nomination; and he, as was then evident, and is still abundantly so, had been foremost among the aspirants to your lordship's see. Yet even he was soon shamed out of his opposition, for every one saw through his ambition and impudence. Whatever then were his secret intentions, (of these God takes cognizance,) he was one of the first to give his vote in your favour, and the loudest in his praises of the election."

with acclamations of joy: so great was their delight that no language can describe it. But Thomas paid no attention to all these tokens of the public satisfaction: he advanced on foot with humility and contrition of heart, and with his eyes filled with tears, thinking less of the honour than of the burden which he was about to take upon him. He was ordained and consecrated archbishop by Henry of Winchester; for he was the most eminent of the bishops, both for his piety and his high birth, for he was a monk and brother of Stephen of Blois, who succeeded the first Henry on the throne of England, which he held twenty years. For William the bastard was succeeded by William Rufus, who drove into exile the illustrious archbishop of Canterbury, saint Anselm, and was slain while hunting by an arrow from a certain knight, directed not by accident but by Divine Providence, as was generally supposed. To him succeeded his brother Henry, who was the father of Matilda, and was a most magnificent and powerful sovereign. After him reigned the above-named Stephen of Blois, brother of the bishop of Winchester, and of the illustrious Count Theobald the elder. Whilst Stephen was still alive and reigning, Henry, son of the empress Matilda, came over and obtained the sovereignty. It was in the eighth year of his reign that Thomas was consecrated archbishop in the city of Canterbury.[7]"

On the completion of this solemn ceremony, messengers, among whom was the archbishop's clerk and private friend, John of Salisbury, were dispatched to inform the sovereign pontiff of what had taken place. The pope, surrounded by his cardinals, gave them audience, and letters were read from the king, and from the prior and convent of Canterbury. The election met with general approbation, and after a short delay, the messengers returned to England, bearing with them the pall, by which it was supposed that the head of the Church gave power to discharge the archiepiscopal functions. This "mystic government and badge of an archbishop[8]," was deposited on the high altar in the church of Canterbury, from whence it was taken by Becket himself, who advanced, clothed in his pontifical robes, and tendered the solemn oath which was usual on such occasions.

[7] Rog. Pont.   [8] Fitz-Stephen.

CHAPTER XI.

BECKET ARCHBISHOP — PUBLIC OPINION OF HIS ELECTION — HIS PURITY OF LIFE, AND MANY VIRTUES.

Many years after the event related in the last chapter, which raised Thomas Becket to the highest pinnacle of earthly glory, Herbert de Bosham, one of his clerks and constant attendants, occupied the leisure hours of his retirement from the bustle of the world, in writing the life of his illustrious master. His work, of which not a single perfect copy is known to exist, is a curious specimen of biography, and derives its principal value from the writer having been an eye-witness of what he relates. "All my coevals," says he, "who witnessed, as I did, the passion of our master, have been removed from the world, and already sleep in Christ. On me, therefore, who alone survive, this duty has devolved, and therefore I have taken the pen in hand, choosing rather, if it must be so, to err on the side of presumption than of indifference." His notices, however, up to the elevation of his master to the throne of Canterbury, are brief and sketchy, but after that period they become most ample, and abound in curious details, in which his style displays all the pomp of a Johnson, and all the loquacity of a Boswell.

The following passages will describe his matter, and perhaps his style:—" Sinner that I am," says he, " for having undertaken to pourtray his character, without having accompanied Moses to the summit, or Joshua to the declivity of the mountain; but I dwell here in this valley of tears, in the midst of a people in sin and suffering like myself. Wherefore also I am proceeding in my unregenerate state to describe one who had now become a new man: my soul shrinks from the untried subject, and my pen, which hitherto has sufficed in its weakness to describe the manners of a weak man passing through this world of weakness, now finds its powers exhausted. The dignity and bright splendour of the theme strike me aghast, and unnerve me. But I feel comfort, such as it is, in that these eyes have witnessed it; and therefore, not like a novice, but taught by the grace of Him who created and formed mankind, I will alter my style as I best am able, and will describe the heavenly likeness of the heavenly one, even that pontifical form, so conspicuous in Christ's pontiff, that the men of this my time, who are now alive, and all those who live in future ages, and especially pontiffs, may have a pattern to admire and to imitate; yea, which ought rather to be painted in vermilion, than to be written with the pen. For if I may be boastful, nay because I must, and because it is expedient for me to be so, this bright model has been already shown to me beforehand, not in the mountain, but here, even here in this valley of tears: I saw, and followed, and attended on, the archbishop, during the whole time, up to the day of his death, through many and various temptations; and now I may boast of it, for I was honoured throughout the whole of that time by many marks of his favour, in which respect indeed I believe that no one went beyond me. And it is for this reason, I think, that by the secret counsels of the Most High I alone survive, though all the others have been removed out of this world, who with me saw and ministered to the archbishop,—reserved, I believe, for this very task, that as I myself saw the brightness of our master's character more closely and carefully than the rest, so I may hand down his heavenly image to future ages. It is now, whilst I am writing this, the fourteenth year since his death, by the providence of the Most High, who lets not a sparrow fall to the ground without his will, and has spared my life also even to the present hour. And it is well that it is so, for now, with God's aid, shall my pen teach future generations, not only what I myself have seen concerning the life of our master in the flesh, but also those things which have happened since, and through his death, alike precious and triumphant; but let us now proceed with the thread of our history."

The applause of the whole people at the promotion of the chancellor was not, however, unalloyed. The tongue of envy was not silent: some remarked that his election was contrary to the canons, for that the favour of the king, and not the choice of the clergy and people, had secured him his appointment. Others charged him with arrogance and presumption:—" How should a man," asked they, " who had not ventured to put his hand to an oar, now dare to assume the command, and himself to take the helm?—particularly in the Church of Canterbury, where all the convent were of monastic profession, and every prelate had been a regular follower of the religious order. But now they had an archbishop, who in his dress hardly resembled a clerk at all, but delighted in the luxuries of a court, and though all his conversation had been secular, was not ashamed to be exalted to this eminence, nay rather, as they believed, had been eager to be exalted. This did not show him to be a follower of Moses, or of Jeremiah, who had been sanctified to God even from his birth. When Moses was sent to speak to Pharaoh, he hesitated and said, " Who am I, Lord, that I should go and speak to Pharaoh?" In like manner the willingness of the new archbishop was contrasted with the modesty of Gregory, St. Ambrose, and other saints of the Church, when placed in similar situations, and from all these comparisons they draw inferences to his disadvantage. But to meet these hostile murmurs, it was urged by his partizans, that so prudent a man as the chancellor could not fail to have weighed well the matter in his mind, before he undertook so responsible an office: as by accepting it, he would become head of the English Church, so would he bring upon himself the onus of every excess or scandal that should arise; and he must have already decided on bidding farewell to luxury and worldly pleasures, if he intended to discharge his duty as he ought. It was also urged, that he had told the king beforehand what would be the necessary result of his election: it was impossible for him to serve two masters; either he would neglect his God to please the king, or in his zeal for the Lord, he would lose the favour of his earthly sovereign.

This is expressly asserted by Herbert de Bosham, who says, that when the king sent the chancellor into England during the vacancy of the see of Canterbury, he conversed with him privately the night before his departure in the castle of Falaise: the ostensible object was to settle some disturbance on the Welsh frontiers; "But," said the king, "you do not yet know the real reason for your being sent: it is my intention that you shall be made archbishop." The chancellor smiled at these words, and pointed to his gay attire, saying, "You have selected a pretty costume to figure at the head of the monks of Canterbury. If you do as you say, my lord, your mind will very soon be estranged from me, and you will hate me then as much as you love me now: for you assume at present, and will continue to assume an authority in Church matters which I should not consent to, and there will be plenty of persons to stir up strife between us." John of Salisbury also says, that "the chancellor, being a man of much prudence and foresight, and knowing well the duties of an archbishop, saw clearly that he could not accept the office without offending either God or the king—and that he would have finally declined it but for the interference of Henry of Pisa the cardinal, who had no small share in persuading him to come to this decision, for it gave him such an opportunity of promoting the advantage of the Church, as was not likely to occur again. With these arguments were mingled others, all tending in the same direction; and all these were remembered by those who defended him from having forced his way to the mitre solely to gratify his own ambition. It was suspected moreover by some, that Becket seized the opportunity which was offered to him, that he might be in a position to rescue the Church more completely from dependance on the state: for at this period the return of peace and tranquillity throughout the land, had given leisure to attend to matters connected with the courts and administration of justice throughout the country. If this was his motive, it furnishes us with another instance of the fatal blindness which had fallen over the eyes of the king, who is supposed to have elevated Becket, solely that he might depress the Church. Both opinions are, perhaps, equally groundless. The king would think his own attachment to his chancellor a sufficient motive for promoting him, and the chancellor, most probably, hesitated to accept this signal mark of his master's favour on religious scruples alone: when these once began to give way, a revulsion of feeling was easy, and he may have accepted the archbishopric without further hesitation—only that he seems from the moment of his acceptance, never to have done a single act that could disgrace or compromise it.

But the examination of such a question as this, in which the motives and thoughts of individuals are concerned, can be conducted by no uniform standard; we must be content to take the characters of men as best exemplified in their actions, and in the adaptation of their conduct to the sphere of life in which they are placed. It remains, therefore, for us to inquire in what way the new archbishop conformed himself to the solemnity of that high position to which he had now attained: and it is no slight praise that he himself was aware of the somewhat irregular, though not sinful, career by which he had made his way to so high a dignity. This should not be forgotten by those who charge him with an assumption of piety which he did not truly feel: we should ever spare the modesty of those who are aware of their own imperfections, even if they exceed the usual limits in their attempts to make all the atonement in their power.

That a change in his mode of life was expected of him, is not to be wondered at; it is also more than probable that he deeply felt that necessity, and we think it equally certain that he made that change with no greater rapidity than his own sincere and conscientious spirit would acquiesce in; for we do not believe that he could have brought himself to profess an assumption of religious asceticism to which his heart was a stranger. All his biographers and clerks have dilated at considerable length, on the sudden change in his way of life, from the moment of his attainment to his present spiritual eminence. Let us follow the narrative of his secretary Fitz-Stephen, which though it exhausts all the common-places of devout piety and depth of religious feeling, yet is evidently based on facts belonging to the individual character he is describing, and if the same writer's anecdotes, before quoted, tended to show that Thomas Becket was no ordinary chancellor, the account which we shall here lay before the reader, will convince him in like manner, that the chancellor was changed into a no ordinary archbishop.

"The archbishop, in his consecration, was anointed with the visible unction of God's mercy, and putting off the secular man, was clothed in Christ Jesus: he cast aside the temporal duties of the chancellor; and how to discharge the functions of a good archbishop alone occupied his thoughts.

"To this end he kept watch over his mind with all diligence: his words assumed a serious tone so as to edify the hearer; his works were those of mercy and piety; his thoughts, those of justice and equity. Clad in sackcloth of the coarsest kind, reaching to his thighs and covered with vermin, he mortified his flesh by spare diet, and his general drink was water, in which hay had been boiled. He always, however, took the first taste of the wine, and then gave it to those who sat at table with him: he ate a portion of the meat that was placed before him, but regaled himself principally on bread. All things, however, are clean to the clean, and it is not the food but the appetite which is to blame. He often exposed his naked back to the lash of discipline. Immediately over the sackcloth he wore a monk's habit, as being abbat of the monks of Canterbury; above this he wore the dress of a canon, that he might be in conformity with the clerks. But the stole, that delightful yoke which binds us to Christ, was ever, day and night, around his neck. His countenance externally was fashioned like that of the multitude, but in his inward soul he was very different. In these respects, he took for his pattern St. Sebastian and St. Cecilia; the former of whom, beneath the covering of a military cloak, bore the spirit of a soldier of Christ, whilst the latter, subduing the flesh with sackcloth, appeared outwardly adorned in vestments wrought with gold. In his table and his dress he essayed to be really religious, rather than to seem so. Intent on prayer, he endeavoured to reconcile, and in a manner to unite his created spirit to the great Spirit his Creator. As the interpreter between God and men, he in his prayers commended man to God, whilst in his preaching he commended God to man. He was zealous in reading the Scriptures, and had some one to instruct him in its sacred pages. Sometimes after dinner he conferred with his clerks, hearing them, and asking them questions. His messmates were religious men, and his clerks virtuous and learned. In the same way he had a chosen household, with whom all good men were hospitably entertained, and treated with every respect. In almsgiving he was most munificent, for he sometimes sent four or five marks to the hospitals and poor colleges; sometimes he sent meat and provisions.

"His predecessor, Theobald, of blessed memory, had doubled the regular alms of the bishops his predecessors: and now Thomas, in the spirit of pious rivalry, doubled all Theobald's donations. In order to fulfil this holy purpose, he set aside the tenth part of every thing he received, from whatever source it was derived. In his secret cell he every day, kneeling on his knees, washed the feet of thirteen beggars, in memory of Christ: he then entertained them with refreshments till they were filled, and gave four shillings to each of them. If he was on any occasion, though seldom, prevented from doing this in his own person, he took care to have the duty discharged by deputy. In his solitary hours, it was marvellous how plentifully he indulged in tears, and when he was serving at the altar, you would fancy that he had before him our Lord's passion bodily in the flesh. He handled the holy Sacraments with awe and respect, so that his very manner confirmed the faith and conduct of the lookers-on.

"Further: he received into his house the wandering and needy: he clothed many against the severities of winter. At Canterbury he frequented the cloisters, where he sat, like one of the monks who generally sit there, studying some useful book: afterwards he went to visit the infirm monks, and to learn their wishes, that he might gratify them. He was the comforter of the oppressed, the husband of the widowed, the friend of orphans. He was, moreover, humble and affable to the mild, but severe to the proud. Against the injustice and insolence of the powerful he was lifted up like a strong tower looking towards Damascus; nor did he pay respect to the requests or letters of the king or any other person in favour of any one, if contrary to justice.

"The purity of his life was now perfect, seeing that even when chancellor his morals had been pure. He was a second Moses, often entering, and often going out from the tabernacle of the Lord: entering it at the accepted time for the contemplation of his God, and going out from it in order to perform some work of piety towards his neighbours. He was a second Jacob, at one time paying his visits to the more prolific Leah, at another, to the more beautiful Rachel. He was like one of God's angels on the ladder, whose top reached to heaven, now descending to lighten the wants of man, now ascending to behold the Divine Majesty, and the splendour of the heavenly one! Aloof from the transitory things of this world, he gazed with ardour on the things that are above. His mind was bent on those virtues which render happy this present life, and earn for us the life which is to come. His prime counsellor was Reason, which ever ruled his evil passions and mental impulses, as a mistress rules her servants. Under her guidance he was conducted to Virtue, which, wrapped up in itself, spurns every thing that opposes it, and deriving its origin from itself, again returns into itself, and embracing every thing within itself, never looks abroad for any thing additional. He possessed virtue under four forms. Prudence, which gave him discernment in the notice of things, in the estimate of persons, time, and place, in the avoidance of evil, and the choice of good. He possessed Justice, whereby he studied to preserve to God and his neighbour that which was his own. Fortitude, which vindicates in adversity, and protects the mind from the pain of present evils, and the fear of future ones. Temperance, which checked all tendency to immoderate indulgence in prosperity, recalled him from all licentiousness and desire of the things of this world, as well as from indecent mirth. These four virtues form the true four-horse chariot of Aminadab; the first of Diatessarons! the true harmony of man's life! This is that sweet and delectable concert among men, which fills the ears of the Deity, and brings us to that happy state of being, where apart from every evil, we shall enjoy the accumulation of every thing that is good.

"This state of being was the archbishop's, and by it was he supremely blessed: in all his actions he studied firmness, grandeur, gravity, and decorum: to refer all things to the test of wisdom; to govern himself; to listen to the voice of wisdom, not of the mob; to fear no snares of fortune; to show himself strongly guarded and impregnable against adversity; to believe himself born not for himself, but for all who needed his assistance, and especially for his own Church, the government of which was on his shoulders; to contemplate divine things, even whilst he was on earth; to imitate Jesus Christ, who was born and came down from heaven to suffer; to love him and to keep his commands; and to seek the salvation of himself and the souls committed to his charge. From this it came to pass that Thomas obtained grace in the sight of God, and solid glory among men; all the good bearing testimony in his praise, and passing an unbought judgment upon his worth. This is that which responds to virtue, as the echo answers to the voice, as the image corresponds to its model. Glory is the companion of those who live well, and as it is not to be sought, so is it not to be rejected, but to be ascribed to God. The apostle says, "For if I shall wish to glory, I shall be foolish, but I will speak the truth. Thomas feared this glory and rejected it; lest pride should creep in; seeing that it is written, however just, yet you never can be secure. There is also another vain and false glory, which the proud and vain, rich men and hypocrites, seek; a specious likeness of true glory, but with no recommendation such as is derived from solid virtue. To the eye, indeed, it appears like it, but it is not so in reality. As the good fear the approach of true glory, so do the evil court that which is spurious; or, if they do a work of praise, by their seeking to derive from it glory or reward, they lose both the name and the merit.

"The glorious archbishop, Thomas, contrary to the expectations of the king and of all men, so abandoned the world, and so suddenly felt that change which is the handwork of the Most High, that it filled all with astonishment."

CHAPTER XII.

HIS CHANGED MODE OF LIFE—FIRST ACTS—RESUMPTION OF ILLEGAL GRANTS—THE KING'S RETURN AND INTERVIEWS WITH BECKET.

From the lofty descriptions in which Becket's biographers have related his entrance on the duties of the archbishopric, it has been taken for granted that a sudden and extraordinary change was made in his whole deportment; that on entering the sacred office he assumed the garb and habits of a devotee: and on this assumption his admirers have founded their belief in his miraculous conversion and wonderful sanctity, whilst his enemies have designated his conduct as gross and palpable hypocrisy. But both opinions are untenable. The acts of mortification, which the foregoing accounts disclose, were incumbent on all the ecclesiastics of that period: to wash the feet of thirteen beggars would be thought, in the present day, an offensive assumption of humility, if it were not actually still practised in some countries where the Catholic feeling of perpetuity still exists[1].

[1] In the cathedral at Brussels this ceremony is still publicly performed on Ascension-day.

In the same way, to neglect the person and suffer it to be overrun with vermin was not unusual with ascetics, even from the days of St. Cuthbert. So far from affecting a sudden change of external deportment, and beyond what was practised by other ecclesiastics, "Thomas Becket[2] carried with him on his entrance into the Archiepiscopate, far more of the display of worldly splendour, for which he was remarkable as chancellor, than the custom of the times, and the general expectation of his contemporaries required of him—*after* his advancement, as *before*, his dress and retinue were remarkable for their magnificence—his table for its almost fastidious delicacy,—his companions, for their rank and intellectual accomplishments, —his studies, for their political and philosophical, rather than their religious character—and the only change discernible in his pursuits and manner of living, was such as the change of his rank and occupations would necessarily suggest to a refined taste.

"The facts on which this belief is founded are as follows:—

"1. A letter is extant, written from John of Salisbury to the archbishop, in the spring of 1165, *i.e.* two years after his consecration, pressing on him in strong terms the duty of disen-

---

[2] Froude's Remains, vol. ii. p. 2.

gaging his mind from the class of studies in which he suffered himself to be absorbed, and of concentrating his hopes and thoughts on matters of more lasting concernment. The passage is an interesting one, and shall be quoted entire.

"'My advice to your lordship,' says this excellent man, 'and my earnest wish, and the sum of my entreaties, is this; that you commit yourself with your whole soul to the Lord and to your prayers. It is written in the Proverbs, 'the name of the Lord is a strong tower, the righteous runneth into it, and is safe.' In the mean time, to the best of your ability, put aside all other business; other things are important and necessary; but what I advise is still more important, because more necessary. The laws and the canons may profit much, but not for us under our present circumstances. Believe me, my lord,

'Non hæc ista sibi tempus spectacula poscunt.'

"'These things are better food for curiosity than for devotion. Your lordship recollects how it is written: 'Let the priests, the ministers of the Lord, weep between the porch and the altar; and let them say, Spare thy people, O Lord.' 'I communed with my own heart,' saith the Prophet, 'and made diligent search'—'in the day of my trouble I sought the Lord ;' thus teaching us, that to cleanse and discipline the spirit is the way to ward off the lash of conscience, and to obtain for us the loving mercies of God.

"' Who ever rose with a feeling of contrition from a study of the laws or even of the canons? The exercises of the schools, too, are more likely to puff us up with the pride of science, than to kindle within us any feeling of devotion. I would far rather see your lordship's thoughts employed upon the Psalms, or on the sermons of the blessed Gregory, than intent upon this philosophy of the schools. Far better were it to confer on serious subjects with some spiritual person, and to warm your feelings by his example, than to dwell upon and discuss the subtle controversies of secular literature.

"' God knows the sincerity with which I speak this—your lordship will receive it as it seems good to you. Yet be assured that if you do these things, God will be on your side, and you need not fear what flesh can do unto you. He knows that in our present troubles, we have no mortal arm to depend upon.'

" I have preferred giving this extract entire, to selecting particular passages from it, because there is something in the very tone and spirit of it, apart from the particular sentiments, which absolutely refuses to be explained on the common hypothesis, respecting the archbishop's assumed character. I think it will be felt at once to be written by a sincere man to one whom he believes sincere; and at the same time, by a man disciplined in the ways of godliness, to one who would acknowledge himself as a disciple. If John of Salisbury believed the archbishop to be a great saint, he never would have thought this advice either necessary or becoming. If he had regarded him as a hollow pretender to sanctity, he surely would have addressed him in a less affectionate and confidential tone. It seems scarcely too much to say, that if this letter stood alone, uncorroborated by any parallel facts, yet, while its genuineness was admitted, it would cast a doubt on all the statements of subsequent historians.

"2. Another letter has come down to us, written to the archbishop a few months later, by another intimate friend of his—John, Bishop of Poictiers; in which the latter remonstrates with him on the unnecessary and impolitic magnificence of his retinue and style of living, urging on him the necessity of husbanding his resources, and at the same time of conforming his habits to those of the religious establishment in which he was at that time living as an exile.

"'It will be necessary for your lordship, as far

as one can judge from the present aspect of your affairs, to husband your resources in every possible way; to let your enemies see that you are prepared for any sufferings to which your exile may reduce you. For this reason I have often warned your discretion, and must still anxiously press you to get rid of your superfluous incumbrances, and to consider the badness of the times, which promises you neither a speedy return, nor a safe one. Your wisdom ought to know, that no one will think the less of you, if, in conformity to your circumstances, and in condescension to the religious house which entertains you, you content yourself with a moderate establishment of horses and men, such as your necessities require.'"

These admonitions would have been inappropriate, if the archbishop were such a model of sanctity as is the received opinion respecting him. But it is not difficult to see the truth, which lies between the panegyrics of his friends and the vituperation of his enemies.

"It is obvious that on so sudden a change of station, a person of nice perceptions would, without any intention to affect a change of character, still perceive the propriety of changing many circumstances in his manner of living. Mere good taste, unaccompanied with any more serious feeling, would at once point out to him the unsuitableness of a chancellor's establishment, to an archbishop's office; and a degree of seriousness, even short of what he had already evinced, might, on a crisis of such importance, prompt the reformation of other levities. If Thomas Becket, on his sudden promotion from a mere secular office to the highest post in the English Church, had not entirely changed his external demeanour, he must have been a person of worse taste than there is reason to think of him; and if he had remained the same person internally, of worse feeling. And looking at the external change which actually did take place in his conduct, and the internal change which seems indicated by his professions, neither appear greater in degree, or in any way different from what his previous character would have led us to expect. In short, under each set of circumstances, he exhibits to us the same man."

These quotations may serve to counteract the opinion respecting his extraordinary sanctity, which is alike offensive to truth, and to the character of the man: let us proceed to show what were his first public acts in the new situation in which he was now placed.

It will be remembered that King Henry was in Normandy during the election and consecration, which had been completed according to his instructions by the young prince, his son. The first communication he received from the new archbishop was to resign the chancellorship as incompatible with the office and spiritual duties of a bishop [3]. This message made impression on the mind of the king, who apparently had intended that Becket should retain the highest civil, as well as the highest ecclesiastical, dignity in the kingdom; and he was mortified at this renunciation of it. There can be no doubt that those of the courtiers who were jealous of his superior talents and rapid promotion, would avail themselves of this act, which was at least more hasty than prudence would warrant, to make a breach between him and the king: for "the enemy had already begun to sow tares [4]," and it was already whispered about, that " though the king had made him first his chancellor, and next Archbishop of Canterbury, yet he, nevertheless, now withdraws himself from obedience to the king, and even opposes him in many things. The king's courtiers, studying to please their master, whispered these insinuations into the king's ears, detracting from the archbishop, and treating him as an enemy, though he had never given them cause [5]."

This act of the archbishop, which would seem to be the natural consequence of his late election, was probably executed with too great haste; for the king, it is said, vexed at this unexpected event,

[3] Ralph de Diceto.   [4] Fitz-Stephen.
[5] Fitz-Stephen.

called on him to resign the archdeaconry of Canterbury also, and though the archbishop for a long time delayed to do so, yet in the end he consented. This is another point of which modern historians have availed themselves to malign his character; but the account of the transaction which has come down to us is so meagre, that it is difficult to ascribe to the affair its true character. The archbishop may have been unwilling to sanction the king's interference in a matter which he thought to belong exclusively to the Church, but this defence of his conduct is quite as gratuitous as the imputation which has been, on the other hand, made against him, of an inordinate wish to engross the emoluments of the Church.

These however were points at issue between the archbishop and the king, and as the latter took no further notice of them than the slight displeasure which the resignation of the chancellorship created, we are justified in the inference that no disunion would have arisen from this cause only. But Becket had already, and perhaps with equally imprudent haste, entered on questions of wider moment, which were morally certain to array against him many, and even all of the courtiers and the temporal peers, and even some of the bishops also. The necessities or negligences of former archbishops had led to the alienation of many of the manors and estates belonging to the see of Canterbury: these Becket determined to resume, and in doing so he would have the strict law of the case in his favour, for the alienation of freehold property was fettered with such restrictions as made it very difficult for estates to pass legally from one hand to another. In the case of Church property, the same difficulties exist even to the present day. Some of these lands Becket at once claimed and took possession of: these were principally fee-farms, as they were called; and he resumed his rights over these in a summary manner, by excluding the farmers and taking possession of the lands, without waiting for a decision from the courts[7]. An attempt was made to call him to account for these proceedings, but he replied that he should not plead in the case of estates which were notoriously the property of his see, and had been unjustly alienated[8]. In this way he recovered many estates, and retained them in his possession until his exile, when both these and others reverted to lay hands.

Among those from whom he claimed the restitution of property that had been unlawfully

[7] Herbert de Bosham.

[8] Fitz-Stephen states positively that Becket had previously applied to the king for a licence, which was granted him, to revoke all the estates that had been alienated from the see by previous archbishops.

granted away, was William de Ros, who held seven knight's fees, that had been in some way or the other confiscated on the death of Theobald. But in this instance the archbishop, considering the importance of the estate, or the power of the holder to defend his possession, was content with asserting his claim, and for the prosecution of it awaited the return of the king, who was absent in foreign parts. But this claim fell to the ground altogether, for matters of greater moment arose, which distracted the archbishop's attention, and William de Ros remained in possession of the estate.

Another claim of a similar nature enlisted many of the nobility against the archbishop. Roger Earl of Clare held Tunbridge and its honour, which had formerly been alienated from the see of Canterbury. The archbishop now called on Earl Roger to do homage for the castle and domain, and in particular for that portion of the territory which lay within a league of the walls, and was called the *ban-lieu*. The earl replied that he had no objection to do homage to the archbishop, but he objected to state for what lands the homage was rendered. The matter consequently remained in suspense; but harm resulted to the archbishop from the business, for the Earl of Clare was connected with most of the nobility, and had a beautiful sister, with whom the king had been in love: and many a knight and baron were indignant at an attempt to spoil their kinsman.

The custody of Rochester castle was another subject of contention. Becket claimed this by virtue of a grant of William the Conqueror, and this claim also procured him enemies. As yet, however, no one dared openly to profess his enmity to one who was still supposed to possess a large portion of the king's favour. Some, however, of the parties aggrieved crossed the sea into Normandy, and vented their complaints and their indignation before the king; who pacified them for the moment, and deferred attending to their complaints until his return to England, which was likely soon to happen. This was, no doubt, the conjuncture of things to which Fitz-Stephen alludes as causing so much alarm to many of the chaplains of the king's court. "Moreover," says he, "certain persons about the court, clerks of the king, thinking it more likely that the archbishop's rigid justice would deprive them of certain churches which they had unjustly obtained, than that they would be inducted to any fresh ones, or be promoted to higher benefices during his time, endeavoured both by their means, and by the agency of some of the bishops, to excite the king and the court against the archbishop."

These events, particularly the unexpected resignation of the chancellorship, were no auspicious preliminaries to the meeting of the king and his powerful subject. This interview took place at Southampton, where the king landed soon after Christmas-day, and about seven months after the election of his favourite to the archbishopric[9].

The archbishop, informed by couriers of the king's intention to visit England, hastened down to Southampton, in company with prince Henry the son, to meet him. On their entering the king's lodgings a shout of joy was raised by the by-standers: the archbishop and his sovereign, forgetful of every thing but their former friendship, rushed into each other's arms, and strove to out-do one another in professions of their regard. The king seemed to pay no attention to his son's presence, but gave vent to his satisfaction at meeting his former favourite for the first time since his promotion. Among the things which caused him pleasure were the reports which had reached his ears, of the piety and regard for religion which had characterized all the new archbishop's actions. This may be admitted as likely to have called forth the king's satisfaction; for it was he who had thrust Becket into his present exalted station, and he must have been conscious of the responsibility which would rest on his own

[9] Herbert de Bosham.

shoulders, if his nominee should disgrace or fall short of his high dignity. The archbishop, on the other hand, addressed a few words of congratulation at the king's safe return, and to allow him time for repose after the fatigues of the voyage, withdrew to his own quarters.

They again met at an early hour the next morning, and passed the whole day riding together, apart from the rest of the court, talking over the events which had happened since they had parted. When they had thus enjoyed one another's company for several days, the archbishop, accompanied by his pupil, the young prince, withdrew; and his enemies seeing the favour with which he had been received, dared not open their mouths against him.

CHAPTER XIII.

THE ARCHBISHOP ATTENDS THE COUNCIL OF TOURS

At the time of which we are now speaking, there were many abuses in the Christian Church, and these had been much aggravated by the schism which divided Europe into two great parties. The aspirants to the papal throne were Octavian and Alexander III., the former supported by

Frederic, the emperor of Germany, the latter by the kings of France and England. But the cause of Alexander finally prevailed, and a general council was meanwhile called in the city of Tours. The archbishop of Canterbury made preparations for attending the synod, and first waited on the king to restore the young prince, his pupil, to the custody of his father. After spending a few days in private with the king, at a village called Rumnel, on the Kentish coast, and belonging to the see of Canterbury, he set sail, accompanied by his favourite clerk, Herbert de Bosham, who has given us a narrative of the journey. They landed at Gravelines, on the coast of Flanders, and were received with much respect by Philip, earl of that country. On the following morning, the nobility and gentry flocked from all sides to meet their illustrious guest, offering their houses, their services, and every thing they possessed to do him honour. The same reception awaited him in Normandy, Maine, and the other dominions of the king of England, through which his road lay. He arrived at Tours the third day before the opening of the council, and at his approach all the city was moved, and went forth to meet him; not only the citizens and natives, but the strangers also and foreign ecclesiastics, who had come to take part in the proceedings of the council, thronged the roads to obtain sight of a man whose fame had spread so widely. It was even remarked that the cardinals hastened without the gates of the city to meet him, except two only, who stayed behind, that the pope might not entirely be left alone. At the entrance of the archbishop into the audience-chamber, the throng was so great that the apostolic pontiff was afraid of being crushed, and withdrew into his private apartments. When the archbishop had at length reached the pope's presence, his holiness received him graciously, and having addressed to him a few words of courtesy, dismissed him. "Go now, my brother," said he, "and refresh yourself, for you require rest after the toils of your journey." Upon this the retinue of the archbishop retired to the king's castle, which had been appointed for them to lodge in.

On the following morning his doors were crowded by the numerous ecclesiastics who were in the town, and who came to offer their salutations. The nobles also and magistrates of the city and neighbourhood came to visit him and to do him honour. And the Roman court considered him as by far the most distinguished person of all who had come to attend the council. Their proceedings[7] lasted several days, during

---

[7] The council directed its animadversions in particular against the sale of benefices, abbacies, &c., and other simoniacal practices.

which archbishop Becket procured the confirmation of many privileges which had been granted by former popes to his Church. At length he took his departure, and arrived safely in England, where he was received by the king with the usual tokens of favour and approbation.

CHAPTER XIV.

GILBERT FOLIOT, THE RIVAL OF BECKET.—HIS ORIGIN.—IS FIRST PRIOR OF CLUGNY, THEN OF ABBEVILLE.—ABBOT OF GLOUCESTER, BISHOP OF HEREFORD, AND FINALLY OF LONDON.

WHILST these events confirmed the opinion which universally prevailed of the address and talents of the archbishop, and seemed to justify the king in having promoted him, an individual of whom we must now take some notice, was silently advancing through the different stages of ecclesiastical preferment, and destined to play a prominent part in the events which led to the tragical termination of Becket's career. This was Gilbert Foliot, a man apparently not only of foreign extraction, but born also in King Henry's continental dominions. He was first prior of Clugny, afterwards of Abbeville, and in the year 1139 was raised by the influence of Milo, constable of Gloucester, and Robert Bethune, bishop of Hereford, to be abbat of Gloucester. He held this dignity nine years, and was then advanced to the bishopric of Hereford, which became vacant by the death of his benefactor, Robert de Bethune. The abbacy of Gloucester and the bishopric of Hereford being situated on the Welch frontiers, it was considered of much importance that these offices should be filled by men of talent and high character; for the Church of Wales, at all times refractory against the jurisdiction of the Roman pontiff, was not always submissive to the metropolitan rights of the see of Canterbury.

A collection of letters is still preserved, which attest the zeal of Gilbert Foliot, and the ability with which he administered the duties that devolved on him in both these high stations. Nothing however occurred which demands notice, as being in any way connected with our present subject. But in the year 1161 or 1162, the bishopric of London became vacant by the death of Richard; and now, after a vacancy of more than a year, the bishop of Hereford was selected to succeed him. In consequence of this decision of the Church of London, the following letters were addressed to him by king Henry, the archbishop of Canterbury, and pope Alexander, inviting him to acquiesce in the decision which they had made in his favour:—

LETTER VII.[9]

"THOMAS, BY GOD'S GRACE HUMBLE MINISTER OF THE CHURCH OF CANTERBURY, TO HIS VENERABLE BROTHER GILBERT, BY THE SAME GRACE BISHOP OF HEREFORD, HEALTH.

"THAT the city of London surpasses in grandeur all the other cities of this kingdom, is well known to all of us, my brother: for the business of the whole realm is therein transacted; it is the residence of the king, and frequented more than any other by his nobles. For this reason, it is important that the Church of London, which has now lost its ruler, should receive for its new bishop a man whose personal merit, attainments in learning, and prudence in managing public business, shall not be unworthy of the dignity of that see. After much deliberation in this matter, it is the unanimous opinion of the clergy, the king, ourself, and the apostolic pontiff, that the general welfare of the kingdom, and the interests of the Church, will best be promoted, by your being translated to exercise the pastoral care over the diocese of London. To this end I have received the instructions of our lord the pope, and I enjoin you, by virtue of his authority, to give your assent without delay to

[9] Gilberti Fol. epist. tom. I. ep. 145.

the Church of London, passed in presence of our lord the king, and with the consent of the whole clergy and ourself; and to take the government of the aforesaid Church into your hands with promptitude corresponding to the necessity which exists for its interests to be committed to such an able person. And I entreat of you, my brother, that whereas yon are bound to this by virtue of your obedience to ourself, so you may be led by your own inclinations to undertake the duties of this important trust. Thus, not only sincere affection, but also proximity of place will unite us both in the same good work, to give one another mutual assistance in ministering to the necessities of God's Church."

LETTER VIII.[1]

" HENRY, KING OF ENGLAND, DUKE OF NORMANDY AND AQUITAINE, AND COUNT OF ANJOU, TO GILBERT, BY GOD'S GRACE BISHOP OF HEREFORD, HEALTH!

"Your excellency has been recommended to my notice by the many sound virtues of your mind, and the irreproachable purity of your life. And not to me only, but to every one that knows you, though I have had more occasions than other men to commend you, on account of the

---

[1] Gilberti Fol. epist. tom. I. ep. 147.

sound spiritual advice which you have so often given me, about matters touching my own personal dignity, as well as the state of my kingdom, and public matters in general. For this reason, influenced by the wish that you should be, if possible, always at hand to give me your advice, and considering that this will tend much to the maintenance of my own honour and dignity, as well as to the benefit of my heirs and of my whole kingdom, I pray you earnestly to acquiesce without delay, in the decision which the whole Church of London has lately come to, and which is backed by the mandate of our lord the pope: for you will not only gratify me by so doing, but will, if it be possible, considerably augment the love and favour which I and all my barons already feel towards you. Thus your company will relieve me when I am fatigued both in mind and body by the cares of state; for whenever any thing of moment happens in the kingdom, it is at London that councils are held, and the barons and myself transact public business. Wherefore, that your goodness and virtues may be more widely diffused and made known, our lord the pope has with much propriety assigned to you the charge of the Church of London, to the benefit of the Church itself, which needs such a ruler, and in no small degree of myself, my heirs, and the whole kingdom. Let nothing therefore, prevent you from immediately fulfilling the wishes of our lord the pope, and of ourself, with the addition, as we trust, of your own honour and advantage. Witness, Thomas the archbishop, at Windsor."

LETTER IX.[1]

"ALEXANDER, BISHOP, AND SERVANT TO THE SERVANTS OF GOD, TO HIS VENERABLE BROTHER GILBERT, BISHOP OF HEREFORD, HEALTH AND HIS APOSTOLIC BLESSING.

"From the letters of our dearest son in Christ, Henry, the illustrious king of the English, and of our venerable brother, Thomas, archbishop of Canterbury, as well as by the report of our beloved son Ralph[2], archdeacon of London, we learn that you have been translated to exercise the pastoral care over the episcopal Church of London, good cause and necessity for the same having been shown by the king, because that at London is his royal residence, where he spends the greater portion of his time, and where his barons and nobles assemble to deliberate on the business of the state. Wherefore, inasmuch as the aforesaid city is pre-eminent above the other cities of his kingdom, it is the king's wish that the Church

---

[1] Gilberti Fol. epist. tom. I. ep. 146.
[2] Radulphus de Diceto the historian.

of that capital should be intrusted to the charge of a bishop, whose learning both in canon and in civil law is superior to that of his contemporaries. For as he has committed the custody of his soul to your keeping, he wishes to have you near his presence, that he may consult you when necessity requires. Wherefore, we also, wishing to gratify him who is our dearly beloved son in every way we can, consistently with God's service, and in respect of your reputation for religion, honesty, and learning, have assented to the king's wish in this particular, provided always that the Church of London has unanimously required it, and we do hereby signify to you, my brother, by this our apostolical letter, to acquiesce in the recommendation of our brother, the archbishop aforesaid; and without delay or excuse, to undertake the charge of the aforesaid Church of London, and provide for its necessities, both spiritual and temporal, as you best, with God's assistance, may be able. For though we know that your religion and honesty would lead you rather to minister in an humble station than to preside over a large and famous diocese, yet you will not hesitate to take upon you a burden which God's providence demands that you shall bear. For though the sacred canons forbid translations from one Church to another, without sufficient and manifest cause, yet we, considering the reasons which the king has propounded to us, as aforesaid, and in regard to the personal wishes of his majesty, have acquiesced in your translation, for we entertain no doubt that much benefit will, by God's grace, result from your zeal to the whole Church of London aforesaid. Given at Paris, the 18th day of March."

Under these favourable circumstances, Gilbert Foliot assumed the pastoral care of the Church of London; and his high favour both with the king and the archbishop, rendered the accession of future honours more than probable. It cannot, indeed, be said with certainty that Foliot was an ambitious man, or that his advancement at any one stage had been effected by other than lawful means. He had been brought into notice at first by the patronage of Milo and Robert de Bethune, but he was afterwards promoted in consequence of his talents for business, and his own great personal virtues; among which, not the least was the ascetic abstinence which he practised in his mode of life. The rigour with which he repressed all carnal affection was a matter of public notoriety, and had reached the ears of the Roman pontiff, who addressed to him a letter on the subject, cautioning him not to push his severities to such an extreme as to endanger his life, and so deprive the Church of his valuable services.

This letter, however, belongs to a later period, when the mortification of defeated ambition had possibly passed away from his mind, and at a time when he might perhaps have no temptation to relax his austerities, from the prospect of a second chance of obtaining the archbishopric being held out to him.

But, whatever might be the views of Gilbert Foliot when he was bishop of London, there can be little doubt that while bishop of Hereford, he was at first opposed to the election of the chancellor, or that he withdrew his opposition when he perceived the unanimity with which all concurred in his rival's promotion. Among the historians who have written of this period, is Gervaise[a], the chronicler of Canterbury, who was admitted a monk of St. Augustine's on the very day that Becket was consecrated primate: his words are as follows:—

"A.D. 1161, died Theobald, of blessed memory, archbishop of Canterbury, primate of all England, and legate of the apostolic see, on the 18th of April, and in the twenty-second year of his pontificate. At this time," adds the same historian, "flourished Thomas, archdeacon of Canterbury, and chancellor; the most influential person in the whole kingdom : he was glorious

[a] Scrip. Hist. Ang. Trysden, p. 1418.

in name, supereminent in wisdom, the admiration of all men for his nobleness of mind, the terror of his enemies, the friend of the king, and second in magnificence to him only; nay, he was the lord and master of the king himself."

This death of the archbishop was a conjuncture which all had expected, and which could create surprise to no one. If, however, there was one man who might be led to view this event with excited feelings, that man most assuredly was Gilbert Foliot. The sound and regular advance which he had hitherto made—and apparently without much seeking on his part, certainly with no inordinate seeking—towards the highest station of the English Church, was no doubt a subject of satisfaction, if not of pride to him; and if he had commenced his career free from the suggestions of worldly or even of spiritual ambition, he might well be excused if the present event gave birth to feelings that had as yet been strangers to his bosom.

The position of things at the death of Theobald was of a most critical nature; and the crisis is one of the greatest importance to the true and impartial consideration of the character of him who forms the subject of our narrative: for the transactions of the year which intervened between the demise of Theobald and the election of his successor, led principally to those animosities, which a few years later had so fearful an issue. That king Henry had already given some intimation of his intentions to raise the chancellor to the vacant archbishopric, may be inferred from the allusions which had already been made before Theobald's death, whether seriously or in jest, to his probable appointment; but we unfortunately are left almost entirely without information of what passed in the interval which occurred before the king's intentions were carried into effect. There is no doubt that the usual cabals respecting the appointment of a new archbishop would begin among the monks of Canterbury, who claimed the right of electing: and if we may judge from a letter of Gilbert Foliot, written apparently after Becket's death, when there was a contest between the monks and the English bishops about the election, we shall hardly doubt that there were similar cabals on the death of Theobald, about the most proper person to be raised to the vacant dignity.

This letter, which has never before been quoted in reference to a question on which it seems to throw some light, is as follows:—

LETTER X.

"TO OUR LORD THE KING, THE BISHOP OF LONDON, HEALTH AND AFFECTION FROM THE BOTTOM OF HIS HEART.

"I HAVE delayed, my lord, to write to your highness, because I knew that you would be informed by your messengers of what has been done in the matters of the Church of your kingdom, even before I should be able to write. At length, however, I write to you, though somewhat tardily, and I beseech you, by God's mercy, not to listen to my calumniators, nor to pay any attention to the slanders which the monks of Canterbury have spread abroad concerning me. They say that I aspire to the archbishopric of Canterbury, and for this reason impede them by every means in my power, and prevent them from electing any other person. God, who is the Truth, knows that this is not true. When I received my first promotion, I was made prior of the Church of Clugny, and afterwards prior of Abbeville. From thence I was elected to the abbacy of Gloucester, and then to the bishopric of Hereford. I am now by translation Bishop of London, and I assert with confidence that I never sought to obtain either of those dignities, to which it nevertheless pleased God to raise me. I therefore, from the inmost recesses of my conscience, declare to my Lord God, that I am satisfied with his bounties, and I say to you also, my lord the king, that your grace has been most abundantly and most sufficiently exhibited towards me in all things. God forbid that I should be thus grasping. God forbid that you yield your assent in this matter. Whether I have impeded them in their election, you, my lord, can yourself determine. Remember what took place in the case of his lordship of Bayeux. The bishops of your kingdom viewed the matter as grave and serious, yet, with God's aid, I persuaded them to acquiesce in his election. The monks alone opposed, because they saw you were particularly bent upon it. The next case was that of Bec. Here again the bishops were most averse, but by my instance and intreaties I procured their assent, which they yielded contrary to their own wishes. We come next to the case of Chertsey. Not only the bishops and abbots, but almost every body in your kingdom viewed the matter with indignation; yet, in order to preserve the peace, and to forward the election which you so much wished, I prevailed on them, though with much difficulty and opposition, to consent, that if the monks of Canterbury would show the least respect to the bishops in pronouncing the election, they would acquiesce in the choice, and so put an end to your anger against them. If, however, they should show a grasping spirit, and should exclude the bishops altogether from being consulted, or taking part in the election, they would in that case be obliged to put it off to a later period; whereas, by gentle conduct, they might at once bring it to a satisfactory termination.

"Consult your own honour, my lord the king, and consider well whether it is most advantageous for yourself to give up the matter wholly to the monks, who are bound to you neither by homage, fidelity, nor personal attachment, or to pay respect to the bishops, by electing the highest person in your kingdom, who are bound to you either by homage or allegiance, and whose duty it is, under God, to support your honour. It would be well, therefore, if so please your highness, that you should adopt some means best known to your modesty and wisdom, to check this arrogance of the monks, who presume so much on your humility, and to direct their attention to some eminent person in your kingdom; that so, whilst the claims of both parties to have the first voice in the election remain to be settled at a future opportunity, whenever it shall arise, the election may now be made by the prior, and some one of the bishops, or by any other mode that God may point out to you, and to your council; whereby the state of the Church may be tranquillized by your wisdom, and the clouds which hang over the kingdom in consequence of this dissension, may, by God's grace, be dispersed."

In this letter the bishop of London wished to point out to the king some particular person for the office, or any person in general who might be deemed best qualified to be placed at the head of the English Church. If he had no individual specifically in view, we should be led to interpret it as a hint to the king in his own favour; but this hint is at variance with his own protestations, that he did not seek promotion: so that it is left to us to conjecture, that the prominent part which Gilbert Foliot had taken against Becket, for ever precluded him from occuping that high station in the English Church, which his great rival, by his untimely death, had relinquished.

These observations seem of importance, to clear the character of Henry II. from the imputation of having thrust into the government of the Church of England a man who was notoriously unequal to the duties required of him, and whose character and whole previous course of life would justly disqualify him for so sacred and so responsible an office. The same remarks will, probably, lead the reader to another inference, which seems to stand forth from the obscurity in which, from our want of more minute information, the history of the years 1161 and 1162 is involved, that at the time when Becket was raised, confessedly by the royal influence, to be archbishop of Canterbury, there was another individual, whose high rank in the Church, and great personal merits, pointed him out as an eligible candidate for the vacant dignity; that this individual was so strongly opposed, as we shall see, to the elevation of the chancellor, that, whether justly or unjustly, his opposition to another's election has been not unnaturally ascribed to a desire of obtaining the honour for himself[5].

[5] The appointment of Gilbert Foliot to the see of London is surrounded by many difficulties. The biographers of Becket are almost entirely silent on the circumstances attending Foliot's promotion, and we are informed by allusions contained in the letters of the period, that he refused from the first to make the profession of obedience to the archbishop: this is hardly reconcilable with the friendly tenor of the letter given in page 145, and still less so with another letter preserved in the Cave manuscript at Oxford, which runs thus:—

"THOMAS, BY GOD'S GRACE, HUMBLE MINISTER OF THE CHURCH OF CANTERBURY, TO HIS BROTHER GILBERT, FORMERLY, BY GOD'S GRACE, BISHOP OF HEREFORD, BUT NOW BY THE SAME GRACE OF LONDON, HEALTH!

"BE not vexed, my dear brother in the Lord, that we have imposed a heavier burden on you, and called you to the care of a larger Church, for the Divine mercy has so ordered it, and we do not doubt that it is for the best. It is, moreover, due to your character, to your good deeds, by which you have distinguished yourself in the diocese of Hereford, that it should now be said to you: 'Friend, go up higher: you have been

CHAPTER XV.

DEDICATION OF READING ABBEY — TRANSLATION OF EDWARD THE CONFESSOR—FIRST MISUNDERSTANDINGS BETWEEN THE KING AND BECKET—COUNCIL OF WOODSTOCK — SHERIFF'S DUES — CHURCH OF EYNESFORD—CLERICAL OFFENDERS —FILLING UP OF THE SEES OF HEREFORD AND WORCESTER.

THE year which elapsed immediately after the elevation of Becket to his high office, passed away in comparative tranquillity, and is marked by two of those brilliant ceremonies with which our ancient Church occasionally gratified the eyes of the people. The first of them was the dedication of Reading abbey, the scanty ruins of

---

faithful over a few things; and have deserved to be made ruler over many things!'

" We have not committed the helm of St. Peter's vessel to a man inexperienced, as your humility expresses it, in the art of spiritual navigation ; but he who has long steered his bark upon a river, should now be called to launch it on the ocean. The lighten candle, which was hidden under the bushel, is now placed upon the candlestick, that it may give its light throughout the Lord's house. . . . . Fear not then to come, whither your own merit calls you, for you shall experience from us all the aid and consolation that you require. . . . . . Farewell, my dearest brother in Christ."

which in our own times, declare how massive and substantial were the works of our ancestors. The king himself attended the dedication of a Church, within whose walls his grandfather lay buried.

The other ceremonial was held at Westminster, for the purpose of disentombing and translating the body of the "glorious king Edward the confessor." To assist in this pious duty, the king and all the nobles and prelates of the realm were assembled: the corpse of the saintly monarch was raised from the ground and deposited in the shrine which still passes under his name, and all classes congratulated themselves on the amity which existed between the head of the Church and the first civil magistrate.

It was evident that the revocation of his Church's property had not estranged from him the affections of the king, and his progress to and from the council of Tours was sufficiently gratifying to the king; for the whole of Europe, with the apostolic pontiff at its head, had publicly expressed their approbation of the man whom he had chosen to fill the highest archiepiscopal see of the west. But the year in which Becket made this triumphal progress through his master's continental dominions did not reach its close, before the fatal storm began to blow, which swept before it all the ties of former friendship between him and his sovereign, all the respect and homage of the world, and left him in solitary dignity, alone to support what he considered the cause of his Church, and to experience a reverse of fortune as sad as his rise had been glorious. Let us trace one by one the causes which led to this unhappy issue.

The archbishop, before his journey to Tours, had conducted his reforms with even-handed justice; and the king, though appealed to by the parties aggrieved, felt evident reluctance to interfere. A case now occurred of downright opposition on the part of the archbishop to the will of his royal master, whereby, also, the king was baffled in attempting to possess himself of a fertile source of revenue. A council was convoked at Woodstock, and among other matters that came before it, was a request from the king to alter a custom which had long existed in the kingdom. The sheriffs of every county used to receive two shillings annually for every hide of land, and the earls and barons enforced the payment of this sum from their vassals, as a compensation to the sheriffs for the benefit of their services [1]. The king now proposed that this

---

[1] E. Grim. Rog. Pont. who states what this service of the sheriffs was, "quatenus tali servitio et beneficio eos a gravaminibus et calumniis hominum suorum cohiberent."

payment should be made into the royal exchequer, and not to the sheriffs. At this proposal all were thunderstruck, and said not a word, except the archbishop, who answered, " My lord, your highness ought not to convert this payment to your own use, for those two shillings are not paid by compulsion or as a due, but by our own choice: and if your sheriffs conduct themselves peaceably towards our people, we shall continue to pay them as before, but if otherwise, no one can compel us." At this the king grew angry, and exclaimed, using his customary oath, " By God's eyes, it shall be enrolled on our exchequer forthwith; and you have no business to oppose my will in this respect; for no one attempts to injure your people without your leave." "Nay," replied the archbishop, " by those same eyes of God, none of the men on my estate shall ever pay it as long as I am alive." This opposition annoyed the king, who said no more on the subject, "but," says the historian Grim, "immediately began to turn his anger against the clergy, because any obloquy which he might throw on them would redound more especially on the archbishop as their head."

About the same time another circumstance occurred, which added to the king's anger: the Church of Eynesford was in the gift of the see of Canterbury, and had been bestowed by Becket on one of his clerks, whose name was Lawrence. The lord of the manor of Eynesford, whose name was William, objecting to his right of nomination, expelled Lawrence's people; the archbishop instantly excommunicated the offender, who applied to the king for protection. His majesty wrote to the archbishop, commanding him to grant William absolution. To this it was replied, that it was not competent for the king to issue such a command, for that excommunication and absolution were matters of spiritual jurisdiction. The king rejoined, that it was an infringement of his royal dignity for any bishop to excommunicate one of his tenants in chief without first consulting him. At length, to pacify the king, for he was become very angry and refused to see the archbishop, the man received absolution. The king, who was then at Windsor, said, "He has done it so tardily, that I now do not thank him for it[2]."

This case would not, perhaps, in itself have given the king much uneasiness, but his royal prerogative was touched, and the turn which the thing took was disagreeable, so that on the whole the king was offended. Other cases were brought before him of a similar description. In the

---

[2] Fitz-Stephen.

diocese of Salisbury, a priest was accused of manslaughter by the relations of the deceased. The priest pleaded his orders and appealed to his bishop: the king's official called on the bishop to inflict justice on the criminal: the accused persisted in denying the charge, and the bishop called on him to disprove it in the way which the canons required, because common report concurred with the voice of the accusers in declaring his guilt, and evidence against him seemed to substantiate the accusation. The prisoner failed to clear himself, and the bishop applied to the metropolitan to pass sentence upon him. The sentence of the archbishop was the same which was usual in such cases: "Let him be deprived of orders, and of every ecclesiastical benefice, and be confined in a monastery, where he may be kept to strict penance during the remainder of his life!" This was the sentence which the Church generally passed on its members for the more flagrant crimes, a sentence sufficiently dreadful, one would suppose, to deter from crime, and equally consistent with the principle of humanity which the Christian faith inculcates. "This is the usual sentence which is passed on clerics," says Herbert de Bosham, "without any mutilation or lopping of the limbs," such as, we may infer, was the barbarous practice of the lay-tribunals.

In the midst of these transactions, Becket did not cease to remind the king that two bishoprics had now been vacant some time, and that the interest of the Church as well as the king's reputation required that they should be filled up as speedily as possible. The see of Hereford had been vacant since the translation of Gilbert Foliot to London[3]; that of Worcester, since the death of John the preceding bishop: and the king showed some intention of long delaying to appoint successors, in order that he might himself enjoy the revenues. This pernicious custom had acquired strength during the preceding reign; but it is one against which Becket stedfastly set his face, not only as archbishop, but when he was chancellor. By his intervention the king had been induced to forego his cupidity, and to deal honestly with the Church. This was the result of the archbishop's interference in the case of Hereford and Worcester. The former see was given to Robert of Melun; the latter to Roger, son of Robert, earl of Gloucester. But the concurrence of this matter with the foregoing causes of uneasiness to the king, could not but produce its natural effect, of augmenting the coolness which had begun between him and the archbishop.

[3] See Godwin de præsulibus Angl. The chronology of these dates 1161, 1162, 1163, as connected with these sees, is involved in great uncertainty.

A case now occurred at Dunstable. Philip de Brois, a canon of Bedford, had been accused of the murder of a knight, but was acquitted in the court of the bishop of Lincoln. But the sheriff, who had an old quarrel with the canon, renewed the charge, and Philip, provoked at this persecution, used opprobrious language, not only of the sheriff but of the king also, before Simon Fitz-Peter, one of the king's travelling justices, and a large audience. For this offence he was immediately convened before the archbishop, and acknowledging himself guilty, pleaded that he had spoken in anger, and was sorry for his offence. The king was urgent on the court to pass sentence, and in order to satisfy him, if possible, Philip de Brois was condemned to have his benefice sequestrated for a year, and to be banished during that time from the kingdom. This harsh sentence was carried into force, and "yet the king was not satisfied [2]."

Two other cases are recorded, one of a clerk [3] in

---

[2] Fitz-Stephen and Herbert de Bosham.

[3] The reader is here cautioned against supposing the word clerk to mean a clergyman in every case. The word is applied indiscriminately to priests, deacons, and a host of inferior officers, and classes of men, amongst whom were included students, men of letters, and generally such as could read and write. It is unnecessary to point out the calumnies to which the clergy specifically have been liable from the misinterpretation of this name.

Worcestershire, who debauched a young lady and murdered her father: the other of a clerk in London, who stole a silver cup. The king wished to have them tried by the lay-courts: the archbishop opposed, on the ground of their being *clerics*. The sentence of the latter is recorded: "he was deprived of his orders, and branded into the bargain to please the king [4]."

All these occurrences recalled to the king's mind what had happened to himself some years previously at York. A burgess of the town of Scarborough, came and informed him that a certain dean had got twenty-two shillings out of him, and gave much annoyance to his wife, whom on his own single evidence he charged with adultery. Now this was in express defiance of a law which the king had recently passed. The dean was accordingly cited, and appeared before the king in presence of the archbishop Theobald, the bishops of Durham and Lincoln, and John, the treasurer of York, who was afterwards bishop of Poitiers. His defence was, that the accusation had been made by two other men, one of them in deacon's orders, the other a layman, and that on her denying the charge her husband had given the money, two shillings to himself, and twenty to his archdeacon, in order to ensure her better

---

[4] Fitz-Stephen.

treatment. This statement, however, he was unable to substantiate, and the king called on the court to condemn him, saying, in great anger, that the archdeacons and deans got more out of his subjects in this manner every year than his own revenue amounted to. When they went to hear the sentence, John the treasurer said he must refund the money, and then, by privilege of his orders, be handed over to the mercy of the archbishop. "What then," said Richard de Lucy, "will you say to the king, whose law has been infringed?" "Nothing," replied John, "the man is a clerk." "Then I will have nothing to do with the judgment," said Richard de Lucy, and immediately went to the king. The clergy soon after returned, and John read aloud the sentence: but the king declaring in great wrath that it was unjust, appealed to archbishop Theobald. But within twenty-four hours he heard of the death of his brother Geoffrey, so that he soon forgot the matter, and never prosecuted the appeal.

Some years had passed since the last affair had happened at York, but the king had not forgotten it, and would perhaps have brought his plans against the privileges of the Church to maturity much sooner, if the see of Canterbury had not been filled first by the mild and placable Theobald, and then by his own bosom-friend and nominee. But at length the subject was brought with renewed importance to his consideration, and the ability with which the new pontiff wielded the powers of the Church, was not inferior to the zeal with which he defended its privileges. This was an unfortunate state of things, when we consider that the sword of the state was at this time in no less able hands, and that its dignities were in no less safe keeping. If, therefore, a contest arose between the two, it would be a war even to the knife. This issue might have been anticipated, and it turned out accordingly. The crisis had arrived: the tie which held the king and the priest together was broken; the antagonistic principles of Church and State were so diametrically opposed, that bosom-friends separated in deadly strife, each to maintain the privilege of his order! The recent charges against ecclesiastics, and the leniency of their sentence,—so it seemed to the king,—excited his indignation, and he set himself to consider in what way he might humble the very man whom he had before taken so much pains to raise to his present elevation.

It was not long before an opportunity offered for inflicting a blow, and it was a mode of showing his anger, to which unfortunately the king, impelled by his bitterness in remembering and resenting injuries, did not hesitate to condescend.

Clarembald, recently elected to be abbat of St. Augustine's, professed to hold his dignity independent of the archbishop: and the king thought it not beneath him to support the abbat in his contumacy: the act of consecration therefore was not performed, because the usual oath of obedience was withheld. At the same time, he encouraged the bishop of London in the design of claiming metropolitan honours for his see, founded on the ecclesiastical constitutions of the ancient British Church.

These events no doubt caused much annoyance to the archbishop, whose prediction, that by accepting his present office, he should lose the king's favour, began so speedily to be verified. Still, however, no open attack had been made either upon him, or upon the rights of the Church; but he received a letter at this time from John, bishop of Poictiers, who in his former quality of treasurer in the Church of York, had offended the king by his pretended leniency towards the ecclesiastical offender. If he had not anticipated open measures of hostility on the king's part, this letter would have removed his doubts, for the first step had already been made by the officials in the diocese of Poictiers.

LETTER XI.

"TO HIS REVERED LORD AND HOLY FATHER, THOMAS, BY GOD'S GRACE ARCHBISHOP OF CANTERBURY, JOHN, BY THE SAME GRACE HUMBLE PRIEST OF THE CHURCH OF POITIERS, HEALTH AND THE BLESSED VIRTUE OF PERSEVERANCE.

"Scarcely one day, my lord, was given to make preparations for my journey, after I received your lordship's letter; for every hour seemed tedious, which delayed the important business that you urged me to undertake. Indeed, the letter drew tears from my eyes: for the earnest style in which it is written implies, I fancy, some little distrust of my friendship; but with your leave, my lord, I would rather your confidence should be wanting than my own zeal. However, I have done as you bade me, and cared nothing what my good people of Poitiers might say about my journey, though I endeavoured to give their suspicions a wrong direction. For this reason I gave out that I was going to Tours to meet the bishop of Evreux[5], Richard de Hamet, the constable, William Fitz-Hamon, and the other officers of the king, who were to assemble there about that time, to arrange terms of peace with the counts of Auvergne. And, indeed, it really was my wish to ascertain how far

---

[5] Rotrou, a son of the Earl of Warwick, and afterwards Archbishop of Rouen.

they were to be relied on, because our friend Luscus, (whose mental vision God has wholly extinguished,) and Simon de Tournebu, constable of Thouars, have just brought certain harsh and unheard-of ordinances from our lord the king. They came to Tours a little before St. Peter's day, and calling on Henry Panatarius to witness, if necessary, that they had faithfully executed their commission, took me apart a little, as if they had private business with myself. Seeing this precaution on their part, I also demanded that one of the abbats, or, at least, some clerk or canon, should be present; but this they refused, on the plea that their business concerned no one but myself.

"They then began with forbidding me, in general terms, and under severe denunciations, to interfere with such things as concerned the king's royal dignity; and when I readily promised to do so, they came to more specific points, forbidding me, 1. To summon before me any inhabitant of my diocese, at the suit either of widow, orphan, or cleric, till the king's law-officer, or the lord of the manor, had failed to award justice. 2. To hear any complaint in cases of usury; or, 3. To pronounce sentence of excommunication against any baron, without first either consulting themselves, or obtaining his consent to my judgment. These were the principal points in which I was said to interfere with the king's prerogative, and this especially in the case of clerics, whose patrimony, however inherited, I was charged with exonerating from all servile obligations. Moreover, a penalty was attached to my persisting in any such usages for the future. They stated too, that in all this they had not gone to the extent of their commission, but that out of respect for my person they had ventured to suppress much on their own responsibility; that the penalties, which in their instructions attached to myself, they would undertake to transfer to others; *i.e.* to the persons who should attend my summons, at the suit of the parties above mentioned; and in cases of usury, to the accused, if he dared to appear before me, as well as the accuser. If, however, I should proceed to excommunicate either of these persons in case of contumacy, or any tenant in capite of the king's whatsoever, without first consulting themselves; such persons should be informed, that the king would not interfere with any retribution they might think fit to exact, either from myself in person, or from my goods, or from the person or goods of any cleric who should dare either to publish or act upon my sentence. To all this I answered humbly and respectfully, that though I had no witness of what they stated to me, still I must refer the whole matter to the judgment of my Church: for that I could not myself resign a right which the Church claimed upon prescriptive usage. Afterwards, when on my having conferred with the Church, it was found that I meant to persist in upholding its privileges, he published these ordinances, first to the barons of Poitiers, and then to the citizens in general. Such was the transaction in which I found an ostensible reason for going to Tours. I added also, that in case I failed to obtain full information, it would be necessary for me to proceed to Sens[e].

"On my arriving at Tours, I found that the officers, whom I mentioned above, having fully determined on proceeding to Auvergne, had that very day set out for the castle of Loches: so I followed them without delay, and at the castle found William Fitzhamon and Hugh de Cleers. The others had started before daybreak for Chateaux-roux. From these I obtained information on my own affair: but what I most rejoiced at was the accident which thus enabled me to lay your letter before Hugh de Cleers. On finding that his Chaplain G—— was not with him, I stated that in case of his absence I was commissioned to supply his place by reading it myself, and interpreting its contents; and afterwards, if he pleased, by writing any answer he might wish to dictate. But as he had not time then for

---

[e] Alexander III. was now residing at Sens.

saying all he wished, I allowed him to retain both your letter to G——, and also that which I had read to himself, until he should have time to reply to them, exacting from him a promise that no one but G——, the chaplain, should see them. He seems to me to feel much for the wrongs which the Church of God is suffering, not generally perhaps, but I believe as regards his master, whose actions he fears will be visited by a judgment.

"The bishop of Evreux and the others I have only pursued by letter. I send the bearer from this castle of Loches, where I am. I have sent a courier to the abbat of Pontigny to beg that he will meet me at Sens, to back the solicitations of the abbats of Clairvaux and Fossa Nova[7], in case they should happen to be at court.

"As soon as any thing has been effected, I will take care to inform you by a trusty messenger. In conclusion, I entreat your lordship to allow your chaplain, my friend Turstan de Burins, to visit me for any time, however short. If you are in want of his services, I will send him back directly."

This letter reached the archbishop barely in time to give him warning of what might be expected: for within a week or fortnight the king followed up what he had begun in Touraine, by

---

[7] A Cistercian Monastery in Latium.

issuing a hasty summons to the prelates and barons to assemble in council at Westminster on the first day of the ensuing October.

CHAPTER XVI.

COUNCIL OF WESTMINSTER.—KING'S MEASURE REJECTED BY THE CLERGY. — HIS ANGER. — HE LEAVES LONDON.—STATEMENT OF THE QUESTION AT ISSUE.—POWER OF THE CHURCH.

The bishops and abbats assembled at Westminster, according to the king's summons, in expectation of having to decide some dispute for precedence between the sees of Canterbury and York; for, notwithstanding the numerous cases in which the claims of the former had prevailed, the successive prelates who ruled the Church of York, had from time to time asserted their independence and separate jurisdiction. It was not likely that Roger, the old enemy of the primate of Canterbury, would yield more readily than his predecessors. The assembled bishops were, however, not very agreeably surprised at the subject which came before them[1]. For the

[1] This account is taken from a contemporary writ Herbert de Bosham's narrative is not so complete, though as usual more declamatory.

king began suddenly to pass some severe censures on the conduct of the clergy throughout his dominions. In the first place he complained of the rapacity of the archdeacons, who made gain of the people's sins, and gratified their own luxurious propensities instead of correcting crimes. To remedy this evil, he required that the archdeacons should be compelled to call in the assistance of his own officials before they took cognizance of offences, and after some more remarks to the same purport, he concluded thus: " I am bent on having peace and tranquillity through all my dominions, and I am much annoyed at the disturbances which the crimes of the clergy have occasioned: they do not hesitate to commit robbery of all kinds, and very often murder also. I therefore demand your consent, my lord of Canterbury, and the consent of all the other bishops also, that when clerks are detected in crimes, and convicted either by the judgment of the court or by their own confession, they shall be stripped of their orders, and given over to the officers of my court, to receive corporal punishment, without protection from the Church. I also demand, that whilst the ceremony of stripping them of their orders is performed, some of my officials shall be present to seize the culprit immediately, lest he should find an opportunity of escaping."

The archbishop of Canterbury requested, before giving an answer to a demand which so closely affected the privileges of the Church, that he might have until the next day to deliberate; but this being refused, he withdrew with the rest of the bishops to consult with them at once in private. The following has transpired as the nature of the deliberation which took place:—

The bishops were disposed to yield; because, as they argued, if clerks were not deterred from committing crimes by their greater privileges, they deserved to be punished more than laymen, and could not complain if, in addition to degradation, they underwent the usual sentence afterwards: and in support of this view of the case, they adduced the authority of the Old Testament, in which it was read that Levites when convicted of the greatest offences were punished with death, and in the case of inferior crimes, with the loss of their limbs.

To this the archbishop replied, that he admitted all they had said, but urged the injustice, both before God and man, of inflicting two punishments for the same offence. "God," said he, "never punishes twice: now the sentence of the Church is either just or unjust. You will not allow that it is unjust: it must therefore be just: furthermore, as it cannot be said to be an acquittal, it is a condemnation. If then the culprit, by being degraded, undergoes this condemnation, he ought not to be submitted to another trial or judgment for the same offence. Besides which, the liberties of the Church are in our keeping, and it is incumbent on us to guard them, or they will be subverted; and we are taught by the example of our great High Priest, that it is our duty to defend them even to the death: now as yet we have not done so."

"But," replied the bishops, "no danger will result to the Church from the loss of her liberties; let them perish at present, rather than that we should all perish: let us do what the king requires, for our escape is cut off, and there will be no one to avenge our death. If we consent, we shall enjoy the inheritance of God's holy sanctuary, and take our rest in the secure possession of our churches. Many points must be waved and dispensed with, in consequence of the depravity of the times in which we live[2]."

At this argument, suggested by their fears, the archbishop's patience was exhausted. "It is evident," replied he, "that you conceal your timidity under the name of patience, and suffer the liberties of Christ's Church to be destroyed. Foolish bishops, who has so blinded you? How can you

[2] This alluded to the schism which had so long distracted the Church.

suffer this pretext of granting dispensation to the wickedness of the times to lead you into open guilt? Do you designate the sacrifice of Christ's Church by the name of dispensation? Let things be called by their proper names, and do not pervert both the one and the other. I grant that much is to be conceded to the times, but I do not admit, on that account, that we may add transgression upon transgression. God can ameliorate the condition of his Church, without our deteriorating our ownselves. Can the gain of the Church be made by the crimes of its teachers? God is only trying you. When is the moment for bishops to face danger? In the time of tranquillity? You blush to say so. It must be then in the time of trouble that the shepherd should expose himself for his flock. It was no greater merit in the bishops of old to found the Church in their own blood, than it is for us to die supporting her liberties. I assert, and call God to witness, that it is unsafe for us to recede from that form of government which we have received from our fathers. We are not justified in exposing any one [of our clergy] to death, for it is unlawful for ourselves even to be present at a trial of life and death."

This speech of the archbishop appears to have been conclusive: the suffragans, who had commenced the debate by a most important argument drawn from the superior intelligence of the clergy, and their consequently meriting, if possible, two-fold punishment for their crimes, were yet unable to reply to the broad statement of the Church's liberties, which their metropolitan urged upon them. They broke off their deliberations, and, returning to the king, told him that their duty to the Church forbade them to give their unqualified assent to his demands. The king, hearing this, and finding that he was likely to be foiled in his attempt, abandoned the immediate point in dispute, and asked the bishops generally whether they would in all things observe the royal constitutions of his ancestors. The archbishop of Canterbury answered for them:—"We will," said he, "in all things, SAVING ALWAYS OUR OWN ORDER." The king, turning to the other bishops, put the same question to all, and received from each, as if by mutual consent, the same answer. Not baffled at this, he pressed them still more urgently, beginning with the archbishop: but all, except one, again returned the same qualified reply. The exception was made by Hilary, bishop of Chichester, who omitted the objectionable words, but he failed in his object, for the king, instead of being appeased by the concession, vented on him some opprobrious language, and left the assembly in a furious passion, without completing any of the matters for which the council had been summoned. The day had already closed in, when the prelates returned to their quarters, and the bishop of Chichester was rebuked by the metropolitan on their way home for having conceded to the king, for by doing so he had broken the unanimity with which their deliberations had been conducted. The next morning the king sent to the archbishop to demand the surrender of the castles and honours which he had received whilst he was chancellor, and had not yet given up. His majesty then, deeply offended with all the bishops for their opposition to his wishes, left London early in the morning, without holding any communication with them, or giving them notice of his intentions.

Thus was an open breach at length effected between the king, on the one hand, and the clergy, with the archbishop at their head, on the other. The quarrel had begun, as we have seen, with certain particular cases of crimes charged against ecclesiastics in different parts; and the attention of the king, who at that time engrossed all the legislative as well as executive functions, had been gradually narrowed from the individual cases, until it was centred on the first principles by which ecclesiastics were exempted from the same jurisdiction as the rest of the community. It is necessary to pause here, and to inquire into the validity of this privilege; or rather into its nature; for however popular opinion may have misrepresented the plea by which Becket resisted the king, as no more than one of those arrogant assumptions which, at a later period, were too common in the Church, the validity of the archbishop's plea has been vindicated beyond a doubt, for it was founded, as the able author of the History of England[3] has shown, not merely on the prescriptive usage of centuries, but on a formal grant of William the Conqueror[4]. It is, therefore, unnecessary to adduce arguments in support of what the legislature itself had made valid: and it will be more to our purpose to inquire what was the nature of the privilege to which Becket attached so much importance; what was the mode in which the immunity was exercised; and, thirdly, the general constitution of the Catholic Church in the twelfth century, and the machinery which it could set in motion to defend itself from the aggressions of the state, from which it claimed to be independent.

1. The tendency of the Christian institution was to soften the enmities, and mitigate the violence of man towards his fellow-man: but when it was first introduced into Europe at large, human passions enjoyed perhaps a freer scope for

---

[3] Turner. [4] See Wilkins's Concilia, vol. i. p. 363.

gratification than at any other period in the history of the world. The brute force of the north had gained sovereignty over all the civilized countries of the south. The temporal sword of Rome had fallen from her venerable grasp: she had found safety in the spiritual weapons of Saint Peter, and the inundation of the barbarians was leavened, ere it had reached its height, by the mollifying influence of religion. An empire of the mind replaced the empire of force, and in every country where the Roman legions had of old sustained the majesty of the Cæsar, the name of the Eternal city was still held up to the veneration of the people by a thousand ecclesiastics, holding their commission from the sovereign pontiff. This order of men comprehended not only those whom we at present call the clergy, but a multitude of persons of inferior rank, similar to the parish-clerks and sextons among ourselves, who indeed are only the remains of a more numerous list of officials. All such were formerly comprised under the name of clerics, and no individual of this extensive class, either in civil, or criminal, or any causes, was amenable to any other tribunal than that of the bishop of the diocese.

But besides this separate privilege of judging its own members, the Church asserted its right of trying all causes in which the plaintiff was a widow or an orphan, and all which related to usury, breach of faith, the right of advowson or presentation to Church benefices; and, lastly, the payment of tithes. We shall see presently in what way such extensive claims were enforced. That they not only had been made by the Church, but acquiesced in by the civil power, is evident from the charter of the Conqueror, to which we have made allusion. This then is a most important fact, and a fact decisive against those who have charged Thomas Becket with claiming powers to which he was not entitled, and of throwing every kind of vexatious impediment in the way of his sovereign. Nor does this conclusion tend to lower the character of that able monarch in our eyes. He was a man of enlarged views, who turned all his own personal triumphs to the benefit of his people: his reforms were unfortunately in advance of the spirit of the age: those of the chancellor and the archbishop were free from this imperfection. Hence it is that though, like many a victorious leader, his premature death prevented him from witnessing it, his cause finally triumphed, and the verdict of posterity must be given according to the laws which existed at the time when the contest took place, and not as they have been modified by the increasing intelligence of succeeding centuries.

Thus much then for the privileges which the Church enjoyed: if however these privileges were abused, and served only to expose the laity to be spoiled and oppressed by the clergy, no legislative enactment can maintain them, no prescriptive right be heard in their defence. How then stood this matter? it has been observed that Christianity was a religion of peace: it looked with horror on the punishment of death: for the principles of the New Testament were opposed to severe punishment: "Let him who is without sin cast the first stone at the offender," was the principle of its humane penal code. Now the Church did not claim jurisdiction over lay-offenders, but only over its own members: hence the latter became exempted by their orders from the punishment of death. But short of this were many grades in the penal law of the twelfth century, from all which clerics were equally secure by the privilege of their order. Mutilation of the person and loss of limbs were favourite punishments with the king's justices. Will these inflictions be viewed with favour by the legislators of the present times? It is, perhaps, hardly too much to say, that those who inquire minutely into the merits of the civil and ecclesiastical codes of penal law prevailing in the days of Henry II., would wish rather to see the clerical immunities extended to all the people, than taken away from those who already enjoyed them. But we have already seen in the award passed by Becket himself, what was the nature of the punishment awarded to clerical offenders. Let us add one more instance, taken from a letter of pope Alexander in answer to a case that was referred to his decision [6].

"Concerning Adam, the forger, about whom you wrote to us, our reply is, that you deprive him immediately, whether present or absent, of every ecclesiastical office or benefice for ever; and if he ever returns into the country, you will arrest him and place him in a monastery to spend the remainder of his days in solitary confinement."

A host of such instances might be adduced, and it is curious to remark, that the experience of seven hundred years has not led the most humane and benevolent of our modern reformers to advance in penal legislation one step beyond the point to which the Church attained so long ago.

But what was the machinery which the Church possessed, and which she could put in motion, to give effect to her ordinances, and to preserve her privileges? In the first place, it must be observed [7], that in the time of Henry II., the catholic Church was one compact machine, of which no

[6] Gilb. Fol. Epist. II. p. 67.
[7] The following remarks to the end of the chapter are taken almost verbatim from Froude's Remains, vol. II. p. 49.

individual part could move without giving an impulse to the rest. The Churches of Italy, France, Germany, and England, were cemented together by closer ties than now unite any two dioceses in this country. Men of letters from all parts of civilized Europe talked a common language; intermingled with one another in the course of their education; expended large sums of money in keeping up their correspondence; frequently met one another at the great centre of ecclesiastical intelligence, the court of Rome; were in many instances promoted from one country to another; and now and then were concentrated at once by the calling of a general council. A large number of persons so united could not fail to act in some degree as a body; especially as there was recognized throughout the whole mass, a strict system of subordination, which secured a union of action, even where there did not exist a union of opinion. Inferiors were subjected to superiors by well-defined laws, through which they seldom dared to break, however audacious might be their attempt at evasion. In the case of Thomas Becket, for instance, as we shall see throughout the whole of this history, his suffragans profess in all stages of their disobedience to be acting in accordance with law; and the necessity which obliges them to this, very materially interferes with the efficiency of their opposition. If he gives an order which they are determined to resist, their first endeavour is to prevent its delivery; and for this they have recourse to the most violent measures; the ports are blockaded along the coasts of England and Normandy; the persons of all who embark or debark are carefully examined; and the most savage penalties are inflicted on any who are found with letters, either from the pope or the archbishop. If by chance the messenger escapes their vigilance, and duly delivers his orders in the presence of witnesses, an appeal to the court of Rome is their next resource; and that not with any prospect of obtaining a favourable sentence, but because by so appealing they procure, (1.) a respite from the obligation to immediate obedience; for by the ecclesiastical law any time short of a year from the delivery of the sentence was allowed to the appellant for collecting his evidence: and (2.) a chance of intercepting the second messenger, who, after the term of appeal had elapsed, would have to convey the repetition of the order. If both attempts fail, an embassy is sent to Rome from Henry; and this last expedient succeeds on more than one occasion. But whatever are the partial successes of Becket's opponents, the complicated process by which they are obtained, sufficiently attests the difficulty of obtaining them, and the magnitude of those impediments which the Church system opposed to independent action on the part of its inferior officers.

Again, the machinery of the system was so arranged, that the punishments with which the Church visited individual offenders, indirectly affected large masses of people: each sentence caused a general commotion. The obedient were made the instruments of punishing the disobedient, and thus two purposes were at once answered; the faithful were themselves more closely united by acting together against the aliens. To go into particulars:—the process of excommunication, or, as it was then styled, of drawing the sword of St. Peter, was so contrived as to cause the greatest possible sensation within the circle where the offender was known. The sentence itself was pronounced by torch-light; at its conclusion the torches were extinguished, and the bells tolled; a messenger was then forwarded to all the clergy within the jurisdiction of the dignitary who pronounced it; it was repeated in all the Churches, and posted on the Church doors. And all those to whose knowledge it came, were forbidden, on pain of a similar punishment, to hold any communion, *i.e.* friendly intercourse, with the excommunicated person. Thus it was at any time in Becket's power to create a sensation through the whole province of Canterbury, and if the pope echoed his sentence, throughout civilized Europe.

But the sentence of excommunication was resorted to very sparingly. It was kept in reserve against great occasions, or as a last resource when milder methods had proved ineffectual. If a noble committed any offence against the Church, his first warning was conveyed in a studiously temperate remonstrance: if this failed, it was intimated to him in a courteous but very serious tone, that in case he persisted it would be necessary to proceed farther. The next step was a formal notice, that unless he repented before a certain day, his property would be put under an interdict, —a threat which, according to circumstances, might be executed with various shades of severity. But such a sentence, even in its mildest form, could not fail to create a very strong impression.

And if the sentences of the Church were calculated to do this of themselves, there was something still more striking in the manner of delivering them to the offender. On this point the instructions given by the archbishop to Idonea, a nun, to whom on a very critical occasion he entrusted a sentence against the archbishop of York[a], will speak more vividly than any description. He writes to her as follows:—

[a] Epistolæ S. Thomæ, I. ep. 196. ed. nos.

"God hath chosen the weak things of the world to confound the mighty.

"The pride of Holophernes which exalted itself against God, when the warriors and the priests failed, was extinguished by the valour of a woman: when Apostles fled and denied their Lord, women attended Him in his sufferings, followed Him after his death, and received the first fruits of the resurrection. You, my daughter, are animated with their zeal, God grant that you may pass into their society. The Spirit of love hath cast out fear from your heart, and will bring it to pass that the things which the necessity of the Church demands of you, arduous though they be, shall appear not only possible but easy.

"Having this hope therefore of your zeal in the Lord, I command you, and for the remission of your sins enjoin on you, that you deliver the letters, which I send you from his holiness the pope, to our venerable brother, Roger, archbishop of York, in the presence, if possible, of our brethren and fellow bishops; and if not, in the face of all who happen to be present. Moreover, lest by any collusion the original instrument should be suppressed, deliver a transcript of it to be read by the by-standers, and open to them its intention, as the messenger will instruct you.

"My daughter, a great prize is offered for your toil, remission of sins, a fruit that perisheth not,—the crown of glory, which, in spite of all the sins of their past lives, the blessed sinners of Magdala and Egypt have received from Christ their Lord.

"The Lady of Mercies will attend on you, and will entreat her Son, whom she bore for the sins of the world, God and Man, to be the guide, guard, and companion of your steps. He who burst the bonds of death, and curbed the violence of devils, is not unable to restrain the impious hand that will be raised against you.

"Farewell, bride of Christ, and ever think on his presence with you."

Nor was the danger slight which Idonea was thus summoned to incur;—if, at least, we may judge from what happened on another occasion of much less importance. In the summer of 1166, search was made in the neighbourhood of Touque in Normandy, for certain messengers of the pope and the archbishop, who had delivered to some of the courtiers letters at which the king took offence. "Here," says one of the archbishop's correspondents, "the pope's messenger was taken. He is still imprisoned, and in chains. Here, too, the Lord saved master Herbert out of the hands of his pursuers. Surely he should not have exposed himself so on a matter of such little importance." And this is explained still further by another correspondent, who writes, "You know in what a strait the messenger was who delivered the letters to the king. His finger was thrust into his eyes; as if to tear them out, till the blood flowed; and hot water was forced down his throat, till he confessed that the letter came from M. Herbert. He is not yet released from prison, though the king has received an order to that effect from his mother."

The extent of the machinery here described, and the severity with which those were visited who dared to set it in motion, prepare us to believe that its effects could not have been regarded with indifference. And this we shall find to be the case most fully in the sequel. What has been mentioned, however, may be of advantage, as giving us some idea, to begin with, of the kind of warfare by which an unarmed Church was enabled to maintain its ground, and assisted by the good wishes of the peasantry, to withstand the united efforts of a powerful king and an incensed nobility.

Let us now return to the point of the history from which we digressed.

CHAPTER XVII.

JOHN OF SALISBURY BANISHED.—CORRESPONDENCE WITH THE PAPAL COURT.

THE first person who felt in his own person the ill effects of the king's anger after the council of Westminster was John, surnamed of Salisbury, the confidential friend of the archbishop, and elevated after Becket's death to the bishopric of Chartres. He was now exiled from England, as we learn from a letter of the abbat of St. Remy [1].

"There is a clerk from England living in exile here among us, a great friend of mine, in whose fortune, whether good or bad, I have long felt much sympathy. He is a man of great literary attainments, and the more one knows him the better one likes him. He is at present suffering from the displeasure of the king, and, as I think, most undeservedly, as all he has done is, that he has served the archbishop most faithfully. This person is John of Salisbury, so well known on both sides of the water. You would much oblige both me and him if you and the count of Flanders would petition the king in his behalf,

[1] Epistolæ Joan. Sares. XIX.

and get him pardoned, so that he might return home and enjoy his property again."

Other causes of uneasiness preyed upon the archbishop's mind: the archbishop of York and the bishop of London still continued their endeavours to undermine the metropolitan rights of his church; though it is difficult to imagine how they would have divided between themselves that preeminence which they used all their combined exertions to extort from their common enemy. The archbishop in these straits looked to the pope for consolation, and availing himself of a letter just received from his holiness, which required an answer, he poured forth his grievances in these terms.

LETTER XII.

"TO HIS HOLINESS POPE ALEXANDER.

"THE letter of consolation, which your holiness has vouchsafed to send me, would be a balm to a mind less deeply wounded than my own: nay, if my sorrows had proceeded from a single cause, I should have seen a ray of hope that they would soon be over. But the malice of the times increases daily; our wrongs, and Christ's, which makes us feel them still more, become greater and greater, and wave follows wave so fast in this sea of calamity, that we see nothing but shipwreck before us. There is no chance left for us, but to arouse Him who is sleeping in the vessel, and say, 'Lord save us, we perish!' The iniquity of our persecutors vents on us its malignity the more freely, because of the attenuated condition of the holy Roman see: so that what they heap upon our heads, be it good or bad, runs down over our beards even to the skirt of our clothing. Christ is despoiled even of that which He earned for himself with his own blood: the secular power has wrested from Him his inheritance; the authority of the holy fathers is set at nought, and the canons of the Church fail to protect even the clergy. But it would weary your holiness to relate in writing our sufferings; we have, therefore, sent master Henry, whose fidelity is known to you as well as to us; and what he will tell you by word of mouth is entitled to your belief, as much as if we ourselves had spoken it. And would to God, holy father, that we could address you by our own mouth, rather than by another's. We speak to you as to our father and to our lord; let this not be told in public, for whatever is said to you in the conclave, is brought to the king's ears. Woe is me, that I am reserved for times, in which such evils have come upon us. What privileges did we once enjoy, and with what bitter bondage are we now atoning for them! Truly we would have fled, that our eyes might not see the violation of the Crucified One! But whither should we flee, save to Him, who is our refuge and our strength?

Let your consideration be directed, my lord, to the matter of the Welsh, and Owen who calls himself their prince;- for our lord the king is most excited and indignant on this subject. Dearest father and lord, farewell[3]!"

This plaintive epistle was accompanied with others which he addressed to four of the cardinals. Master Henry, the bearer, hastened with all speed to the papal court, which was at this time held in Sens, Italy being still occupied by the emperor and the rival faction. Before many days he dispatched the following missive to inform the archbishop of the success of his mission.

LETTER XIII.

"MASTER HENRY TO THE ARCHBISHOP OF CANTERBURY.

"I DID not see the count of Flanders, and thought it neither safe nor worth my while to lose time in trying to find him.

"At Soissons the French king listened to my business with much pleasure, and forwarded the abbat of St. Mard, a man of gravity and discretion, in my company, with letters to the pope:

[3] Epistolæ B. Thomæ I.

but the more important parts of his instruction were committed to him by word of mouth, for the king would not trust his secretary to write them. On taking my leave, his majesty, holding my hand in his, pledged himself on his royal word, if ever you visited his dominions, to receive you, not as a bishop or even as an archbishop, but as a brother-sovereign. The count of Soissons, also, assured me solemnly, that if you ever came into his territories, all his revenues should be placed at your lordship's disposal, and if I would take Sens on my way back, he would write you a letter to the same effect.

"Having finished my business at Soissons, I hastened to court in the prior's company, through the estates of Earl Henry, because this way was the shortest, and my companion was a guarantee for my safety. Two days before I was admitted to the pope's presence, the prior delivered the king's letters, and the commission with which he was entrusted by word of mouth. At length I had an audience: His Holiness, on receiving me, sighed deeply, and betrayed other signs of dejection. He had already heard all that took place in the council,—the persecution of the Church, your lordship's firmness, which of the bishops stood by you, how he went out from among you who was not of you, and the sentence passed upon the cleric; indeed every thing, even what had been done most secretly, was known before my arrival to the whole court, and even talked of in the streets. A private interview was then granted me, in which I laid before His Holiness the several heads of our memorial. He, on his part, praised God without ceasing, for vouchsafing to the Church such a shepherd: indeed the whole court loudly extol in your lordship that courage, in which themselves are so lamentably deficient. As for themselves, they are lost in imbecility, and fear God less than man. They have just heard of the capture of Radicofani in Tuscany, and in it of the pope's uncle and nephews, together with several castles belonging to the fathers of certain cardinals, which have surrendered to the Germans. Besides this, John de Cumin has now been a long time at the emperor's court, and count Henry absents himself from the pope's presence, and no messenger has of late arrived from the king of England: and other concurring events have so terrified them, that there is no prince whom they would dare to offend; nor would they, if they could, raise a hand in defence of the Church, which is now in danger all over the world. But of this enough.

"What has been the success of your lordship's petitions, you will doubtlessly hear from the prior, and from the bishop of Poitiers, who by God's grace arrived here the day before myself, and has laboured in your lordship's cause with most friendly zeal. His Holiness declines altogether to offend the king, and has written to the archbishop of York, in a tone rather hortatory than commanding. However, he will send over a brother of the Temple, to mediate between your lordships on the subject of the Cross, and to settle any dispute that may arise in the interim. At all events, the archbishop of York is not to carry his cross in your diocese; this we obtained by dint of perseverance. To the bishop of London he has written in the same strain, and the only effect of the letter will be to make his pride insolent. Indeed, the pope feels this, and sends your lordship a copy of the letter, that you may judge for yourself whether to forward or retain it. As to the profession, his lordship of Poitiers has debated this point with the pope repeatedly, and we have at last obtained a promise, that if on being demanded, it is formally refused, then his holiness will extort it. The bishop will explain this in his second letter; the subscription will distinguish the second from the first. In the matter of St. Augustine's we can obtain nothing. The pope asserts that he has himself seen grants of his predecessors which he cannot revoke, securing the privileges now claimed by that monastery. Lastly, on our requesting that His Holiness would send your lordship a summons to appear before him, he answered with much apparent distress, 'God forbid! rather may I end my days, than see him leave England on such terms, and bereave his Church at such a crisis.'

"May God preserve your lordship in all your ways. At Citeaux, Pontigni, and Clairvaux, by the pope's request, prayer is offered daily for yourself, and your Church. May my lord inform me shortly how he fares, that my spirit may be consoled in the day of its visitation."

LETTER XIV.

"THE ABBAT OF ST. REMY TO JOHN OF SALISBURY.

"TRULY, my dear fellow, you have fixed on a most agreeable place of exile: all kinds of pleasures, however vain, abound in Paris; rich entertainments and choice wines, such as you cannot get at home, and the most charming society. But all this is nothing new: did you ever know a man who did not like Paris? it is a most delightful place, a perfect garden of pleasure. However, many a true word is spoken in jest. O Paris, what a place art thou to beguile and fascinate! what snares hast thou to catch people with! what enticements dost thou hold out to draw men into temptation! what shafts dost thou launch forth to pierce the hearts of the foolish! And my own John thinks so too, and so he has made Paris the place of his exile! I hope he may find it insufferable in good earnest, and get back home again, as soon as possible, to his own country!"

LETTER XV.

"JOHN OF SALISBURY TO ARCHBISHOP BECKET, OCT. 1163.

"EVER since I have been on this side of the water, I seem to have been breathing an entirely different atmosphere: and the country round is so rich, and the inhabitants so happy, that it is quite a change to me after my late troubles. The count, at the request of Arnulf his uncle, had sent some of his men to receive me on my landing: they treated me with the greatest civility for your lordship's sake, and conducted me through the earl's territories, as far as St. Omer's, without charging me any of the usual duties. At this town I met a monk who had known me formerly at Chilham and Trulege, and now introduced me at the monastery of St. Bertin's. The ecclesiastics of this country are generally well disposed to your cause, and you must thank the earl and monks for their good-will when you have an opportunity.

"On arriving at Arras I found that Count Philip was at Castle Ecluse, before which the tyrant of Ypres was so baffled. Thus far God protected me on my journey, and now I found the very man I was seeking for almost in the very road. Count

Philip was out in pursuit of wild fowl, like most men of his fortune, and was eager to learn from me the state of things in England: for my part, I was glad to have so easy an opportunity of fulfilling your commission without further loss of time or expense. He asked many questions about the king and the nobles, and I answered him without offending him, and yet without deviating from the truth. He sympathizes with your troubles, and promises his assistance. When you require ships, he will furnish them: if you are driven to this, send your steward Philip to make a bargain with the count's sailors.

"The next day I reached Noyon, where, to my astonishment, every body knew what had taken place in England, and many things were talked of as having happened at the councils of London and Westminster which I did not know myself, though nothing was exaggerated or perverted. I pretended not to know all they talked about, but they would not believe me. You will be surprised when I tell you that the Count of Soissons told me all the articles of the so-called London council, as minutely as if he had been there himself: not only of what passed in the palace, but in almost every private circle. The French must have had some very active agents among us. The dean of Noyon, a most excellent man, is much concerned to hear the situation in which you are placed: he will receive you hospitably, and place his services and his property at your disposal. Before he had heard of the difficulties in which you are involved, he intended to visit the pope on your behalf, but now he will wait till he hears from you again. I was told at Noyon that the French king was at Laon, and that the archbishop of Rheims was not far off, waiting to have an interview with his majesty, but I was prevented from going to see them by the wars which the archbishop is carrying on against the count de Ruzero and others: so I came to Paris instead. The people here seem to enjoy abundance of every thing: the church ceremonies are performed with great splendour, and I thought, with Jacob, ' Surely the Lord is in this place, and I knew it not;' also in the words of the poet,

> ' Blest is the banish'd man who liveth here!'

"After having settled myself in my lodgings, I went and laid your business before the king: he expresses great sympathy in your sufferings and promises you assistance. He said he had already written to the pope in your favour, and will, if necessary, write again, or see the pope in person. The French are much afraid of our king Henry, and hate him most intensely, but this between ourselves. As I could not see the archbishop of Rheims, I sent your letters to the abbat of St.

Remy[4]; but you had better write to him yourself by one of the monks of Boxley, or some other person, and send him a present. He may be of great use to you, for he is an important man in this country, and through this, and the favour of the king, has much influence with the court of Rome.

"I did not go to court, because I would not excite suspicion, and the bishop of Poitiers tells me the pope is acquainted with my motives. On the receipt of your letter I told Lord Henry of Pisa, and William of Pavia, how detrimental it would be to the Church to concede what is demanded of you. When I hear from the bishop of Lisieux, and the abbat of Saint Augustine's, I shall go to court. Master Henry, who is there, will send me information of their arrival: though I hardly know what I shall do when I get there, for you have so many things against you, and so few in your favour. Great men will very soon be there, bestowing their bounty with a lavish hand; and Rome never yet was proof against bribes, and none of them would like to offend the king. Moreover, there are grants from the Church of Rome in their favour, and in a cause like this, bishops and friends are alike disregarded. The pope, indeed, has hitherto himself opposed us, and

[4] Formerly Abbas Cellensis.

is always complaining of the privileges which his predecessor Adrian granted to the see of Canterbury. By the way, Adrian's aged mother is still living in penury amongst you.

"Now what can we do, needy as we are, against such powerful enemies? We have only words to offer, and the Italians will not listen to them: for they have learnt from their own poet not to buy empty promises. You tell me in your last letter to offer them two hundred marks, but the others will immediately offer three or four.

> ' 'Tis vain, for if we offer all our store,
> In hopes to win, Iolas offers more.'

I will answer for the Italians, that their respect for the king and his messengers will lead them to take a large sum from them rather than a small sum from us. Not that they do not sympathize with your lordship, and the interests of the Church in general, but that your enemies endeavour to undermine you, and say that you are guided by obstinacy rather than a laudable perseverance; and, what is more, I have heard it whispered about, that the pope is to be invited to England to crown the young king. It is even added that his holiness will take possession of the see of Canterbury, and remove your lordship's candlestick out of it; but this I do not believe, for he is certainly grateful to you for your exertions in the Church's cause. When the bishop of Lisieux comes, he will stick at nothing, for I have already had a specimen of his tricks, and, as for the abbat, who can have any doubts about him? They tell me that the bishop of Poitiers cannot succeed in the matter of Saint Augustine's, though he has tried hard in the business: but as your lordship wishes it, I will go and see what I can do. If, however, I fail, it will not be my fault, for as the poet says,

> 'The doctor cannot always cure
> The patient's gaping wound,
> Which sometimes, baffling all his art,
> Inveterate is found.'"

LETTER XVI.

"JOHN, BISHOP OF POITIERS, TO THE ARCHBISHOP OF CANTERBURY, FROM SENS, NOV. 1163.

"REPORT had anticipated the arrival of your messenger, and I was already on my way to the court, but not in time to convey thither the news. All was known, and every body thanked God that you were bold enough to speak the truth before princes. You have not only sustained but surpassed the fame of all previous archbishops. The Church was more powerful in their days, and kings more submissive, and there was no schism to distract our holy Roman mother. God will give you courage to persevere, and reward your perseverance; but it is vain to look to Rome for support against the king.

"Your messenger and I have hitherto got an answer to only one of your requests, and that not in writing. But Henry of Pisa thinks the bishop of London will be compelled to renew his profession of obedience; but he is more sanguine than I; for my own part, all my arguments have failed. I urged that his translation put an end to all former obligations; that he had vacated his former see before he could accept his present, and that consequently, by vacating, he had severed his connexion with Canterbury; that in a translation from one province to another, a new profession is required as a matter of course; that his late conduct at the council showed the necessity of exacting from him a new profession; and lastly, that all persons who received a second fee from the same lord did homage a second time for it. To all this they replied, that a new profession was unnecessary, except in case of a translation from one province to another, and that your lordship could have no plea for requiring a fresh profession, except that the former was made to the former archbishop individually, and not in virtue of his office. In the matter of the abbat of St. Augustine, you will in vain look for either support or sympathy.

"Wherefore, my dear lord and father, you must bow to God's will, and look only to the Church over which He has appointed you. This is your only hope, as it seems it is mine also. God grant that I may precede you in exile, or at least share it with you. Nor can we complain thereof, for we once, through the vain love of this world, together abused prosperity, and it is but just that we should together suffer adversity. Cardinal Henry is preparing for us a place of refuge, and he tells me that he has informed you, through the abbat, that he will do the same for you. I am going to ask the prayers of the monks of Pontigny in our behalf. Human aid is denied; let us ask aid from above. The pope himself has ordered the Church of Clairvaux to intercede for us. Farewell, my lord!"

CHAPTER XVIII.

CABALS AND ATTEMPTS TO SHAKE THE ARCHBISHOP'S RESOLUTION.—INTERVIEW WITH THE KING AT WOODSTOCK.—COUNCIL OF CLARENDON.

THE evil results of a contest of principles are much aggravated when the contending parties are men of superior minds, each used to triumph in what he undertakes, and therefore equally averse to make concessions. This was the nature of the strife which had now begun between Henry II. and his former favourite: each of them had hitherto run a career in which their own great abilities and the favour of fortune seemed to vie with one another in ensuring their success, and both were now embarking in a contest wherein their talents were to be equally baffled, and success might seem to both from the first to be hopeless. That this is a correct view of the state of things can hardly be doubted, when we consider the rapidity with which both parties made their moves at the beginning of this eventful game of hazard. The month of June, 1162, first saw Becket seated on the archiepiscopal throne; in the following April, *i. e.* ten months after his election, the king and he were still on terms of amity, combining to promote Gilbert Foliot to the see of London. Within six months of this period, how many important events had happened! the king had been foiled in his attempt to appropriate to himself the fees paid to the sheriffs; numerous cases of ecclesiastics accused of crimes and sheltered by the Church, and other events tending to set the king and his favourite at utter variance, had been crowded into this brief interval; and to crown the whole, the king had held a council at Westminster, at which had been propounded a change in the constitution, the most extensive that had ever been attempted since the first existence of the English monarchy. For it must not be forgotten, that the Church in England is older than the throne: when a variety of petty princes divided its broad plains into separate jurisdictions, the archbishop had already achieved an empire over the united minds which no temporal prince could compass over the persons of the English nation. St. Augustine and his successors had held councils and courts, which bound all the Saxon people of England, three centuries before any of the kings of the country could claim the same privilege for his parliament of barons; and though many a minor point of ecclesiastical privilege had from time to time been contended between preceding kings and archbishops, none had ever been instituted involving so wide a principle as that which had now begun. The result of the council of Westminster had sufficed to show the king how firm he would find the archbishop in defending the charge which he had been mainly instrumental in confiding to him. The report of a deliberation so deeply affecting the Church had already spread over all Europe; and in the correspondence which passed between Becket and his emissaries, we may form some notion of the position in which things stood. The pontifical court of Rome was not exempt from the venality which is ascribed to all courts, but which may not unnaturally be supposed to be greater from the extensive connexion between Rome and all Christian Europe.

The consciousness of possessing influence at the court of the sovereign pontiff emboldened the king to take active measures from the very outset of this important contest, and the prospects of the archbishop, as developed in the answers which he got from his correspondents, appeared equally gloomy.

Meanwhile, intrigue was busy at work to undermine the champion of the Church; he was assailed on all sides. The bishops seemed at the best to be mere passive instruments of his will, and, as far as regarded their real sentiments, would have yielded to the king in order to secure peace. They had intimated, indeed, as much at the council which had been held at Westminster, and nothing but the firmness of their chief had kept them from dispersing at the first alarm. The proceedings of November and December, in the year 1163, are involved in much obscurity; and the vague language of the biographers is ill-calculated to give us an exact or definite idea of the cabals and negotiations which were carried on. They lead us, however, to infer, that the lukewarmness of the bishops had not been diminished, though it is equally evident that they did not entirely desert their leader, as some of the contemporary historians appear to intimate. That an attempt was made at this time to deprive him of their support, was due to the insidious counsels of Arnulf, bishop of Lisieux, who had lately incurred disfavour at the king's court, and was come to England to endeavour to effect a reconciliation[4]: "My lord," said he to the king, "it will be impossible for you to succeed in the contest in this manner: if you wish to get the better of the archbishop, you must detach some of the bishops from him, and get them to espouse your interests; thus you will either make him give way when he sees himself deserted, or defeat him by main force, if he still persists in opposing you." This hint was not lost on the king, who immediately set about doing as his wily adviser had suggested.

But Arnulf did not scruple, after this, still to communicate with the archbishop, whose severe censures upon his double dealing at a later period proved that he saw through much which he was compelled by the temper of the times to put up with.

The king was not long in practising his new

[4] E. Grim. Rog. Pont. Will. Cant.

line of conduct, for three of the bishops, Roger of York, Gilbert of London, and Hilary of Chichester, had little difficulty in going over at once to his party. As far as themselves were concerned, they did not hesitate to promise absolutely that they would observe the king's royal dignities, and they expressed their regret that the primate should make such a dissension on account of mere words. The king, on the other hand, assured them, that though he objected to the clause, "Saving their own order," yet it was far from his intentions to require any thing which should militate against their canonical vows.

Thus reinforced, the king's emissaries again assailed the archbishop on all sides, both in public and in private. They urged on him every argument which the nature of the case admitted, the benefits he had received from the king, and the obligation he was under to promote his majesty's pleasure, whereas he was now the only one who opposed him; and they always concluded their reasonings with a pledge and solemn assurance, that nothing would be required of him which should strain his conscience or interfere with his vows to the Church. An emissary arrived at the same time from the pope[s], Philip, abbat of Charity, bringing with him letters from

[s] E. Grim.

his holiness, the import of which was, that the archbishop should yield to the king's pleasure for the sake of peace. Moreover, the abbat explained to him, by word of mouth, that the business was no longer in his keeping; the sovereign pontiff had removed him from all responsibility, and he had now only to consent: he also produced letters from the cardinals[a], asserting that they had received a pledge from the king, that he sought only to have a verbal assent from the archbishop, in order that he might be honoured, as became a king, in the presence of his nobles, and not to strain the conscience of the primate, or to exact from him any thing contrary to the canons. "In this manner," continued the abbat, who was an adept in the art of persuasion, "honour will be done to the king, who will not have the appearance of being defeated; the kingdom will again be at your beck and command as before, and all memory of this quarrel will soon be totally effaced. You know how the king has always been attached to your person, and you have hitherto been devoted to his service. Do not let this bond between you be severed, or all its good results will be lost." These arguments were backed by others, suggested by the numerous

---

[a] The legates, perhaps, who were in Normandy.

parties who endeavoured to lead the archbishop to acquiesce in the king's wishes; and at length his resolution gave way. It would, indeed, have been wonderful if he had still kept his ground against such powerful solicitations. It must however be remembered, that he was not driven from his position by force; for the negotiations had assumed the character of petition and of entreaty, rather than of fair argument; and the assurances which were given him of the king's honest intentions would, he might hope, secure him from any unjust advantage being taken of his concession. In this state of mind he hurried to Woodstock, where the king then was, and coming into his presence, promised to assent to his majesty's royal constitutions and dignities, without any reservation of the rights of his own order. The king, pacified by this submission, received him less coldly than before, but not with all his old energy of kindness, and replied, " You must make this statement in a public audience, for it was in public that you opposed my wishes, and in public you must assent to them. Let us therefore summon a council on a certain day; I will convoke my barons, and you, the bishops and clergy, so that for the future no one may dare to contravene my laws[7]."

In consequence of this interview, a council

[7] E. Grim.

was forthwith convoked, and assembled in the month of January, 1164, at Clarendon castle, one of the royal manors. Some days elapsed before the different barons and ecclesiastics could be assembled. At length the business of the council was commenced. The greater part of the first day was occupied with preliminaries, after which, they proceeded to enumerate the prerogatives which the sovereigns of England had enjoyed by prescription from time immemorial. Several of these were already recited, when the archbishop observed, that there were many men in the kingdom much older than himself, and that for his part he was ignorant what privileges belonged to the crown; and that, as the day was so far advanced, it was better to adjourn the meeting till the next morning. This proposition was agreed to, and the bishops and temporal peers retired to their quarters. The next day the proceedings of the council were resumed: a large number of ancient laws were recited, many of which, bearing hard upon the privileges of the Church, did not properly "belong to the dignities of the crown of England, but were invented and brought forward through hatred of the archbishop, by the malice of his enemies, to enslave the Church[s]." It is not doubtful that the king's partizans would carry

[s] Herb. de Bosham.

out to the utmost the instructions which they had received, for many of them had not forgotten the attack which had been made upon their own privileges, in the resumption of the Church-lands; and they would not be likely to forego this opportunity of taking vengeance. The proceedings of the second and third days of this famous council are involved in considerable obscurity: the language of the biographers, some of whom were present, is more than usually vague and declamatory, and all regard to the order in which the events happened is entirely neglected. The best interpretation which can be put upon their words would lead us to infer that the whole of the second day was spent in reciting such laws and customs as the oldest and most learned men present declared to have been in existence in the kingdom from time immemorial. Among these were many which directly impugned established practice, and tended to deprive the Church of what were considered to be her undoubted rights. The ecclesiastical courts were no longer to decide questions concerning advowsons and the presentation to livings: appeals to the pope were forbidden: excommunication was no longer to be passed against tenants in chief without the king's licence: clerics accused of criminal offences were to be tried in the king's courts, and no one, either bishop or other person, was allowed to cross the sea without first obtaining permission from the king. Besides these there were other constitutions equally objectionable and equally repugnant to the canons of the Church. The archbishop commented on each in succession as they were proposed; and the deliberations of the council were again adjourned at evening.

On the third day the recapitulation of the king's royal dignities being completed, his majesty, who was present during the whole business, made an announcement which seems to have taken the archbishop and even all the suffragan prelates by surprise, and to have at once given a very different character to the whole previous proceedings of the council. "It is my wish," said he, "that these royal constitutions of my ancestors should be now reduced to writing, and signed by the archbishop and others present, in order to prevent any further misunderstandings from arising, either now or at any future time: let the elders of the kingdom, therefore, withdraw at once with my clerks apart, and again return with these laws reduced to writing." This order was immediately complied with, and a roll, containing the laws copied out at full length, was produced and read before the meeting. "Now," resumed the king, "to avoid disputes hereafter, it is my wish that the archbishop shall set his seal to these constitutions."—" And I," replied the archbishop without delay, "declare, by God Almighty, that no seal of mine shall ever be affixed to constitutions such as those[9]." This sudden announcement threw the assembly into confusion. It had been evident that the archbishop was reluctant to give his consent, even by word of mouth, to their deliberations: he had expostulated against the greater part of the constitutions as they were propounded, but had been to a considerable degree fettered by the promise which he had given to observe the king's laws. Now, however, that they were reduced into regular form and specified in writing, he declared that this was contrary to every pledge which had been given him, and he refused his assent accordingly. The king seems to have withdrawn in anger from the apartment, accompanied by some, if not all, of the barons. This, probably, is the critical moment which Gilbert describes somewhat rhetorically, in a letter which will be hereafter quoted entire in its proper place, and in the following terms[1]:—

"We stood by you then, because we thought you were standing boldly in the Spirit of the Lord; we stood immovable, and were not ter-

---

[9] E. Grim: Rog. Pont.
[1] Gilberti Fol. epistolæ 194.

rified: we stood firm, to the ruin of our fortunes, to encounter bodily torment or exile, or if God should so please, the sword. What father was ever better supported by his sons in adversity? Who could be more unanimous than we? We were all shut up in one chamber, and on the third day the princes and nobles of the kingdom, bursting into fury, entered the conclave, where we sat, threw back their cloaks, and holding forth their hands to us, exclaimed, 'Listen, you who set at nought the king's statutes, and obey not his commands. These hands, these arms, these bodies of ours, are not ours but king Henry's, and they are ready at his nod to avenge his wrongs, and to work his will, whatever it may be: whatever are his commands, they will be law and justice in our eyes; retract these counsels then, and bend to his will, that you may avoid the danger before it is too late.' What was the result of this? Did any one turn his back to flee? Was any one's resolution shaken? .... Let the truth then be told; let the light of day be thrown on what was then done in presence of us all. It was the leader of our chivalry himself who turned his back, the captain of our camp who fled: his lordship of Canterbury himself withdrew from our fraternity and from our determination, and after holding counsel for awhile apart, he returned to us and said aloud, 'It is God's will that I should perjure myself: for the present I submit and incur perjury, to repent of it hereafter as I best may!' We were thunderstruck at these words, and gazed one upon another, groaning in spirit at this fall of one whom we had thought a champion of virtue and constancy." This is the account which Becket's enemy gives of the memorable proceedings of the last day at Clarendon, tinctured with the animosity which inspired the writer, but evidently based on truth. We find in the other contemporary documents allusions to the peril with which the bishops of Salisbury and Norwich were threatened, if the king should fail in obtaining the consent of the bishops to his laws[2]. Elsewhere, William, earl of Leicester, and Reginald of Cornwall, are said to have expostulated with the archbishop, and to have represented the danger of driving the king to extremities. Again, Richard de Hastings, grand master of the templars, and another brother of the same society, appear to have used their exertions in the same way to induce the archbishop to consent; but all these negotiations are so inaccurately described, that it is next to impossible to reduce them into their proper order. The council, however, was shortly after broken

[2] E. Grim: Rog. Pont: Herb. de Bosham: Will. Cant.

up. The constitutions were committed to writing but, from the expressions used by all the biographers, it is probable that the archbishop did not sign them after all. The words of Herbert de Bosham are these,—" The king demanded, as a precaution, that the archbishop and his colleagues should affix their seals to them; but the archbishop, though greatly excited, did not however wish to exasperate the king, wherefore also he dissembled for the moment, and did not flatly refuse, but interposed delay, for that the business was of too much importance to be hastily concluded, and the wise man saith that nothing weighty should be done without consideration, whereby he and his bishops could decide better on this matter after a little deliberation. Yet he took one of the writings containing the constitutions, with forethought, as one may say, and by premeditation, to keep by him as a voucher of the cause which he had maintained. The archbishop of York took another copy of the writing, and the king a third, to be deposited in the archives of the kingdom. And thus we turned our backs upon the king's court, and rode off towards Winchester."

As they journeyed along, the archbishop's clerks began to make remarks on the events of the day. Some of them lamented the evil temper of the times in which they lived, others expressed their indignation that one man, even though he were an archbishop, should be able to draw the whole Church after him at his own caprice. One among them gave his opinion still more freely. "The government," said he, "seem disposed to upset every thing: Christ Himself is not safe, nor his sanctuary, from these devilish machinations: the pillars of the Church are shaking, and whilst the shepherd flees, the flock fall victims." He who vented these free expressions of his opinion was the archbishop's own cross bearer: the others said nothing. Meanwhile the archbishop appeared to be in low spirits, and rode apart from his attendants, all of whom were as little disposed to conversation as himself. At length, Herbert de Bosham, taking courage, approached by his side, and addressed him, "My lord," said he, "why are you so dejected? you did not use to be in bad spirits, but now you do not say a word to any of us." "And no wonder," replied the archbishop, "for I cannot help fancying that my sins are the cause why the Church of England is thus reduced to bondage. My predecessors governed the Church successfully, and conducted her through many and well-known dangers; but now instead of reigning triumphantly, she is reduced to servitude, and all for me, miserable wretch that I am. Would that I had perished, and no human eye ever beheld me! But it is all right that the Church should suffer these things in my time, for I was taken from the court to fill this station, not from the cloister, nor from a religious house, or from a school of the Saviour, but from the palace of Cæsar,—a proud and vain man,—I was a feeder of birds, and I was suddenly made a feeder of men—I was a patron of stage-players and a follower of hounds, and I became a shepherd over so many souls. I neglected my own vineyard, and yet was entrusted with the care of so many others. My past life was most undoubtedly alien from the way of salvation,—and now these are my fruits! It is evident that I am entirely given over by God, and unworthy even to be ejected from the hallowed see, in which I have been placed." As he spoke these words the tears burst from his eyes[3], and in this melancholy mood he continued his journey to Winchester.

CHAPTER XIX.

THE ARCHBISHOP SENDS INTELLIGENCE TO THE POPE.—TWICE ATTEMPTS TO LEAVE THE KINGDOM.—UNSUCCESSFUL ATTEMPTS TO EFFECT A RECONCILIATION.

A FEW days after the events which took place

[3] Herbert de Bosham.

at Clarendon, the archbishop dispatched a messenger to inform the pope of what had been done, and meanwhile, according to the spirit of the age, he inflicted every kind of personal privation upon himself by way of penance for his supposed crime, and abstained wholly from performing his sacred duties at the altar. The papal court was still at Sens, so that the messenger returned after an absence of only forty days, bringing with him letters from the supreme Pontiff, in which much sympathy was expressed for the trials to which the archbishop had been exposed, absolution was granted for the weakness of which he had fancied himself guilty, and he was encouraged to bear up with confidence under all his sorrows [1].

On the receipt of this letter the archbishop made a journey to Woodstock, where the king then was, and asked to be admitted into his presence [2]; but he was repulsed from the gates by the attendants, and continued his journey to Canterbury. Here he did not long remain; for report informed him that the king was resolved to enforce compliance with his wishes, and some said that the archbishop's life was in danger. This was doubtlessly false, for even when the dissension had been much aggravated by later events, nothing

---

[1] Herbert de Bosham, Grim, &c.   [2] Fitz-Stephen.

was done on the king's part to show that he ever had entertained an idea of attempting the archbishop's life. It is not necessary to account for what was now done, that we should suppose there was any real foundation for this suspicion; for in the letter which passed between the archbishop and his envoys abroad, frequent allusion had been made to his wish to leave the kingdom. The events at Clarendon had not lessened this desire, and he now determined to put it, if possible, into execution. On the sea-coast of Kent was a manor called Aldington[a], belonging to the see of Canterbury. Hither the archbishop withdrew privately, for by the late constitutions it was forbidden to leave the country without the king's licence, and one night, rising unperceived by his household, he embarked with only two attendants in a small boat which they found on the sea-shore, and attempted to cross over into France. The wind, however, was adverse, and they were driven back, just as day dawned, to the coast of Kent. A second attempt, made in the same stealthy manner, was attended with a like failure: but the servants finding that their master was gone, dispersed, and the household was broken up. One of the clerks returned to Canterbury the next day, and took possession of one of the

[a] Alan of Tewkesbury. Fitz-Stephen calls the place Rumeneye, or Romnel. See page 141.

apartments in the palace. In the evening, after supper, he expressed great sorrow for the sufferings to which his master was exposed, and after sitting to a late hour, he said to the servant in waiting, "Go and shut the outer door of the court, and let us go to bed." The servant, in obedience to his orders, lighted a candle and opened the door to go out, when, to his astonishment, he saw the archbishop alone, seated in one of the corners. At this unexpected vision, the servant ran back in a fright and told the clerk, who would not believe what he heard, until he went out and saw it with his own eyes. The archbishop, who had returned privately, called together those of the monks who were there, and explained to them what he had attempted, and how it had pleased God to defeat his purpose.

The morning had hardly dawned, when some officers of the king appeared at the palace, and stating that they had heard of the archbishop's flight, were proceeding to confiscate his goods and furniture: but they were soon informed of his presence, and retired in great confusion. The news, however, of what had happened spread throughout the kingdom, and the king was much exasperated at this attempt to contravene one of the laws which he had been so eager to have ratified. Some writers have described the conduct of the archbishop in this particular as savouring of treason and rebellion; but this is hardly just: the forms of legislation were not so regular in those days as they are now, and the whole tenor of the narrative declares explicitly that the consent to these ordinances which had been extracted from the archbishop was extorted, was verbal, and consequently incomplete. As the head of the English Church, he represented the English people, the third estate in the constitution. The king and nobles were agreed, but the consent of the Church, which was superior to both, was wanting, or was gained by threats, and, as we have seen, had not been ratified, either by the seal of the archbishop, or by the confirmation of the sovereign Pontiff. The archbishop's wish to leave the kingdom was therefore, in this respect, not illegal.

All parties, however, looked with dismay at what they deemed the rashness with which he maintained the cause that he had espoused, and it was generally reported that the king in particular was offended.

That his majesty might not be deceived by the misrepresentations of his enemies, the archbishop himself went to Woodstock, where the king was, and was this time admitted to an audience, not indeed with the cordiality which had characterized their ancient friendship, but yet with politeness and decorum. In alluding to his recent attempt to cross the sea, the king with some degree of pleasantry, and perhaps irony, observed, "So, my lord, you wish to leave my kingdom: I suppose it is not large enough to hold both you and me." Nothing of importance resulted from the interview, save that each party saw clearly that the spirit of the other was as unbending as his own.

After this, affairs took a different turn by the intervention of the bishop of Evreux, who came to the king's court, then held at Porchester Castle, for the express purpose of effecting a reconciliation between the parties. The king cut him short in the discussion with these words, "It is in vain to talk on this subject, my lord bishop: there is but one way to make peace between us, which is this, that both you and the archbishop shall do your best to procure the ratification of the pope to my constitutions." The bishop accepted the offer, and setting off to the archbishop, urged him by all means to comply with the king's suggestion. He represented to him that by these means he would either remove the responsibility of compliance from himself to one who could much better support it, or he would return to the strife, if the pope should refuse the king's request, with redoubled energy and better prospects of success, knowing himself to be supported by the sovereign Pontiff. The archbishop consented without much difficulty to the advice which was offered him; "for," says his biographer, "he had no doubt whatever that the pope would refuse his consent."

All these negotiations had been carried on within two months after the council of Clarendon, as sufficiently appears by the dates of the following letters, the purport of which makes it unnecessary to state what was the result of this application to the pope.

LETTER XVII.

"THE POPE TO THE ARCHBISHOP OF CANTERBURY, SENS, FEB. 27.

"ALTHOUGH your great prudence and integrity entitle you always to our regard, and make us ever anxious to maintain your honour, yet we must watch the temper of the times, and endeavour by prudent management to mitigate the wrath of kings. You know how much zeal our dearly beloved son Henry, the illustrious king of England, has shown in attending to the affairs of his kingdom, and how desirous he is that his arrangements should receive our ratification. Wherefore, when his late messengers, our venerable brother Arnulf, bishop of Lisieux, and our dear son, the archdeacon of Poitiers, petitioned us to grant the legation of all England to the Archbishop of York, and to command you, and all the bishops, to observe the ancient constitutions and dignities of his kingdom, and we unexpectedly modified his petition, he hardly listened to their report, but dispatched Geoffrey, your archdeacon, and Master John, to request the same things again, and even more: and he accompanied his petition with letters from yourself, and the Archbishop of York. In the matter of the dignities, though you and others had given your consent to them, yet we could not grant his request. But that we might not altogether exasperate him against us, and also for your own sake, and considering the evil nature of the times, we have granted the legation to the above-named archbishop. And, forasmuch as condescension must be shown to the will of princes, we advise, and in every way exhort your prudence, to consider well the necessities of the times, and the perils which may befall the Church, and so endeavour to please the king, saving the credit of the ecclesiastical order, that you may not, by doing otherwise, set him against both you and us, and cause those who are of a different spirit to mock and deride us. We will not fail, when an opportunity offers, to speak to the king in every way that may tend to maintain and to increase your honour, and the rights and privileges of your Church. Given at Sens, the 27th of February."

LETTER XVIII.

"THE SAME TO THE SAME.

"Let not your heart fail you, my brother, because the legation has been granted: for the ambassadors gave us beforehand an assurance from the king, and offered themselves to confirm it on oath, that the letters should not be delivered to the archbishop without your knowledge and consent. You cannot believe that it is our wish to humble you or your Church, by subjecting it to any other than to the Roman pontiff. Wherefore we advise your prudence, as soon as ever the king shall be known to have delivered the letters, which we cannot easily believe he will do without your knowledge, to inform us at once of it by letter, that we may, without delay, declare you and your Church and city to be exempt from all legatine jurisdiction."

LETTER XIX.

"TO THE ARCHBISHOP FROM HIS ENVOY.
(SENS, AFTER EASTER, 1164.)

"By the mercy of God, who never abandons those who trust in Him, the king's ambassadors R. and H. arrived at court on the very day that his holiness heard of the death of Octavian, (the antipope,) and they seemed so humble and modest in their communications from the king, whether by letter or by word of mouth, that some of the cardinals, as well as the pope himself, were moved in their favour. They explained at length to his holiness how their master had shown him hitherto the greatest reverence, and would always continue to do so, and they put into his hands the letters about the legation which your archdeacon obtained so dishonourably, whilst I was still with you in England. But as for the conditions on which he obtained them, our lord the king declared, through these his messengers, that he had never made or sought them. Our lord, the pope, took the letters so eagerly, that even some of them who were on his side were surprised at it. How I conducted myself in this matter, and what instructions the pope gave me, I was unable, consistently with my fidelity, to communicate to you until the ambassadors left the court. Afterwards, however, they pretended to be anxious to depart, and then the three cardinals, who are so hostile to you, of Naples, Portus, and Pavia, endeavoured to obtain general letters granting the legation, or at least the same, which had been sent back, made absolute in order to pacify the king. In this, however, they failed, as the pope had before assured me that they never would come into his hands; whereupon they turned the discourse to the matter of St. Augustine, and how they succeeded therein, you will learn from the letters of my colleagues. It is now incumbent on you to protect yourself boldly, and not to be wanting, when God's grace is held out to you so plainly. Farewell, my father.

"The king's envoys said that I was especially obnoxious to their master, and that they would not, for all the gold of Arabia, be in my shoes, if he were to get hold of me. But my fidelity will not be terrified at this, for I say with St. Peter, 'I am ready to go with thee to death and to prison.'"

The negotiations which form the subject of these letters occupied several months, and the death of Octavian, the anti-pope, which happened just after Easter, by relieving Alexander from the anxiety which the existence of a rival had hitherto caused him, was not likely to make him more pliant to king Henry's wishes. But the attention of his holiness was by this very circumstance called off from the controversy to matters of a more agreeable nature, and ultimately his return to Italy removed him to a greater distance from the scene of action. The communication with England was therefore protracted to an indefinite length, and it will not be necessary for us to enter into all the petty intrigues which were carried on by either party; for the third act of the tragedy was now begun at home, in the events which took place at a council summoned to meet the king, and to hear a charge made against the archbishop as oppressive as it was unexpected.

CHAPTER XX.

COUNCIL OF NORTHAMPTON.

In order to understand the nature of the attack which the king—to his disgrace it must be said—now made upon the archbishop, we must bear in mind that when Becket was chancellor, almost all the royal revenues were in his keeping: he had repaired the king's palace in London, besides several other royal fortresses: he had been entrusted with the sole management of the supplies raised to carry on the war at Toulouse, and there is no doubt that in all these different employments more money had passed through his hands than had ever before been committed by a king of England to a subject. The reader will remember that, when he was made archbishop, he had been declared "free from all civil obligations," at the request of Henry, bishop of Winchester, who, according to the usual custom, demanded on the part of the Church that this step should be taken, expressly, as it would seem, to prevent the possibility of so high a dignitary being placed in the humiliating position to which he now was to be reduced. It was no doubt by the mischievous advice of the archbishop's enemies that, though nearly two years and a half had elapsed, he was now accused of malversation during his chancellorship, and required to substantiate his accounts, wherein they said he would turn out to be a defaulter to a considerable amount. Besides this more serious charge, others of a lighter nature were to be made against him, resulting from the attempt which the king had made to enforce the constitutions of Clarendon. The protracted nature of the correspondence with the Roman court, had led his majesty to see how little success he should meet with in that quarter, and he gladly availed himself of this new mode of crushing his enemy by a proceeding totally unconnected with the subject of their previous quarrel.

A general council was summoned to meet at Northampton on Tuesday the 6th of October, in the year of our Lord 1164, for the ostensible purpose of calling the archbishop to account for an alleged injustice to John Marshal, one of the king's retainers, but in reality to prosecute the illiberal proceedings by which the king hoped at length to crush his antagonist.

"On the day appointed (says Fitz-Stephen), we came to the council, but the king, who had amused himself on the road by hawking along every river and stream he came to, entered the town so late that the archbishop did not see him that night[4].

"The next morning, after mass and prayers had been said, the archbishop went to the court, which was held in the royal castle. Having entered the first apartment, he took his seat, waiting for the king, who was not yet come from mass. When at length he appeared, the archbishop rose, and bowing to him with a cheerful countenance, stood ready to salute him on the cheek if his majesty should be willing, but the king made no offer of doing so. The archbishop began the conversation by saying that William de Courci had occupied one of the houses which had been allotted for himself, and requested the king to order him to leave it. The king assented, and gave orders to that effect. The next subject was in reference to a summons that had been sent him to reply to an action brought against him by John Marshal. This man had commenced a suit in the archbishop's court for the recovery of some land that formed part of the archbishop's manor of Pagaham, and during certain days that were devoted to hearing

---

[4] Roger de Pontigny adds that the archbishop's party lodged in the monastery of St. Andrew's.

the cause, he had come with a brief from the king into the court; but the law being against him, he had failed in his cause, whereupon he urged a defect in the archbishop's court, but used for taking the oath required a book of jests, which he took from under his cloak, though the judges of the court would not allow such a book to be used for that purpose.

"The man went to the king, and obtained a summons for the archbishop to appear in the king's court, on the day of the elevation of the Holy Cross. The archbishop, however, did not appear on the day appointed, but sent four knights with letters both from himself and the sheriff of Kent, specifying the injustice which was done by John, and the failure of his evidence. The king, indignant at the archbishop not coming to state this himself, treated the messengers rudely, and uttered severe threats against them for bringing false excuses to him, whereby his summons had been evaded, nor would he let them go till he had made them give bail. After this, at the instance of the same John Marshal, another day had been appointed by the king, who sent the summons to the sheriff of Kent, for he did not choose to write to the archbishop, because he would not put the usual salutation at the beginning of the letter, and this, said the archbishop, 'was the only summons he had received to attend the council; but he was now come, in consequence of the king's command, to answer in this matter of John Marshal.' To this the king replied, that John Marshal was engaged in his court of Exchequer at London, with the collectors and other officers of his majesty's revenue, but that he would arrive the next day, when the cause should be heard. In consequence of this, no more business was done that day : and the archbishop, with the king's leave, withdrew."

On the morning of Thursday, October 8th, which was the second day of the council, all the temporal peers were assembled, and all the bishops, except the bishop of Rochester, and another, whose name is not mentioned, also several of the Norman bishops, when the archbishop was publicly, and without any more delay, accused of treason, because he had neglected the king's summons in the matter of John Marshal, and had given no valid plea for his nonappearance. The archbishop's defence was not listened to, and the king called on the peers to pronounce judgment. It was the opinion of all present, that considering the respect due to the king's majesty, and the oath of fealty and homage which the archbishop had given to pay all due honour to the king, his defence was not admissible, for that he had not pleaded either bodily sickness or such pressing ecclesiastical business as would not admit of his obeying the summons; wherefore they condemned him to have all his goods and moveables confiscated, subject to the king's mercy. But it was necessary that this sentence should be formally pronounced by one of the peers, and bishops and barons were alike averse to discharging this duty; each party trying to shift it off upon the other. The barons urged that they were laymen, and not competent to pronounce sentence on an ecclesiastic and a bishop; to which the bishops replied, and with greater justice, "Nay, this is not an ecclesiastical but a secular court; this office cannot belong to us in particular: we sit here as barons, not as bishops; you are barons, and we are barons, each the peers of the others. If you pay respect to our ordination now, you should have done so before to the archbishop; for if you cannot pass the sentence, still less can we, on one who is our archbishop and our lord." This discussion had begun to wax warm, when the king in anger interfered, and at his command, Henry of Winchester pronounced the sentence. The archbishop, by the advice of his colleagues, bowed to the decision in silence, and all the bishops, except Gilbert of London, who refused, pledged their security for its being submitted to. But though the archbishop made no public opposition to this harsh sentence, he said to those near him, "Though I hold my tongue, all posterity will speak for me, and will exclaim against this iniquitous condemnation!" The same day another charge was brought against him, of having received three hundred pounds from the wardenship of the castles of Eye and Berkhamstede. To this he replied, by disclaiming all obligation to plead on this charge, as he had not been summoned for that purpose; however, he so far would observe gratuitously, that he had spent the money and a great deal more out of his own pocket on repairing the palace at London, and the other castles before-mentioned, as was easy for any one to see. The king rejoined, that this expenditure had been made without his authority or sanction, and demanded that judgment should be passed on that head also. The archbishop anticipated a sentence, by saying that no question of money should ever lie between him and his sovereign, for he would immediately give security for the payment of the three hundred pounds. His sureties were the earl of Gloucester, with two of his own men, one of whom was William of Eynesford. At this stage of the proceedings the council was adjourned till the morrow.

Friday, October 9th.—Third day. The archbishop was informed by a message, that there was a claim on him for five hundred marks, which had been lent him during the war at Toulouse, and also five hundred more advanced him at the same time by a Jew, to whom the king had become surety for the repayment. He was next arraigned, by action of wardship[1], for all the proceeds of the archbishopric while vacant, and of all the bishoprics and abbacies, which had been in his keeping during vacancy in the time of his chancellorship. And he was now ordered to give an account of all to the king. To these demands he replied, that he had received no notice whatever on the subject, and had come entirely unprepared; but that at a fitting time and place he would satisfy the king, if required. The king demanded security of him on the spot; in reply to which, he requested a little delay, that he might communicate with his bishops and clerks: "I do not deny," continued he, "that I received five hundred pounds from the king, but I assert that it was a gift and not a loan, and it is unworthy of his highness now to require payment; it would be more gracious of him to remember the many services which I rendered him at that time, when I was chancellor." But the king turned a deaf ear to all this, and demanded that judgment should be pronounced forthwith.

[1] *Actione tutelæ*, Fitz-Stephen.

The court, both bishops and barons, decided, that as the archbishop admitted having had the money, he must make it good, unless he could prove that it was a gift: they, therefore, called on him to find surety for the payment. To this he replied, that he had property in the kingdom to a much greater value than the sum in question, and it was alike unbecoming the king's majesty to ask for surety, as it was indecorous to himself to be obliged to find it; but the peers reminded him that all his personal property had been confiscated by the sentence of the council, passed on the first day of their sitting, and they added, with acrimony, and to his very teeth, that he must find bail or remain a prisoner. This shameless proceeding was fully countenanced by the king, who urged it on with the most indecent haste, utterly forgetful of the dignity of a king or the generosity of a man. In this emergency, however, five noble spirits were found even in this servile meeting, who stood forward, in open opposition to the king, and became bail each for a hundred pounds of the money in question. Thus terminated the proceedings of the third day[6]; and from this time the temporal nobility looking upon him as marked out by the king

[6] Herb. de Bosham, who calls this the second day of the council, because he combines the proceedings of Wednesday and Thursday in one.

for destruction, no longer went near him, or paid him visits at his lodgings as they had done before, and as many knights continued still to do.

Saturday, Oct. 10. Fourth day.—All the dignitaries of the Church, both bishops and abbats, came this morning to the archbishop's lodgings, to consult what was to be done. The noble-minded bishop, Henry of Winchester, proposed that the king's avarice should be gratified, and he accordingly went himself to the king and offered to pay him 2,000 marks if he would abandon these proceedings; but the offer was not accepted. The council opened the proceedings of the day by calling on the archbishop to reply to the claim, which had been stated the preceding morning, respecting the vacant bishoprics and abbacies. The archbishop replied that he wished to consult his brethren on so important a subject, and for that purpose withdrew with them into a private room. The king, meanwhile, ordered the gates of the castle to be secured, and that no one should leave it without his orders. All now seemed to think that imprisonment, if not worse, would be the archbishop's fate. In the interim, the consultation among the bishops began. Some of the clergy present, and among them Henry of Winchester, said, that the archbishop was bound to resist these oppressions, for that the whole Church was endangered in his person, and that whilst he showed honour to the king, he should not forget the respect due to God and his Church, and that he had no cause to fear, for his enemies could not charge him with a single crime or dishonourable act. He had been delivered over by the king's authority to the see of Canterbury free from all civil claims and obligations, which was no more than was always done, even in the case of a monk taken from one abbey to be made the abbat of another: the brethren always claimed an act of indemnity for him, to save their fraternity from future scandal or annoyance. There were others, however, among the clergy, who leaned towards the king's party, and seemed, indeed, to have had some hint given them by the court how they were to act, for their arguments ran thus: "It is plain that the king's anger is directed against his lordship of Canterbury: he wishes him, no doubt, to resign the see, and throw himself altogether on his majesty's mercy." To this party belonged Hilary of Chichester, who added, "Would to God that you were not the archbishop, but plain Thomas Becket! You must know the king better than we, because you were so intimate with him formerly: but it appears to us that there is no doubt of his meaning: besides, who can be expected to become surety for you to an uncertain, and perhaps a most alarming amount. The king is reported to have said, that either he or you must resign, if both remain in England together. It is better, therefore, to throw yourself entirely on his mercy." This opinion was urged still more forcibly by Gilbert of London, who addressed the archbishop thus: "If you would only remember, my father, the condition from which his majesty raised you, and what benefits he has conferred on you, also the ruin which hangs over the Church and all of us, if you persist in your opposition to the king, you would not only give up your see, but ten times as much, if it were in your power: and, perhaps, the king would recompense your humility by giving it you back again." "It is enough," replied the archbishop, "your opinion is evident: so are its motives."

The argument was now resumed by Henry of Winchester. "This discussion," said he, "is most pernicious to the Church of Canterbury, and ought to make us blush for shame. If our archbishop, the primate of all England, shall set us the example of resigning the cure of souls committed to his charge at the beck and nod of a temporal sovereign, what will become of the whole Church: there will be no more regard paid to rights and privileges; but anarchy will ensue, and the priest will be no better than the people." "True," replied Hilary of Chichester, "but the times are such that the whole Catholic Church is thrown into confusion: the authority of the canons is shaken, and if we act with too much rigour, severity may utterly destroy, what a little mildness and dispensation would have remedied. It is therefore my opinion that we should yield for the moment to the king's pleasure, lest, if we adopt stronger measures, we may be called to a severe account, and suffer worse handling hereafter." The conversation was here interrupted by Robert of Lincoln, a plain, blunt man, though not very famous for discretion. "It seems to me," said he, "that this man's life is in danger, and that he will lose it or his bishopric: what good his bishopric will do him if he loses his life I do not clearly see." "It is indeed too evident," said Bartholomew of Exeter, "that the times are very bad, and if we have it in our power to dissemble a little, and so pass through the worst of it, there is no doubt of the propriety of our doing so; but to effect this, we must not be too unbending: this persecution is against one only, and not against our whole body: it is better for an individual to be in jeopardy, than for the whole Church to suffer." After this, some one asked Roger of Worcester, a near relation of the king, what was his opinion of the matter. "I shall give no opinion," said he, "for if I say that we have received the cure of souls, to resign it at the king's bidding, I shall speak against my conscience, and be guilty of my own damnation: if, on the other hand, I advise to resist the king, there are plenty of his men who will hear me, and will carry word to the king, and I shall be put out of the synagogue, and treated like a public enemy. I have made up my mind, therefore, to say neither the one nor the other."

Thus, then, every one had given his views on the position in which the bishops were placed, but they could come to no decision, and sat some time in silence. All then seemed anxious to adjourn, but they found that the door had been fastened upon them. At last the archbishop said, that he wished to speak to two of the earls who were with the king. The earls were immediately sent for, and the doors were hastily opened to give them admission, for it was suspected that the king's will was about to be complied with. When they had entered, the archbishop said, "We have discussed the whole matter for which our lord the king has convened us; and we wish to consult certain persons, who are better informed than ourselves on this subject, but are not now at hand: we therefore request that this meeting may be adjourned till tomorrow, when, if it please God, we will give our answer." The bishops of London and Rochester were deputed to carry this message to the king. But the former of these, who was the spokesman for the two, gave the message a false interpretation, saying that the archbishop wanted a little delay, in order to make the necessary preparations for complying with the king's request; thus binding the archbishop down to acquiesce. The two earls returned granting the required adjournment, on condition, however, of the archbishop doing as the bishop had said: but on hearing this he was indignant, and explained his meaning, namely, that on the morrow he would give for answer, not necessarily what the king might choose, but whatever should be dictated to him from heaven. The bishop of London was confounded at this failure of his stratagem, and the council broke up: but the numerous knights and others who had all along adhered to the archbishop, and dined in his hall, were now deterred by fear of the king, and no longer went near him. His table would, in consequence of this defalcation, have been almost empty, but in the true spirit of the age, he sent out his servants to call in the poor neighbours, the diseased, the lame, and the blind, saying that they would be a more powerful aid to him in his adversity, than the retainers who had deserted.

The next day was Sunday the eleventh of October, and the archbishop did not leave his lodgings, but his attendants passed the day in deep thought and serious deliberation, for they anticipated on the morrow a renewal of the strife, with but little prospect of its favourable termination.

Early the next day the archbishop was seized with a complaint[7] to which he had been liable, and which deprived him of the use of his legs, insomuch that it was necessary to place heated pillows to his loins. The king hearing this, thought that it was a deception, to avoid coming to the council, and sent to inquire whether it was his intention to appear. The bishops informed the messengers that the archbishop was ill, and unable to get up: but the king was not yet satisfied. Wherefore the earls of Leicester and Cornwall took upon themselves to ascertain the truth, and went to his lodgings for that purpose. Here they found him in bed as had been reported, and unable to move. "Let no one," said he, "suppose that this is a device on my part to avoid going to the council; for to-morrow I will go at all hazards, even if I am carried thither in a litter[8]."

The next morning, which was Tuesday the 13th of October, the archbishop rose early and went to mass, giving orders for the introit, which begins with the words, "Princes sat together against me," to be used on the occasion. Some of the

---

[7] Morbus Iliacus.   [8] Roger Pont. E. Grim.

courtiers were present, and reported this to the king, signifying that he looked upon himself as a persecuted man, like the first martyr Stephen, from whose mass that introit was taken. Others, who were of a superstitious turn, recollected that this was the hundredth anniversary of the Conqueror's landing [9] in England, and anticipated that some signal event would happen. After mass, he took off the pall and mitre, but kept on his other pontifical vestments, and putting on his clerical cape, and secretly carrying with him a portion of the consecrated bread [10], prepared to attend the council.

But first he held a hasty conference with the bishops, all of whom seemed lukewarm, and willing that he should submit to the king's pleasure. "My brethren," said he, "our enemies, as you perceive, are pressing upon us, and the whole world is against us: but my chief sorrow is, that you who are the sons of my mother do not take my part. Though I were to say nothing, yet all future ages will declare that you deserted me in the battle, me your father and archbishop, sinner though I am, and for two whole days you sat as

[9] The Conqueror landed in England in the year 1066.

[10] It was not unusual in the middle ages to carry about a portion of the consecrated elements as a viaticum, or preservative against danger.

judges over me, and were a mote in my eye, and a goad in my sides,—you, who ought to have taken part with me against my enemies. And I doubt not, from the words which have dropped from you, that you would sit as judges over me in criminal causes, as you have already done in civil matters, before this secular tribunal. But I now enjoin you all, in virtue of your obedience, and in peril of your orders, not to be present in any cause which may be moved against my person: and to prevent you from doing so, I appeal to that refuge of the distressed, the Holy Roman See. Moreover, if, as I have heard it intimated, and, indeed, as is already reported publicly, the secular authority should lay violent hands upon me, I command you, by virtue of your obedience, to put forth the censures of the Church in behalf of your father and your archbishop. For be assured of one thing, though enemies shall press hard upon me, and the world itself be against me, though this frail body yield to their persecution, because all flesh is weak, yet shall my spirit never yield, nor will I ever, by God's mercy, turn my back in flight, nor basely desert the flock committed to my care." One of the bishops present, Gilbert of London, protested against this speech, but it is pleasing to find that the noble-minded Henry of Winchester, together with

Joceline of Salisbury, stayed behind after the others were gone, and endeavoured to give him comfort and encouragement to face the dangers which threatened him.

After this, he mounted his horse, and set out to the place of meeting; but on the way he said to Alexander Lewellen, who carried his cross, "I wish I had adhered to my first intention of going in my proper costume, and with the weapons most suitable to a bishop;" for he had at first thought of walking thither barefoot, carrying his cross, and interceding at the king's feet for the liberties of the Church; but his clerks, and two templars who were present, would not allow him to put this thought in execution. When they arrived in the court of the castle, the archbishop dismounted from his horse, and taking the cross out of the hands of Alexander Lewellen, was proceeding to enter the hall on his way to the king's chamber. Here were some of the bishops and others waiting till the business of the day should begin. Amongst them was Robert of Hereford, who seeing the archbishop coming in that fashion, ran up to him, saying, "Suffer me, my lord, to carry the cross, which is much better than that you should carry it yourself." "No, my son," said the archbishop, "suffer me to retain it, as the banner under which I fight." A little further on was Hugh de Nunaunt, archdeacon of Lisieux, who had come in the archbishop's company. On seeing his patron approaching in such guise, he turned to the bishop of London, and said, "My lord, do you allow his lordship of Canterbury to carry his own cross?" "My good friend," replied the bishop, "he was always a fool, and will continue so to the end." All now made way for the prelate, who entered the apartments still carrying the cross. Upon this the bishop of London going up to him, tried to take it out of his hands, but was unable. "Look now, my lord archbishop," said he, "such conduct as this tends only to disturb the peace, for the king will arm himself with the sword, and then we shall have a king and an archbishop well matched one against the other." "Be it so," said the archbishop, "my cross is the sign of peace, and I will not let it go: the king's sword is an instrument of war:" and with these words he took his seat in a room within the castle-hall.

The bishops were now called into the upper chamber, whither the king had retired, when he was informed of Becket's arrival. Amongst these, Roger of York entered last, preceded by his cross-bearer, in defiance of a mandate that he should not carry his cross in the province of Canterbury. This prohibition he had set aside for a time by an appeal to Rome. The Archbishop of Canterbury was now left in the outer chamber with no one but his clerks about him, and endeavoured to keep up his spirits in the arduous position in which he was placed. "My lord," said Herbert de Bosham, who was seated near his footstool, "if they lay violent hands on you, it is still in your power to excommunicate them all." "Far be it from our lord," answered Fitz-Stephen, "to do as you say: rather let him follow the pattern of God's ancient confessors and martyrs, and pray for his enemies and persecutors: if it please God that he shall suffer in this righteous cause, his soul will enjoy happiness in heaven, and blessings will be bestowed upon his memory on earth." Ralph de Diceto, the historian, John Planeta, and others, who were present, were much moved at these words; and William Fitz-Stephen was again about to speak, when one of the king's marshals touched him on the shoulder with his wand, and said that it was forbidden to speak to the archbishop, whereupon Fitz-Stephen made a sign to his master, pointing to his cross, as if he would recommend him to make that his sole dependence. Many years afterwards, when both of them were in exile together at St. Benedict's on the Loire in France, the archbishop reminded Fitz-Stephen of this little circumstance.

During this conversation, the bishops were with the king and barons in the upper chamber, relating to his majesty the reprimand which they had received for having joined in the condemnation of the archbishop: and they repeated to the king the arguments which he had used to them, to prove the injustice of his being amerced in all his goods and chattels. This, he argued, was contrary to established custom: in London, the customary fine was a hundred shillings; but in Kent, which was exposed to the first attack of foreign enemies, and consequently had heavier burdens to bear, it was only forty shillings; now, as his lands lay in Kent, he ought in fairness to have had the advantage of its laws. Moreover, they told the king of the appeal which he had this very day made to the pope against the sentence, and of the solemn prohibition which he had given against their presuming again to sit in judgment on him. The king, hearing this, was beyond measure indignant, and sent out some of the earls and barons to know if he admitted having done all this, seeing that at Clarendon he had promised in good truth to observe all the king's royal dignities, one of which was, that the bishops should attend his tribunals, except in causes of life and death. They were directed also to ask him explicitly if he would give in the accounts of his chancellorship, and abide the decision of the court. The archbishop having heard all they had to say, returned them an answer to this effect:—

"My lords and brethren, earls and barons of our lord the king: I acknowledge myself bound by oath and fealty to his majesty, as his liege man, and it is my duty to show him all earthly honour and fidelity, saving my obedience to God, the dignity of the Church, and my own episcopal character. I am summoned here to answer in the matter of John Marshal, but am bound to nothing else whatever, neither to answer to any other charge, nor to render any pecuniary accounts. I confess indeed that I had many commissions intrusted to me by the king, wherein I rejoice that I served him well, and not only spent all my own revenues in his service, but became surety for his debts. When I was archbishop elect, before my consecration, the king gave me indemnity for all previous transactions. Most of you are aware of this fact, and all the ecclesiastics of the kingdom know it well. I pray you to make this evident to the king, for it would be unsafe to produce witnesses of the fact, nor am I indeed willing to do so, for I will not litigate the matter. Since I have been archbishop, it has been my sincere wish to benefit the Church; if I am not permitted to do so, I impute it to my own sins, and not to the king. God grants his grace when and to whom he will. As to rendering the accounts, I cannot give surety for doing so. I have already, since I have been here, bound all the bishops and all my friends: nor is it just to compel me to do so, because the decision has not yet been given. I am summoned here to answer in the cause of John Marshal only. As regards the bishops, I blamed them for passing so severe a sentence on a single instance of neglect of court, which did not amount to contumacy. I also appealed from their judgment: I forbade their proceeding any further to judge me: I still appeal from the sentence, and place myself and my Church under the protection of God and the Sovereign Pontiff."

This pointed and pithy speech silenced the nobles, who returned to the king in haste, to report what they had heard, and to consider what was next to be done. Some of them, however, as they retired, talked aloud, so that the prelate might hear them, of the summary and, we may add, barbarous punishments by which former monarchs had treated refractory ecclesiastics [9].

The king now endeavoured to force the bishops to join the court in passing sentence: at this they were all thrown into the greatest consternation, and pleaded the prohibition of the archbishop, which they dared not disobey. In this emergency Roger of York left the council-chamber, calling

---

[9] "Stigandum... nigranti injectum puteo, perpetuo carceri damnavit... Goffridus, comes Andegaviæ... eunuchatorum ante se in pelvi afferri membra fecit," &c.—Fitz-Stephen.

out to his clerks, Master Robert Grandis and Osbert de Arundel, " Let us be off, and not wait here to see what will be done with his lordship of Canterbury." "No," replied Master Robert, " I shall not go, for if his lordship of Canterbury loses his life in this matter, he cannot lose it in a better cause." Bartholomew of Exeter came next, and threw himself at the archbishop's feet: " My father, pray have some consideration for yourself, as well as for us; for we shall, all of us, this day be ruined through the odium which lies against you. A decree has just gone forth from the king, that all who take your part shall be considered as enemies of the state." These intreaties were enforced by Joceline of Salisbury and William of Norwich, who had been threatened with mutilation of their members on the spot, if they any longer sided with him. The archbishop, addressing himself to Bartholomew, said, " Flee, then, my brother, for your thoughts are not bent on defending the cause of God and his Church."

The other bishops had now come to an understanding with the king: it was agreed that they should themselves appeal to the pope against the prohibition under which they laboured; and they assured the king that there was no chance of their being defeated in the appeal, because the archbishop had at Clarendon given his consent to the very laws which he now attempted to prevent from being put in execution. With this view the bishops now came out in a body to their superior, and whilst they all stood before him, Hilary, of Chichester, addressed him thus, "My lord, we have reason to complain of you: you have placed us in a most unpleasant dilemma, by the prohibition which you have given us: when we were all assembled with you at Clarendon, we were required by our lord the king to promise obedience to his royal dignities, and to save us from doubt, they were placed before us in writing: we pledged our assent to them, your lordship first, and then we the suffragans, by your orders. The king then demanded an oath of us, and also that we should attach our seals to the writing: but we replied that our oath, as priests, to observe his laws in good faith, without dishonesty, and lawfully, ought to be sufficient. The king acquiesced in this: yet now, my lord, you forbid us to take part in the proceedings of the king's courts, which, nevertheless, we are bound to do by the laws which you and we swore to observe at Clarendon. We, therefore, hold that you have perjured yourself, my lord, and we can no longer yield obedience to a perjured archbishop: wherefore, we place ourselves under the protection of our lord the pope, and summon you by appeal to his presence."

To this speech the archbishop replied thus:—

"I hear what you say, my lords, and will meet you on the day of appeal: but what took place at Clarendon, was done SAVING THE HONOUR OF THE CHURCH. For, as you yourselves have just admitted, we attached three conditions to our promise, by which our ecclesiastical dignities are safe. For whatever is against the faith of the Church, and the laws of God, cannot 'in good faith' or 'lawfully' be done; nor can the 'dignity' of a king consist in destroying the liberty of the Church, which he has sworn to defend. But besides all this, the king sent his royal dignities, as you term them, to be confirmed by the pope, and they came back not confirmed, but annulled. This is an example which the holy Father has given us to imitate. If we fell at Clarendon, (for all flesh is weak,) we should resume our courage, and again contend with our foe in the strength of God's Holy Spirit. If we pledged ourselves to what was unlawful, you well know that an unlawful oath is not binding."

The bishops again withdrew, and presently all the barons came out in a body, without the bishops, who had been allowed to withdraw. Two of them, Robert, earl of Leicester, and Reginald, earl of Cornwall, who seem to have been generally deputed to transact business of this kind, approached the archbishop to signify to him the sentence which had been agreed on; and Robert, who was the older, was proceeding to address the archbishop, but when he had got to the words, "Hear, my lord, the judgment of the court——;" the archbishop rising hastily, interrupted him—"The judgment of the court—nay—my son the earl, rather hear you me. I came here in the cause of John Marshal; and you talk of judgment in another cause which has not been tried. Is judgment to precede trial? Besides which, when I gave up the chancellorship, wherein your lordship knows well how faithfully I served the king, I was delivered over to the Church free from every civil obligation. I did not seek my promotion, for I knew my own weakness, but the king was pleased that I should be promoted; and his son, prince Henry, when asked how he delivered me over to the Church, replied, Free from all responsibility for the past. Thus then I am not bound to plead in this cause, and will not hear your judgment."

The earl seemed startled at this statement, and said it was a very different view of the question from that which the bishop of London had given the king. Wherefore he turned to the earl of Cornwall, who was as reluctant as himself to proceed with the delivering of the sentence. After exchanging a few words with one another, they agreed that nothing more could be done without communicating with the king, and they requested the archbishop to await their return.

"Am I then a prisoner?" said he. "By St. Lazar, no," answered the earl. "Then hear but one word more, my lord," continued the archbishop; "as the soul is more worthy than the body, so are you bound to obey God rather than an earthly king. Shall the son judge or condemn his father? I therefore decline to receive judgment from the king or you: the pope alone, under God, is my judge. I place myself and my Church under his protection. I call the bishops, who have obeyed the king rather than God, to answer before his tribunal, and so protected by the Holy Catholic Church, and the power of the apostolic see, I leave this court!"

He rose to depart, and a torrent of abuse and of reproachful epithets—traitor! and perjured! was showered upon him as he left the room. In the court below was a heap of wood which had been placed there to burn, and the archbishop in passing struck his foot against one of the logs, which almost threw him down. The mob at this renewed their abuse, headed by his old enemy Randolf de Broc, and began in derision to shoot at him the straws which were lying about the court. A little further on he was met by Hamaline, an illegitimate brother of the king, who reproached him with sneaking away like a traitor, "Were I a knight," replied the archbishop, "my sword should answer that foul speech."

He now mounted his horse, which had been waiting for him at the castle gate. Herbert de Bosham was with him, but could not so easily get near his own horse for the crowd. Here, however, another difficulty presented itself; for the gate was locked and had no key in it: but one of the attendants, Peter de Mortor, espying a bunch of keys hanging in the corner, took them down, and was fortunate enough to open the gate at the first trial.

Meanwhile the king was informed of the cause of all this bustle and disturbance in the castle, and either the bishop of Hereford or some other person who stood near, pointed out what a scandal it would be upon his majesty, if any harm should be done to their metropolitan within the precincts of the royal palace. Upon this the king dispatched a herald, who made proclamation through the streets of the town, that no one should touch, or in any way molest the archbishop. This notification served in some measure to facilitate their departure. But it was only from the followers of the court that danger was apprehended: with the people generally he was not only safe, but a great favourite, and such an immense multitude[1] followed him out of the

---

[1] In the Bodleian copy of Alan of Tewkesbury, and no doubt in the other ancient copies, are added the words " morbo

town to the monastery where he lodged, that it was as much as he could do to hold the cross, guide his horse, and bestow his blessing on those who asked it. "Look," said he to his clerks, "what a glorious procession escorts me home from the tribunal! These are the poor of whom Christ spake, partakers of my distress: let them come in, that we may feast together," and the doors were thrown open accordingly.

The party proceeded first to the high altar of the chapel, where they made their devotions, and then placed the cross which the archbishop had carried before Saint Mary's shrine. They then proceeded to the refectory to eat after the toils of the morning. "This has been a bitter day," said William Fitz-Stephen to the clerks, of whom not above ten remained faithful in this emergency. "Yes, William," answered the archbishop, "but there is a bitterer still to come." Then after a pause he added, "I hope none of you will suffer himself to be betrayed into any unseemly conduct, or reproachful language; whatever abuse may be vented upon you, answer not a word: let them abuse you as they will. To abuse is the mark of an inferior, to bear it, of a superior. If we would teach them to controul their tongues, let us show

---

regio laborantium, " *of persons suffering from the king's evil*: a curious instance of superstition. These words are omitted in the Quadrilogus.

that we can controul our own ears. It is not I who suffer from their abuse, but he who shows that he feels it."

CHAPTER XXI.

THE ARCHBISHOP ESCAPES BY NIGHT TO LINCOLN, AND FROM THENCE TO CANTERBURY—GRAVELINES—ST. OMER'S—SOISSONS.

THE supper hour passed away without much interruption, and the clerk happened that evening to read to them the persecution of Liberius, from the tripartite ecclesiastical history. In the course of the narrative occurred the text, "If they persecute you in one city, flee to another." As the reader recited these words, the archbishop's eyes met those of Herbert de Bosham, as if the same thought had occurred to the minds of both. After this, some knights of the household requested liberty to depart for fear of incurring the king's anger: this was readily granted, and the clerks alone remained. Two of the bishops now appeared with a message from the king: these were, Gilbert of London and Hilary of Chichester, who said that they had found a mode of restoring peace, if the archbishop would assign over to the king, for a time, his two manors of Otford and Muncheaham in consideration of the pecuniary matters at issue between them. To this he replied, "The manor of Heccham once belonged to my archbishopric, and it is now in the king's hands. There is no hope at present of recovering it; yet I would expose this head of mine to any danger rather than resign even the claim to that manor." This answer vexed the two bishops, and on being reported to the king, served only to increase his indignation.

The archbishop now determined to return to his own diocese, and sent the bishops of Rochester, Worcester, and Hereford, to ask of the king a safe-conduct. They found the king in a very good humour, but he told them that they should have an answer to their message the next day. This was an ominous reply, and the apprehension which it created was confirmed by a hint from two noblemen in whom he could confide, that real danger threatened him.

The hour for saying complends was now at hand; and the archbishop signified to the brethren that he intended to pass the night in St. Andrew's Chapel, behind the high altar. This was a mode of combining devotion with security, for the altar was still looked upon as a sanctuary. The monks, who had once before during this week of danger kept vigil with him, proposed to do so again, but he declined their attendance. His bed was accordingly placed as he directed, and he retired at an early hour, as if satisfied with the events of the day, whilst one of his familiar servants lay without to keep off interlopers. His intentions had already been communicated to three persons on whom he could place confidence, Brother Scailman, Robert de Cave, and Roger de Bracy, who were instructed to procure four good horses, not of his own stud, for fear of creating suspicion. This had accordingly been done, and four capital horses were in waiting outside the door of the convent, as if for the use of some of the inmates. Among other preliminaries, Herbert de Bosham was ordered to set off immediately for Canterbury, where his officers were at that very time collecting the rents, and having got as much money as possible into his possession, to await the archbishop's arrival at Saint Omer's[1].

When all was ready they left the monastery by a postern door, and mounted their horses under cover of the darkness. Several circumstances combined to facilitate their escape. In the first place, the guard had not yet been placed at the

---

[1] Another interesting fact is recorded by Herbert de Bosham. The archbishop, before parting from him, gave him a book which he highly valued, to keep till they met again, lest it should be lost in the spoliation which he thought would follow his escape.

north gate of the town, and so violent a storm came on at the moment of their departure, that this, and the ordinary obscurity of the night, effectually concealed them from observation.

The four horsemen made the best use of the night that they were able[3], and arrived whilst it was still dark at a small village called Graham, or Grabam, about twenty-five miles from Northampton. Here he lay down to sleep for an hour or two, and afterwards continued his journey twenty-five miles further to Lincoln, where they arrived about dawn of day. The archbishop had assumed the habit of a novice, and called himself Brother Dearman. His attendants had an acquaintance in the town, named Jacob, in whose house they lodged. From the city of Lincoln the fugitives continued their route by water in a small boat, which conveyed them forty miles down the river to a hermitage belonging to the monks of Semplingham. In this lonely spot they remained three days, for it was certain that the king would send out emissaries to bring them back, and by this delay they hoped to baffle pursuit. From the hermitage they then proceeded to St. Botulfs, a distance of ten miles, and from thence to a place called Haverolot, also belonging to the abbey of

[3] The rain fell in such torrents, that the archbishop was obliged four times to cut off a portion of his long cloak to relieve himself of the weight.

Semplingham. From this point they travelled by night only, and rested during the day, for fear of being recognized, for they were now approaching the borders of Kent, where he was generally known to the people. After eight days, he reached a place on the sea-coast of that county called Estrey, about eight miles from Canterbury, where he considered himself safe, because the place belonged to his own metropolitan church. Still, however, caution was necessary, and he remained concealed in a house (perhaps the parsonage) near the church, where there was a small secret chamber, with an opening into the parish church. Thus he was able to attend the celebration of the Holy Eucharist, and to receive the kiss of peace from the officiating minister, who was in the secret: here also, when prayers were finished, he bestowed the final blessing on the congregation, though they knew it not. At length, a small open boat was procured, and on the second of November, which was the twentieth day since he left the castle of Northampton, the archbishop, after a most tempestuous voyage, arrived at Gravelines, in Flanders.

During these events, the court at Northampton were engaged in serious deliberation what course, under the circumstances, would be the best to follow. The appeal, which both parties had made, prevented the king from confiscating the archbishop's property, and so every thing was suffered to remain in its existing state, but the bishops of London, Chichester, Exeter, and Worcester, together with certain of the lay nobles, were immediately dispatched to prosecute the appeals at the papal court. By a singular coincidence, these emissaries crossed the straits on the same day as the archbishop, and had so boisterous a passage that his lordship of London lost his cape and hood.

The fugitives, on coming to land, pushed the boat ashore on a lonely spot, and commenced their journey on foot over the pebbles and loose sand. They had not gone far before a party of young men met them, one of whom bore a falcon on his wrist. The archbishop's eye brightened at the sight, which reminded him of his early days, and he showed such manifest interest in the bird, that one of them exclaimed, "What, are you the archbishop of Canterbury?"—"Simpleton," said one of the others, "do you think the archbishop of Canterbury travels in this fashion?" This prompt, though accidental reply, saved him from detection, for the news of his flight had already spread on both sides of the water.

The earl of Boulogne, on whose territories they landed, had an old enmity against the archbishop for having opposed his wish to marry Mary, abbess of Romsey. Orders had been given to keep a look out for him on the coast; and as his person was well known, and his arrival generally expected, it was difficult for him to pass undetected, even in the dusk of the evening, in the disguise of a Cistercian monk, under the assumed name of Brother Christian, by which he passed among his three companions. This adventure served as a warning to him not to expose himself again to be recognized, and thus the four travellers continued their way in silence.

But after walking some distance, he was so overcome with the fatigue of his journey, that he sank to the ground, and said to his attendants, " I can go no further, unless you carry me, or procure me some conveyance." After some delay, they procured for one shilling the loan of a horse, which, instead of a bridle, had a halter of straw round its neck. On this they spread their cloaks, and set the archbishop thereon. In this manner they reached Gravelines, where they intended to pass the night. In the inn, as they sat at supper, their host remarked the great stature, high forehead, fine hands, and noble bearing of his guest, and also the easy liberality with which he gave the most delicate bits of his supper to the children. Knowing that the archbishop of Canterbury was supposed to be concealed in that neighbourhood, he called his wife aside and told her his suspicions. The good woman put into requisition all that penetration for which her sex is remarkable, and came to the same conclusion as her husband. But, fortunately for the fugitive, his entertainers were friendly disposed: the man fell at his feet, and blessed the saints for the honour they had done him of bringing so distinguished a guest to his roof. The archbishop, however, as a precaution, kept the man with him in his own company as much as possible, that his loquacity might not betray the secret.

Thus far Providence had befriended them, but they were not yet out of the enemy's country: wherefore they rose at an early hour the next morning, and for want of other conveyance, pursued their course on foot towards St. Omer's. On their way they reached some farm-buildings belonging to the religious house of Clairmarais, and situated on the bank of a small river. Here they took boat and arrived in the evening at Clairmarais, having travelled twelve leagues that day, principally on foot. They were now at no great distance from the castle and town of St. Omer's, where they knew they had a good friend in the abbat of the monastery of St. Bertin's. But it was still desirable to use precautions against a sudden surprise from their enemies, and to this end they withdrew to a small hermitage, situated among the marshes, called Aldmunster, the original cell of the holy confessor,

St. Bertin. Here they lay in concealment three days, which no doubt passed away the more agreeably from the circumstance that Herbert de Bosham and some other clerks had joined them at Clairmarais, bringing horses, clothes, silver plate, and other valuables, which they had managed to carry off from the palace of Canterbury.

On the fourth day after their arrival at this lonely spot, the venerable abbat of St. Bertin's, whose name was Hodeshall, persuaded them to place themselves under the protection of his monastery. The most ready access to St. Omer's was by water, and as it was now Friday, a fast-day, the attendants of the archbishop began to entertain apprehensions that they should meet with but sorry fare at the abbey. "My lord," said one of them to the archbishop, "we are going this day to enter a most hospitable society, and I should think the toils of our journey might be a sufficient excuse for a little indulgence: suppose your lordship were to give them a dispensation to eat meat for once."—"Do you forget that it is Friday?" replied the archbishop, "it would not be right to do so." "But suppose that there should be a scarcity of fish," rejoined the clerk. "Nay," said the archbishop, "that must depend on God's pleasure." The pious historian who tells us this was not content to end the anecdote with what was so natural a conclusion, but he says that "at these words a large fish, of the kind called a Brenham[5], leaped out of the water into the bosom of the man of God."

The toils and perils of this unhoped-for escape from his enemies were now past: the hospitable abbat and brethren of St. Bertin's received the archbishop with open arms, and provided him and his company with every thing they required. Here also the archbishop had an interview with Richard de Lucy, who was on his return from the court of king Louis. This worthy nobleman, whose only fault was that he was faithful to his master, even when his master was in the wrong, tried to induce the archbishop to return to England, assuring him that he would make his peace with the king: but his arguments were unheeded. Wherefore he revoked the homage which he had formerly sworn to the archbishop, and returned alone to England.

But there remained still one possibility of danger to the archbishop. The king of England, immediately on hearing of his escape, had written to the count of Flanders, who was his relative, requesting him to send back the fugitive. When, therefore, the emissaries of the archbishop ap-

---

[5] Query 'a Bream'?

peared to ask a safe-conduct to Soissons, he hesitated whether he should offend his powerful neighbour and relative, or violate the laws of hospitality. To gain time for deliberation, he returned a doubtful answer, which created some misgivings in the archbishop's mind. Among those who had come to see him at St. Bertin's was Milo, bishop of Terouenne, an Englishman by birth, and a great friend of the archbishop. They deliberated together on the count's reply, and both agreed that it was safest to trust to no one but themselves. Having come to this determination, they admitted the friendly abbat into their counsels, and he willingly offered them his aid to promote their success. The archbishop's party, amounting to forty horsemen, left St. Bertin's by night, accompanied by their hospitable host and bishop Milo, and arrived safely at Soissons.

CHAPTER XXII.

EMBASSIES FROM BOTH PARTIES TO THE POPE AND THE FRENCH KING [6].

It will be remembered, that shortly after the archbishop's flight from Northampton, king Henry

[6] Alan of Tewkesbury, and Herbert de Bosham have been principally followed in this chapter.

sent a deputation, consisting of some of the most influential bishops and nobles of his kingdom, to the papal court. These envoys found themselves but coldly received by the inhabitants of the country through which they passed, and the bishops who formed part of the king's embassy began to entertain fears for their own safety. To conceal, therefore, the character of their mission, it was given out in reply to the questions of the people, that they were the company of the earl of Arundel, and the bishops passed for ordinary individuals of his train. By this stratagem they continued their journey unmolested, and passed so near Clairmarais, that if the archbishop had not retired to the hermitage in the marshes, he would probably have become an object of impertinent curiosity to his enemies.

The king's ambassadors, on their way to Sens, stopped at Compiegne, where the French king then was, and were admitted to an audience. They produced letters from their own sovereign, in which Thomas Becket, described as the "late archbishop of Canterbury," was stigmatized as a traitor and a fugitive, and Louis was requested by Henry, in the character of one of the great vassals of the crown, to give Thomas no protection in his dominions. At the words, "late archbishop," the French king, who prided himself upon his devotedness to the Church, was much scandalized, and said to the ambassadors, "I am a king, like unto your master; but I should not dare to deprive the least clerk in my dominions." "I know him well," continued the king, "the archbishop of Canterbury; he was once chancellor to the king of England—he was a noble-minded man; and, if I knew where he was to be found, I and my whole court would go out to meet him." "But he did much harm to France," said the earl of Arundel, "at the head of the English army." "And that was no more than his duty," said the French king, "and your arguments only make me admire him more: if he had been my servant, he would have done as much for me." Thus the deputation, seeing no chance of success, left the French court, and continued their route towards Sens.

But their movements were no secret to the other party. The archbishop had detached the faithful Herbert de Bosham and another of his company, from St. Bertin's, to follow his enemies and watch their movements, and these two, combining the character of ambassadors with that of reconnoiterers, kept the other party a day's journey in advance, so as not to be detected, and entered Compiegne the morning after the king's messengers had quitted it. The French king was informed that they belonged to the archbishop's company, and came on his behalf, so that he readily gave them audience: but not knowing either of them personally, he frequently asked whether they were of the archbishop's own immediate household. Being answered in the affirmative, and repeatedly assured of the fact, he admitted them to kiss him on the cheek, and treated them with great regard and kindness. He even condescended to tell them the contents of the letter which the king of England had sent him, adding, "My lord the king of England, before he drove away from him so distinguished an archbishop, and his own friend too, should have remembered that text of Scripture, 'Be ye angry and sin not.'" Herbert de Bosham's companion remarked in reply, "He would, perhaps, my lord, have remembered it, if he had heard it so often as we clerks do in the church-service." The king smiled at this sally of wit, and dismissed the envoys with every token of kindness and urbanity. The next morning, with the advice of his ministers, he granted safety and protection to the archbishop throughout all his dominions, adding, in allusion no doubt to king Henry's own form of words, that "it was one of the ROYAL DIGNITIES of France to PROTECT FUGITIVES, and especially ecclesiastics, and to DEFEND them from THEIR PERSECUTORS." With this favourable answer the two envoys left Compiegne, and continued their journey to Sens, where the papal court was held, and, as they hoped for a speedy return, they did not think it worth their while to apprise their master of the success of their mission to the French king. We will imitate the example of the two envoys, and follow them to the court of the pope at Sens, after which we will return to the archbishop at Soissons, where he had just arrived.

Herbert de Bosham and his colleague reached Sens soon after the ambassadors of the king of England, and were doomed to experience, in the behaviour of the cardinals, the difference which is made between men in their apparently forlorn condition, and such powerful adversaries, for they were received with coldness, and without the usual honours of salutation. In the evening, however, of the same day they were admitted to a private audience with the pope, to whom they explained the object of their mission, the contest between the archbishop and the king concerning the liberties of the Church, and all the various perils which they and their master had encountered. The holy father spoke kindly to them, and expressed his pleasure at hearing of the archbishop's safety, and as the hour was now late, he wished them good night, and dismissed them.

The next day had been fixed on for giving audience to the king's ambassadors, and the archbishop's two envoys entered the presence-chamber to see what turn things would take. The pope and cardinals took their seats, and the bishop of London, on the part of himself and colleagues, rose to address the conclave:—

"Holy father," said he, "the Catholic Church looks to you for protection, and for an example of conduct. A dissension has lately arisen in England between the throne and the Church, from a trifling matter which might have been set right by a little timely discretion. But as his lordship of Canterbury, following his own individual judgment, and not our advice, has pushed the matter to extremities, without making allowance for the evil temper of the times, or considering the danger that may result, he has placed all of us, his bishops, in a state of doubt and embarrassment. If we had followed his example, things would have been infinitely worse. But because we would not be led by him, as indeed we ought not, he has tried to throw the blame of his own rashness on the king, on us, and on all the kingdom. To give a colour, therefore, to his own infamy he fled, though no one harmed him, or would have harmed him, as the Scripture has it, 'The wicked fleeth when no man pursueth.'"

"Nay," interrupted the pope, "spare—I entreat you, spare,"—"I will spare him, holy father," said the bishop,—"Not *him* but *yourself*, brother," rejoined the pontiff. At this rebuke the bishop of London was confused, and said no more.

The argument was taken up by Hilary of Chichester. "My lord, it is the privilege of your holiness to bring back to peace and tranquillity all those who have wandered from the path, and to set right whatever is wrong throughout the whole world. The great presumption of one man must not be allowed to cause a schism in the catholic Church. His lordship of Canterbury does not consider this, for he abandons wise counsel and thinks only of himself, and thus annoys the king, the clergy, and the people of the whole kingdom, and surely such conduct ill comports with his character: in fact, it never comported, nor in any case could have comported———" Here he was unable to extricate himself from the involved sentence which he had begun, and the cardinals could not restrain themselves, but laughed outright, one of them observing that the bishop, after floundering about, had got into port at last.

The archbishop of York, seeing the downfall of his two colleagues, took up the debate. "Father," said he, "no one can be better acquainted with the archbishop of Canterbury, his character and motives, than myself; and I can say from my own knowledge, that when he has once set his heart upon a thing, it is next to impossible to make him forego it. It can, therefore, be easily imagined that his present obstinacy proceeds from the ordinary constitution of his mind. It seems to me that the only way for him to be brought to his senses is by your holiness treating him with some little severity."

The bishop of Exeter then delivered his opinion. "It is not necessary to trouble your holiness with many words, for this matter cannot be adjusted without hearing both sides: we have, therefore, to request you, my lord, to appoint legates, who shall hear this cause between the king and the archbishop, and when they have heard, give judgment."

There was a silence for some minutes after this speech, when the earl of Arundel, seeing that none of the bishops were disposed to say more, advanced to the papal throne and asked to be heard. Leave being given, he addressed them in his native tongue as follows:—

"My lord, we who do not know Latin, have not understood a word of all that the bishops have said, and therefore think it necessary to state to you our object, which is not to speak ill of any one, particularly so reverend a person, but to show the loyalty and devotion of our king to your holiness. We are the most powerful nobles and bishops of his dominions, and if there had been any other greater than we, they would undoubtedly have been chosen instead of us. You once experienced our king's loyalty, my lord, in the beginning of your reign; and we dare to say that there is no more faithful son of the Church than he. Nor do we deny that the archbishop of Canterbury is equally able and prudent in every thing that concerns his office; so that if there could only be peace between the throne and the Church, both would flourish under such able leaders, the king and the archbishop. It is, therefore, our petition that you shall devote your most serious attention to discover some way of establishing peace between them."

Such was the tenor of what was said by the king's deputies, as they each addressed the Roman court in succession. The archbishop's messengers were present, and Herbert de Bosham twice rose to repudiate the calumnies which were uttered against his master, but the pope checked him, "Peace, my friend; forbear to defend your bishop, there is no charge against him."

The ambassadors now seeing that the pope could not be made to deviate from the usual course, nor be induced to declare for either party until both should be heard, requested that the archbishop should be commanded to return to England, and that a legate *a latere* should be sent to try the question at issue. It is even said that they were commissioned by the king to promise, that if the pope would side with him against the archbishop, Peter's pence, which had hitherto been paid only by those attached to the soil, should from that time be due annually for ever from all the inhabitants of towns, castles, and cities; but the sovereign pontiff was not thus to be bribed[7]. He consented to appoint a legate, but not until he should first have heard what the archbishop had to say; nor would he command him to return to England, which would, in fact, be placing him in the power of his enemies. The embassies were now on the point of breaking up, when the bishop of London returned and asked the pope, with what authority he meant to invest the legate. "With all that is requisite," replied the pope. "That is," said the bishop, "with full power to decide the question at issue, and without appeal?" "Not so, brother," said his holiness; "to hear appeals is a privilege which we never can consent to forego." This reservation was of essential importance to the cause of justice, for it was notorious that some of the cardinals were less inaccessible to the king's wealth than the head of the Church had just shown himself.

[7] Fitz-Stephen.

The ambassadors had now failed in their principal object, but still had hopes of succeeding ultimately in gaining a victory for the king over his refractory subject. The pope suggested that, as the archbishop was known to be on his way, and would soon arrive, they should wait and be confronted with him before himself. But they were forbidden by their instructions to spend more than three days at Sens; and a significant hint had been given them of an intention on the part of some knights who lived in the neighbourhood, and were friendly to the archbishop, to set upon them and plunder their baggage, which was known to contain a considerable sum of money. This naturally alarmed them, and they hastened their return to England: on the way they arrived at a certain river, where on the opposite banks they saw the archbishop's party, consisting of no less than three hundred horsemen, journeying to Sens. A hasty consultation was held, the result of which was that Guy, dean of Waltham, was sent back to reconnoitre, and give them intelligence of the reception which the enemy should meet with at the papal court. No further particulars of their journey have been recorded.

CHAPTER XXIII.

THE ARCHBISHOP'S INTERVIEW WITH THE FRENCH KING AND THE POPE—HE BECOMES AN INMATE OF THE MONASTERY OF PONTIGNY.

THE archbishop of Canterbury entered Soissons, no longer as a fugitive, but at the head of a large procession of horsemen, worthy of his dignity, and the next day the king of France arrived from Compiegne. He was speedily informed that the archbishop was there already, and he immediately ordered his own cavalcade to proceed to the hotel of so distinguished a visitor. Having heard from the archbishop's own mouth a narrative of his adventures, the king expressed much sympathy at the sufferings he had experienced, and gave orders that ample funds for the maintenance of himself and household should be furnished from the royal treasury. A few days were devoted to compliments and courtesies between two such illustrious personages, after which the archbishop departed for Sens, at the head of that noble escort, furnished by the liberality of the French king, which, as we have already mentioned, was descried by the English bishops returning from their interview with the pope.

At the head of this splendid retinue the exiled archbishop entered Sens on the fourth morning after the English ambassadors had quitted it, and those of the cardinals who were disposed to espouse his cause, came out on horseback to meet him [a]. Others of the conclave, and perhaps the majority, were averse to declaring themselves, and at the first interview received him coldly [b]. It was debated some time among the archbishop's clerks which of them should conduct the argument in the presence of the pope, and then finally decided that the archbishop himself should speak.

When they entered the conclave, the pope assigned him the place of honour at his own right hand, and on the archbishop rising to address the meeting, the holy pontiff requested him to keep his seat. He then, in a modest speech, related the principal facts of his own life, both as chancellor and as archbishop, and concluded with spreading out before the pope and cardinals the roll containing the constitutions of Clarendon. "These, holy father," continued he, "are the laws which the Church of God are called upon to receive."

The perusal of these constitutions, sixteen in number, produced great effect on the whole

[a] Fitz-Stephen. [b] Alan.

audience, for it was impossible not to see that the power and privileges which the Church had hitherto enjoyed, would be reduced to a shadow by the establishment of such ordinances. All concurred with the pope in determining to support the archbishop against his enemies; and the pope, whether in sincerity or in order to produce effect, we cannot say, reprimanded the archbishop for having in a moment of weakness consented to observe the constitutions. "But though your crime, brother, has been great, yet you have done your best to atone for it. You have fallen, it is true, but you have risen stronger than before, and the sufferings which you have experienced are sufficient to obliterate your offence." The conclave then adjourned till the next day, when they again met, not in solemn audience as before, but in the pope's secret chamber. Here the archbishop indulged in the same outpouring of his secret thoughts, which had escaped him on the road when he was returning from the council of Clarendon. "The truth must be told, holy fathers, before God and your own consciences. I say it with sobbing and groaning, these evils have befallen the English Church on my account. I went up into Christ's fold, not through the straight gate of canonical election, but was thrust in by the influence of the government. It was sorely against my will, but nevertheless it was the handiwork of men, and not of God. What wonder then if it has ended in misfortune. Yet, on the other hand, if I had resigned my charge into the king's keeping, as my fellow-bishops urged me, it would have been a pernicious precedent of yielding to the will of princes. I forbore therefore to do so, until I should come into this holy presence. I acknowledge my uncanonical election, and for fear of still worse results, lest I should lead my flock to their own perdition, I resign into your hands, holy father, the burden of the archbishopric of Canterbury, which I have no longer strength to bear!" Saying these words he took from his finger the ring, and gave it into the pope's hands.

This unexpected circumstance led to a long and earnest debate between the cardinals, many of whom saw in the resignation of the archbishop a favourable mode of settling the dispute between the parties; all, however, agreeing that the first high dignity in the Church which should fall vacant, ought to be bestowed upon the archbishop, in consideration of the high preferment which he resigned. But again the pope interfered in his favour, and was seconded by several of the sacred college, who said that the archbishop should on no account be allowed to withdraw from a position in which the interests of the Church now required that he should be maintained.

This deliberation had been held in private, and the archbishop was now called in to hear their decision. "My brother," said the holy pontiff, "we acknowledge your zeal in the Church's cause: it has atoned for the informal election of which you speak: receive now from my hands a new investiture, free from the defects of your former title. We shall maintain you in your cause, because it is the cause of the Church. But whereas you have as yet spent your life in luxury and a high estate, and know not what privation is: we wish you to learn, in company with some of Christ's humblest servants, how to subdue the flesh to the spirit. My brother here, the abbot of Pontigny, will receive you into his holy monastery, where you will fare as a simple monk, and as an exile in the cause of Christ. Be of good courage, my brother, resist the enemy, and await with patience till the day of peace and consolation from on high shall visit you."

In consequence of this determination of the pope, the archbishop set out soon after, in company of the abbat, for the monastery of Pontigny. The brethren of that house were overjoyed at receiving into their fraternity so illustrious a member, and their guest himself hastened to conform to all the monastic usages of the society. One of the brethren, named Roger, was appointed to attend upon him, and this man afterwards compiled a brief memoir of his life. A short time after he had become an inmate of the abbey, he wrote to the pope, requesting the gift of a monastic habit on which the holy father had bestowed his blessing. This was immediately forwarded to him from Sens, and the bearer was ordered to say, that the pope had sent him a dress such as he had, and not so good as he could have wished. The abbat of Pontigny stood by whilst he was putting it on, together with some of his clerks, one of whom observed that the pope was not a very good tailor, for he had made the cape much too small and narrow. "Perhaps," said the archbishop, smiling, "that was done on purpose; for the day before yesterday, when I was dressing for mass, you ridiculed me for sticking out so much behind; and to-day, if I had had a larger cape, you would have called me hump-backed." This anecdote is accompanied by a remark of the biographer, that the archbishop was naturally spare and thin, though very tall, and that he often was taken for a stout man, in consequence of the thick horse-hair shirt which he wore, covering not only his body, but his arms and legs.

It was now the close of the year 1164; and the archbishop remained two years in the asylum which the walls of Pontigny afforded: we shall leave him there for the present, and relate the events which took place in England after the return of the king's ambassadors.

CHAPTER XXIV.

THE HARSH PROCEEDINGS OF THE KING OF ENGLAND.—EXILE OF THE ARCHBISHOP'S FRIENDS.

THE king of England gave audience to the bishops at Marlborough on Christmas-eve, 1164, and though an ambassador from the pope accompanied them to palliate the ill success of their mission, his majesty was greatly indignant at their failure, and early on the morning of the twenty-sixth of December issued orders for confiscating all the archbishop's property, seizing on the revenues of his see, and banishing all his relations. On the 27th his officials arrived in London, headed by the archbishop's constant enemy Randolf de Broc. This ferocious man was commissioned by the king to take the church of Canterbury into his custody, and to execute his majesty's harsh sentence against the archbishop's partizans. All his relations in whatever degree, and of both sexes, were summoned to Lambeth, when they were sentenced to be transported across the sea, and made to swear that immediately after landing they would present themselves before the archbishop, wherever he might be. This was done in order to cause him sorrow at the sufferings of so many of his kinsfolk. The hard sentence was extended to all his clerks, and domestic servants, so that four hundred individuals of all classes were thrown on a foreign coast without food or clothing, and with no apparent means of support. Infants at their mothers' breasts, and others still unborn, were speedily relieved from their sufferings by death, together with their mothers, whilst the more hardy survivors were reduced by cold, hunger, and fatigue, to so emaciated an appearance, that they looked more like ghosts than men. Nor is this picture to be considered as ideal: the accommodations which modern times afford for traversing the country did not then exist. Woods and uninhabited wilds occupied the intervening space between one town and another, and the towns themselves were too small and poor to support, for any length of time, so large a number of exiles. But at this dreadful crisis, the French king, and others of that generous and enthusiastic people, behaved nobly in their cause; the empress Matilda and the count of Flanders protected some, and before long time had elapsed, most of those unhappy people were received into comfortable lodgings, and provided with the necessaries of life.

This was not, however, the only tyranny which was practised against the partizans of the Exile. William of Salisbury was taken prisoner, and kept six months in captivity in Corfe castle: Thurstan de Cromdon was kept twenty-four hours in a filthy dungeon at London, and liberated on paying a fine of a hundred marks: Alfred of Walthamsteade, and Stephen de Elratory were fined one hundred pounds. William Fitz-Stephen would have suffered like the rest, but a curious poem[1], which he presented to the king in the chapel of Bruhull, enlisted the vanity of that monarch in his behalf, and he was let go free.

These measures were all that now remained in the power of the king to adopt: the archbishop was safe under the protection of the pope, and in the hospitable keeping of the monks of Pontigny. The stirring character of our narrative will, therefore, for a while subside; and we shall

---

[1] The commencement of this poem is as follows:—

Mighty Monarch of all ages, king of heaven, king of earth:
King of all things, King of all kings, to whom all things owe their birth.
Thou who stillest when thou willest, all the roar of ocean's wave;
And excitest all the mightiest storms that o'er its surface rave.

place before the reader a selection from the letters which passed during this interval of comparative tranquillity.

LETTER XX.

"CIRCULAR FROM THE KING TO THE BISHOPS OF ENGLAND.
DEC. 24, 1164.

"You are not ignorant, reverend fathers, of the injurious treatment which I and my kingdom have received from Thomas, archbishop of Canterbury, and how basely he has fled the country. I command you, therefore, to cause all his clerks who remained with him after his flight, and all others who have acted in a manner derogatory to myself or my kingdom, to be prevented from receiving any of the proceeds of their benefices in your diocese without my permission, and that you give no countenance or support whatever to the aforesaid clerks. Witness, Richard de Lucy, at Marlborough."

LETTER XXI.

"THE KING TO THE SHERIFFS OF ENGLAND.
DEC. 24, 1164.

"I HEREBY command you, if any one, either clerk or laic, in your bailiwick shall appeal to the court of Rome, to have him arrested and put in ward until my pleasure shall be known. Also that you seize into your own hands all the revenues and possessions of the archbishop of Canterbury, as Randolf de Broc and my other officers shall signify to you. Also to arrest the fathers and mothers, brothers and sisters, nephews and nieces of all the clerks who are with the archbishop, and put them and their cattle in safe-pledge, until my pleasure shall be known, and that you bring this brief with you when you are summoned."

LETTER XXII.

"THE ARCHBISHOP OF CANTERBURY TO THE POPE.
JAN. 1165.

" IN your presence, holy father, is my refuge; that you, who have redeemed the Church's liberties at your own peril, may give ear to me who have followed your example, and suffered equally for the same. The cause of the Church would have sunk before the rapacity of princes if I had not faced the coming evil. The more I loved the king, the more I opposed his injustice, until his highness's brow fell lowering upon me. He heaped calumny after calumny on my head, and I chose to be driven out rather than to subscribe. I was called before the king's tribunal like a layman, and was deserted in the quarter where I had looked for support. My brethren, the bishops, sided with the court, and were ready to pronounce judgment against me. Thus, almost crushed by the multitude of my foes, I have fled to your presence, which is the last refuge of the distressed. Under your protection will I prove that I was not amenable to that tribunal, nor to their judgment. Your privileges, holy father, are at stake: by this pernicious precedent the spiritual power would yield to the temporal. Thus I resisted, for fear that to yield would be a confession of weakness, and bring on me more extensive aggression. They say that those things which are Cæsar's should be rendered to Cæsar. Be it so; the king must, indeed, be obeyed in many things, but not so that he shall cease to be a king: that would make him no longer Cæsar but a tyrant, and those who resisted him would contend for themselves and not for me. The last judgment is admitted to be his who can kill both body and soul: is not then the spiritual judgment final on earth? Why have I been assailed for appealing to him, who cannot, must not judge falsely? They have assailed me unjustly, or else they doubt your impartiality. I wonder not that laics should thus attack the Church, but I wonder much that bishops should have led them on. Could I anticipate the hostility of those for whom I encountered such opposition? If they had been willing, I should have gained the victory. But the head faints when it is abandoned by the other members. If they had been wise, they would have seen that in attacking me they were attacking their own privileges, and serving princes to their own servitude. They left spiritual things for temporal, and so have been stripped of both. They judged me, their father, though I protested and appealed to your holy presence. If they had conspired in the same way with the king against the whole Church, what would your holiness then have said? They plead that they were fulfilling their duty to the king. I reply that their obligation to him is of a temporal nature, to me they are bound in spirituals. What obligation can be stronger than that which binds them to themselves, and the spiritual concerns of their souls? They say that this is not a favourable moment for provoking the king to anger. Alas! this refined sophistry leads to their perpetual servitude! they are even accelerating that catastrophe by lending the king's arrogance wings to fly! Had they paused, he would have paused also. But further, when is constancy required, except under persecution? Are not friends then proved? If they always yield, how can they ever succeed? They must one time or other make a stand.

" Look down then, with condescension, holy

father, on my exiled and persecuted condition: remember that I was once in a place of pride, from which I have been driven by injustice—and in your cause. Put forth your severity, and coerce those who have stirred up this persecution; but lay it not at the king's door; he is the instrument and the agent, not the author of these machinations."

LETTER XXIII.

"POPE ALEXANDER TO THE ABBAT AND BRETHREN OF CLAIRMARAIS.

"For the services which your bounty has rendered to the sister of our venerable brother, the archbishop of Canterbury, and to her children and family, we cannot express our thanks; but we commend you for your zeal in the cause of religion, and will not cease whenever occasion shall offer, to promote the interests of your monastery, and to grant all your petitions, as far as our duty to God's Church will permit us. The archbishop also will lose no opportunity of shewing his gratitude and deep sense of this great service which you have done him."

LETTER XXIV.

"TO HIS SERENE LADY AND DEAREST DAUGHTER IN CHRIST, MATILDA, THE ILLUSTRIOUS QUEEN OF SICILY, THOMAS, BY DIVINE APPOINTMENT, HUMBLE MINISTER OF THE CHURCH OF CANTERBURY, HEALTH, AND SO TO REIGN TEMPORALLY IN SICILY, THAT SHE MAY REJOICE FOR EVER WITH THE ANGELS IN GLORY!

"ALTHOUGH I never saw your face, yet I am not ignorant of your renown, the fame of which is supported by nobility of birth, and by great and numerous virtues. But amongst other perfections which we and others delight in, we owe a debt of gratitude to your highness, which we are now endeavouring to acknowledge, for the kindness with which you have received our fellow-exiles, Christ's poor ones, our relations who have fled into your parts from him who persecutes them. You have consoled them in their distress, which is a great duty of religion: your wealth has relieved their indigence, and the amplitude of your power protected them in their necessities. By such sacrifices God is well pleased, your earthly reputation is amplified and made known, and every blessing is secured to you. By these means you have bound ourself also to you in gratitude, and we devote all that we possess and all we are to your service. As the first fruits of our devotion, we have used our good services with the most Christian king, to second your prayers, as you may know by the requests which he had made to our dear friend, the king of Sicily, and by the words of the venerable prior of St. Crispin's, whose literary attainments, singlemindedness, and fair fame, make him dear to all good men. He is a man of correct life, sound doctrine, and as far as regards human judgment of perfect sanctity; and we beg of your highness to hear him with as much reverence as you would listen to the whole western Church, assembled at your feet. And this I pray, not only out of respect for his person, but in regard of the Church of Clugny, whose necessities he is charged with, and which is reputed throughout all the Latin world to have possessed within its walls all the glory of virtue and perfection from the time of our first ancestors. In other respects also, I pray you, if so please you, to place as much confidence in all that he shall tell you, as coming from me, as if I myself had said it. Farewell!"

LETTER XXV.

"THE ARCHBISHOP OF CANTERBURY TO RICHARD, BISHOP ELECT OF SYRACUSE.

"Your humanity makes us guilty of presumption, and the bounty which you have displayed towards our relations makes us doubly debtors to you and yours. In this interchange of kindnesses we are compelled, and not unwillingly, to contract debts with so kind a creditor, trusting that God will discharge all our obligations, for it is He alone that can release those who fear Him. You have entertained our fellow-exiles and relations; and without doubt have thereby entertained Him who promises to repay all that shall be lent to the poor in his name. You have gained praise among your countrymen, and glory among posterity, and made us your debtors. God does not permit us to meet: receive, therefore, the bearer of this letter as my second self, and trust him as you would trust me. He is distinguished for his literary attainments, as well as his moral conduct, and amongst the monks of Clugny he is a model for imitation. He is charged with commissions from his brethren, from his most Christian majesty, and from me. By receiving him with respect, you will receive us also, that pious king and me, whose agent he is. There is one thing remaining, which I will whisper into your ear, and which I hope you will grant me, to do your utmost with the king and queen to procure the recall of that noble-minded man, Stephen, bishop elect of Panormus, both for reasons which at present shall be nameless, and because by doing so, you will confer a lasting favour on the French-king."

CHAPTER XXV.

INACTIVITY OF THE ARCHBISHOP IN 1165—LETTERS WRITTEN DURING THAT YEAR AND THE EARLY PART OF 1166.

THE monastery of Pontigny afforded a secure and tranquil retreat for the archbishop, who seemed disposed not only to acquiesce in the routine of monastic life, but to push his asceticism beyond the verge of prudence. His table was furnished by the monks on a scale suited to his dignity: but he gave secret orders to his attendants to provide him with the usual hard fare of the brethren: this brought on a serious illness[1], which confined him to his bed, and his medical adviser forbade his continuing a mode of life to which he had not been accustomed.

The remainder of the year 1165 was spent in tranquillity, and the discharge of religious duties. The following letters seem to belong to this period:—

---

[1] Edward Grim adds, that one side of his face swelled to a frightful degree, until it ended in "the disease which they call fistula," and that he was at length cured by having two teeth extracted.

LETTER XXVI.

"HERVEY THE CLERK, TO THE ARCHBISHOP OF CANTERBURY.

"I LAID your lordship's petition before the pope, according to your instruction, with as much secresy as possible, for none of the cardinals but my lord Manfred was present. I afterwards, however, called and showed it to cardinals Hyacinth and Otho, as well as their lordships of Portus and Ostia, with whom the pope is in communication concerning your lordship. On the other matters, about which your lordship is anxious, I am not yet able to send you any positive information. You are not to suppose from this, that our lord the pope, or your friends among the cardinals, have any wish to recede from what they have promised; they are really zealous, and the pope will do even more than he said. But the fact is, it was a very delicate matter to manage his lordship of Portus. I myself was engaged in this matter fifteen days, and so far succeeded, that without seeming to wish it, I prevailed on him to support your cause before the pope at Clermont. His lordship the pope too, with a view to stimulate him and others still farther, and to commit them to a strong part, assumed at first an appearance of coldness, and threw difficulties in the way of their proposals. This has caused delay in our proceedings, but I hope we shall soon find the advantage of it. His lordship of Ostia is especially pleased at the pope's thoughtful manner of proceeding. As soon as the business is settled, I will take care to forward you the documents.

"Moreover, it is the advice of his lordship the pope, that if the king of France makes a serious offer to support your lordship at his own expense, you may accept from him, not merely your bread and wine, but also your meat. From the three counts, he thinks you will do well to receive nothing publicly: from the count of Flanders you may accept whatever he offers, but not unless he really presses you, lest his zeal should tire itself out. Not that his lordship the pope has any fear of this, as he confides in the count's generosity and goodness of heart, and hopes great things from his interceding for your lordship with the king of England."

LETTER XXVII.

"JOHN OF SALISBURY, TO THE ARCHBISHOP OF CANTERBURY.
AFTER JAN. 25.

"A few days since, I had an interview with the pope, in which I took pains to set before him what seemed to me to open a way for peace to himself and us. He answered, that he too had conceived hopes of this from certain words of the emperor's, which had been communicated to the abbat of St. Mary's; *i. e.* that the king of England would willingly consent to terms, if the pope would mediate between himself and the king of France. His holiness evidently inclined to the proposal, and the king of France did not hold back, so an interview was expected; and the king of France had been already invited to spend the feast of purification at Sens. I took my leave, and hastened to Paris, where I had an interview with the king.

"He still sympathizes with your lordship and your fellow-exiles, and reprobates the harshness of his lordship our king. Yet he seemed to me to speak with less warmth than usual. On my continuing to press him, he owned to me, that though he loved your lordship and approved your cause, yet, under all circumstances, he could not take on himself the responsibility of pressing strong measures on the pope, and thus perhaps alienating our king from the Church of Rome.

"He dwelt so much on this head, that on going over everything in my mind, I cannot anticipate much advantage from an interview in which our king is to meet the pope in person. He will state much that is plausible, in his own favour, and against your lordship; he will be liberal too in his threats and in his promises; and the court is too accessible to such influence. Besides, the high steward of the king of France supports his cause; and what is worse, earl Robert, whose wife, a relation of my abbat, sends many presents to England, and among them lately, three hundred ells of Rheims linen, to make shirts: she is a prudent lady; and entertains hopes that, besides the presents she and her husband receive in return, she shall get the king to provide for some of her many children, by marrying them to English nobles. The archbishop of Rheims too loves earl Robert and his family dearly. So that I fear when it comes to the point, fortune will easily shake off such friends as these. It is therefore my advice and entreaty to you, and I press it most earnestly, that you commit yourself with all your soul to the Lord and to prayer. It is written in the Proverbs: 'The name of the Lord is a strong tower, to which if a man flee, he is freed from every tribulation.' Put aside all other occupation, as much as you are able, however important, for what I advise you is more important still. The laws and canons are of use to us, but, believe me,

> 'No curious speculations such as those
> This urgency demands;'

for they excite curiosity, but not devotion. Do

you not remember how that it is written, 'The priest shall mourn between the vestibule and the altar, saying, Have mercy, O Lord, have mercy upon thy people, &c.?' This teaches us that spiritual exercises, and thoughts that purify the conscience, avert the scourge, and secure the mercy of the Lord. Who ever rises with a contrite heart from the study of the laws or the canons? I will say more. The exercises of the schools sometimes swell out and puff up science, but seldom or never inflame devotion. I would rather you should meditate on the Psalms, and study the moral writings of the blessed Gregory, than philosophize in the scholastic fashion. You should confer on moral subjects with some holy man, by whose example you may be stirred up, rather than be studying the discordant subjects of secular learning. God knows with what devout motives I write all this: you will take it as you think proper. If you do as I suggest, God will stand by you, so that you need not fear what man may do against you. God knows there is no man, to whom we can look for aid in our present straits. I have heard that the king of France has been urgent with the pope on your lordship's behalf, and has expressed his thanks to the convent of Pontigny. I hear too that your lordship has written to the archbishop of Rheims, to ask that he will allow your goods to be brought through Flanders in his name, as if for himself. If this is so, I am surprised. It is said too, that Hugh, the monk of St. Benedict's, is returned from England, and certain others, on an embassy from our king to the pope and the king of France; what news they bring I am yet ignorant. It is said too, that there has lately been an earthquake in England, near Canterbury, and London, and Winchester; but I doubt the truth of this. They say too, that the bishops, in whose diocese there are churches belonging to your lordship, claim jurisdiction over them, and that the clergy are too much frightened to resist. Yet I can hardly think this, except that I suppose they would gladly avail themselves of some excuse for underhand interference, which they may at some future time appeal to as an act of ownership. For, as I hear, it was while the see of Canterbury was vacant, that Sefrid, bishop of Chichester, exercised authority over those churches for which his successor now contends. But though I scarcely think it possible, still I recommend your lordship to protect yourself against the chance of it, by procuring letters patent from the pope, declaring that such acts shall not be construed into a precedent.

"But your lordship knows better than I can do what is going on in England. May I entreat you to send me word, by the bearer of these, how your lordship fares, and what is going on at the court, and whether the abbat is yet returned, who was sent to England by the pope.

"Farewell, my lord, and call to mind the zeal of your predecessor, which he retained up to the very day of his death. My best wishes to all your friends. My abbat salutes you, and so does the bishop of Châlons; to whom I spoke lately about receiving one of your clerics. He acquiesces readily, but hopes you will send him some creditable person; yet he will take in whomsoever you will send. When you send him, do instil into him the necessity of a modest deportment, for the men of this country are modest."

LETTER XXVIII.

"JOHN BISHOP OF POITIERS, TO THE ARCHBISHOP OF CANTERBURY [1].

"WE have just received your lordship's last letters, which were brought by brother Simon, and great comfort we have derived from them. They were a set-off against other news which had just been brought us of a less pleasing kind. The place too where we received them was lucky; *i. e.* at Le Mans, and in the presence of my lord the bishop. For that Catholic man, sympathizing

[1] Epistolæ S. Thomæ.

as he does in the distresses of the Church, was comforted by them under the affliction our late information had caused him. We may fairly hope that, if what is now stated be true, the emperor will have too much on his hands to leave him time for tyrannizing over the Church. It surprised us, however, that your lordship should have said nothing of what passed in the conference the king of France held at Auxerre on the octave of the apostles.

"It seems advisable that your lordship should accept the liberal offer the said king and earl Henry are said to have made you. It will make your exile more endurable; and the king will probably feel less scruple in confiding his secret counsels to you, if he hopes to keep you under obligation to him.

"What he would wish most, would be to provide for you out of the revenues of some vacant bishopric or archbishopric, and thus to preserve his own funds unimpaired.

"It will be necessary for your lordship, as far as one can judge from the present aspect of your affairs, to husband your resources in every possible way, to let your enemies see that you are prepared for any sufferings your exile may reduce you to. For this reason I have often warned your discretion, and must still anxiously press you, to get rid of your superfluous incumbrances, and to consider the badness of the times, which promises you neither a speedy return nor an easy one. Your wisdom ought to know that no one will think the less of you, if in conformity to your circumstances, and in condescension to the religious house that entertains you, you content yourself with a moderate establishment of horses and men, such as your necessities require.

"Your lordship should know that you have nothing to expect from the queen, neither advice nor support, for she trusts her whole counsels to Raoul de Faye, who persecutes you as bitterly as ever. Circumstances come to light too every day, which lead one to think that the infamous story I mentioned to you is not far from the truth.

"Among the rumours which are brought from England by those who come from the king to the queen, and boast great things of their own party, one is, that the king has a second time engaged the Welsh; nay, as they boast, has assailed them, and with small loss to himself, has slain an immense multitude.

"We send you a copy of the letter the king has sent his mother. You will also receive by the bearer of these, a writing directed to you by master Hugo, cleric to Richard of Ilchester.

"Of what took place in the conference of Shrewsbury we know nothing, except that the king mocked the bishops whom he had summoned there, and dismissed them at once, retaining their attendants with him.

"If anything comes to our knowledge that seems likely to interest you, we shall take care to send you word, and pray your lordship to do the same for us. Farewell."

LETTER XXIX.[1]

"KING HENRY, TO REGINALD ARCHBISHOP OF COLOGNE.

"I HAVE long wished to have a just cause for leaving pope Alexander and his perfidious cardinals, who presume to support that traitor Thomas, formerly archbishop of Canterbury, in his rebellion against me. Wherefore, by the counsel of my barons, I mean to send to Rome the archbishop of York, the bishop of London, and the archdeacon of Poitiers, John of Oxford, and Richard de Lucy, to warn the pope from myself and my whole kingdom, no longer to support the cause of that traitor, but to release me from him altogether, and let me have another archbishop of Canterbury in his place. They are also required to revoke all that they have done in this matter, and to make a public decree that the pope, for

---

[1] Epistolæ S. Thomæ.

himself and his successors for ever, shall ratify my royal constitutions; and if they do not consent to this request, I and my barons and all my clergy will obey him no longer, but will do all we can against him, and any of his party who are found in my dominions shall be expelled. I therefore pray you, as a friend whom I value, to send to us without delay brother Arnold, or brother Ralph the hospitaller, that they may afford safe conduct to my ambassadors aforesaid through the emperor's dominions, both in going and returning."

LETTER XXX.[4]

"ALEXANDER BISHOP, SERVANT TO THE SERVANTS OF GOD, TO HIS VENERABLE BROTHER GILBERT, BISHOP OF LONDON, HEALTH AND APOSTOLICAL BENEDICTION.

"It will not have escaped your memory, that our beloved son in Christ, Henry, the illustrious king of England, requested of us formerly, with much earnestness, to permit your translation from the see of Hereford, which you then occupied, to that of London. And, moreover, that to secure our assent, he dwelt on the advantages likely to result from your promotion, alleging that London was the seat of the government, and that he wished to have you near his person, for the

[4] Epistolæ S. Thomæ.

benefit of your counsels, as well in temporal matters as in those that concern his soul. We, therefore, looking to the interest of the king and nation, and above all, of God's holy Church, consented to your promotion. A time has now arrived, when we expect to reap the benefits we then proposed to ourselves, and to experience the reality of the hopes which were then held out to us.

"Doubtless you are not ignorant, that the aforesaid king has of late fallen off much from his devotion to the holy Church: he has forbidden appeals, has entered into communication with schismatics and persons excommunicated, and exiled from his dominions our venerable brother the archbishop of Canterbury, by which acts he has become even a persecutor of the Church. Wherefore we command you, in conjunction with the bishop of Hereford, to warn the king that he desist without delay from these evil practices, and make satisfaction for what he has done amiss; admonish him to love his God with singleness of heart; to respect as he was wont, his holy mother, the Roman Church; to withdraw his prohibition on all visits and appeals to it; to recall and reinstate our brother aforesaid, the archbishop, in his diocese; to stand fast in his reverence towards the blessed St. Peter and ourself; to attend on works of piety and religion; no longer to oppress, as he is said to do, or permit others to oppress, the Churches and clergy of his kingdom or his other territories; but to love, maintain, and by his royal protection support them; that by these means he may obtain from Him by whom kings reign, both a continuance of his temporal kingdom here, and the gift of an eternal one hereafter.

"Furthermore, although we ourself, in consideration of his former devotion, and his service shown to us in time of need, still love him with abundant charity, as a noble prince and most renowned king, and still labour for the advancement of his glory (though he himself seems to think otherwise of us) with a fervent zeal; nevertheless, it is fit you should recall to his mind, that unless he repents of his evil deeds, and that speedily, God will most surely visit him with heavy vengeance, and the time must at last come when our patience can no longer endure.

"These things we desire to lay before him, not for our own good, but for his safety, in return for those many and signal services which he has before now rendered to us as a most Christian king. His greatness is our delight; his welfare, and that of his kingdom, is the object of our most earnest wish.

"Lastly, our confidence in your prudence and attachment, induces us to commit to you certain matters of importance. Hereby, therefore, we authorize you to make a faithful collection of Peter's pence throughout all England for the current year, and to transmit the amount to us as soon as possible. We request, moreover, that before the aforesaid collection has been completed, you will furnish us with such a supply of money, as your own resources or your credit can procure, and transmit it before the ensuing first of August. You may repay the loan out of the collection. By so doing you will confer on us as great a favour, as if you handed over the whole sum as a present." Given at Clermont, July 10.

LETTER XXXI.

"THE BISHOP OF LONDON TO THE POPE.

"Beloved father in Christ: we have, as in duty bound, laid the commands of your holiness before the famous and well-beloved prince, the king of England, who is now with his army on the borders of Wales. In conjunction with our venerable brother, Robert, bishop of Hereford, we presented our instructions to his majesty, and both with entreaty and such arguments as we could venture on using, exhorted him to a speedy compliance.

"We pressed him to regard the warnings of

his father, and if in any thing he had done amiss, to return at once to the way of righteousness; to love God with a pure heart, to honour the holy Catholic Church, and not to interfere with its jurisdiction; above all, to recall and reinstate our father, the lord archbishop; to protect our Churches and their ministers, and to persevere in his allegiance to the holy Apostolic See. Moreover, we warned him that, should he persist in disobedience, there was a point beyond which the patience of your Holiness could not endure, and we reminded him of the retribution he might expect from that God who had exalted him, and could also cast him down.

" His majesty, in return, expressed his thanks for your holiness's admonitions, and replied to each of them with the greatest moderation. He said that his allegiance to your holiness remained unshaken, that the very idea of disregarding it had not so much as entered his mind, nor would he in the slightest thing oppose your holiness's wishes, where he could comply with them without compromising his prerogative. That of late, if he had been in any respects wanting in reverence, some excuse was to be found for him in the repulses he had met with, which were scarcely a requital for his past services. Yet that he still relied on your holiness's goodness, in the hope of receiving less harsh treatment at your hands.

That he had no wish to interfere with appeals to your holiness's court: but merely claimed to himself the right, in civil causes, of hearing the case first, according to the ancient usage of the country: should his decision prove unjust, he would place no farther obstacle in the way of an appeal. Moreover, should this claim prove in any way prejudicial to the interests of the Church, he pledged himself to submit it to the judgment of the next general British council. As to the intercourse he had held with the emperor, he protested that, up to that moment, he did not know of his excommunication; and, with regard to the flight of our father, the lord archbishop, he assures your holiness that it was not ordered by him; that his lordship's absence is purely voluntary, and that no one will interfere with his returning whenever he is so minded: only that he will have to answer certain complaints lodged against him respecting a breach of the royal privileges, which he is sworn to uphold. That in any instance where a Church or churchman may be supposed to have received injury at his hands, he will cheerfully abide the judgment of his assembled clergy.

"Such was his majesty's reply, which we forward to your holiness as it was delivered to us. At the same time, we venture to submit to your holiness, that though we could have wished it in some respects different, still, in main points, it seems to vindicate his majesty's conduct; and that, in the present crisis, it might perhaps be hazardous to require a fuller submission. It is written, 'A bruised reed shall He not break, and smoking flax shall He not quench;' and it may be questioned how far it is desirable to risk the alienation of a great king and nation by an ill-timed, though just, exercise of severity.

"A wounded limb may recover as long as it is united with the body; when cut off, its situation is desperate. May your holiness be pleased to try the milder course with us, in our present state of unparalleled distraction. Soon, perhaps, a more favourable opportunity may present itself, and your holiness's commands may take a fuller effect. Just at present, it may be expedient to make some sacrifices with a view to permanent advantages by and by. Even supposing things to end in the continued exile of our lord of Canterbury, and a temporary disaffection of England, still, were it not better to forbear for a time, than to have recourse at once to the desperate step? For although most of us, it is to be hoped, are proof against persecution, still there will be found many to bow the knee before Baal; the pall of Canterbury may be sought from the hands of the intruder, and there would be no want of underlings to occupy our Churches.

"The possibility of such an event is even now openly talked of; and thus the dangers which impend over us concern the whole Catholic Church as well as ourselves.

"As regards Peter's pence, if the king had not backed our applications by a royal mandate, no attention whatever would have been paid to us. However, the money will be all collected by the proper time, and we shall, God willing, forward it to your holiness by the first opportunity."

LETTER XXXII.

"POPE ALEXANDER TO THE ARCHBISHOP OF CANTERBURY.

"Since the days are evil, and since it is necessary to endure much in consideration of our circumstances, we request and entreat of you, that in your whole conduct respecting your own cause, and that of the Church, you act with caution, prudence, and circumspection, doing nothing in haste, but all things with gravity and deliberation; and that in all possible ways, consistent with the liberties of the Church and the dignity of your office, you will labour to conciliate his Majesty the king of England.

"Till the ensuing Easter, you must so far endure the excesses of the said king, as to forbear all proceedings either against his person or territory. After that time God will vouchsafe better days to us; and you, as well as ourself, may adopt more rigorous measures with safety."

CHAPTER XXVI.

THE POPE RETURNS TO ITALY.

THE vicinity of Pontigny to Sens gave the archbishop of Canterbury many opportunities of seeing the Roman pontiff, who continued in all their personal communications to show him respect and kindness: but the difficult situation in which the pope was placed must be considered a very plausible, if not satisfactory excuse for the hesitation which he showed to take decisive steps in his favour. The same reasons led his holiness to wish that a reconciliation could be effected between the contending parties. This laudable object was baffled by the unfair requirements of the king of England; for when both he and the pope were equally desirous of meeting to settle the question at issue, the king was unwilling that the archbishop should attend their interview. This, however, was a point which the pope would not give up; and the reluctance of both seems to have proceeded from their fears of being circumvented; the pope by the king's blandishments, if the archbishop were not there to fortify him against flattery, the king of being defeated by the archbishop's superior abilities for managing such a controversy. Thus the attempt to effect a reconciliation altogether failed. In the latter part of 1165, or the early part of 1166, the pope returned to take up his residence in the ancient seat of empire, and the archbishop accompanied him as far as Bourges, where they took solemn leave of one another, never again to meet on this side of the grave.

But the withdrawal of the holy pontiff from France, only rendered him still more anxious to effect a reconciliation between the king and the archbishop, and before his departure a combined movement was made to bring about this desirable result. King Henry's letter to the archbishop of Cologne had been made public, and his messengers were already on their way to the court of the emperor: letter after letter was sent to the king of England, to remind him of his duty, and of the punishment which fell on schismatics.

LETTER XXXIII.

"TO HIS MOST RESPECTED LORD HENRY, BY THE GRACE OF GOD, THE ILLUSTRIOUS KING OF ENGLAND, DUKE OF NORMANDY, COUNT OF ANJOU, AND DUKE OF AQUITAINE, THOMAS, BY THE SAME GRACE HUMBLE MINISTER OF THE CHURCH OF CANTERBURY, HEALTH AND PROSPERITY IN ALL THINGS.

"To talk of God requires a mind at liberty and at ease. Therefore will I speak to my lord, and pray he may be peacefully disposed towards all men. I entreat you to bear patiently my admonitions, which by God's grace, that never is given in vain, may confer safety on your soul and free mine from blame. Tribulation and anguish encompass me: whether I speak or whether I am silent, evil still awaits me. If I am silent, woe is me, for how shall I escape from Him who says, 'If thou speakest not to warn the wicked from his way to save his life, his blood will I require at thy hands.' Yet if I speak out, I dread the anger of my lord the king, lest it happen to me according to the words of the wise man, 'When one who pleases not is sent to intercede, it is to be apprehended that the mind of the angry man will be excited to still greater anger.' What then shall I do? Shall I speak or hold my tongue? There is danger in both. Since, however, it is safer to incur the anger of man than to fall into the hands of the living God, I will trust in the mercy of the Most High, in whose hand are the hearts of kings, and who can incline them as he thinks best, and I pray it may be for the best! and so I will speak unto my lord the king, even as I have begun.

"Good often falls to a man against his will, and especially when it is his advantage and not his pleasure which is consulted. In your kingdom the daughter of Sion is held captive, the spouse of the great King is oppressed by many, and afflicted by those who have long hated her, and who ought rather to have honoured than afflicted her. But she suffers this more particularly from you, though you cannot but remember the several benefits which God has conferred upon you, in the beginning and in the middle of your reign, even almost to this very day. Release, release her, and permit her to reign with her Spouse, that God may bless you, and your kingdom may revive, and this reproach be removed from your generation, and there may be peace in these your days. Believe me, my dear lord and most serene prince, God is patient in retribution, and waits long; but He is a most severe avenger: listen, I pray you listen, that it may be well with you. But if you will not, it is to be feared, (though God forbid it!) lest the Most

High should gird the sword upon his thigh, and come with a strong hand and numerous troops to free his spouse, not without severe blows upon him who troubles her, for her oppression and for her servitude. But if you will listen to me, for God deems it necessary in this to try your obedience as of a bold and faithful servant, he will do you good, and will add honour to honour upon you and your sons and daughters for many generations. But if not, I fear, (though God forbid it!) that the sword will not fail from your house, until the Most High comes and takes vengeance on them for the wrongs which He and his children have received, even like the house of Solomon, though he was chosen by God, and endowed with so much wisdom and peace that he was called by men the son of wisdom and of peace; yet he departed from the way of the Lord and walked in iniquity after iniquity, so the Lord rent the kingdom from him and gave it to his servant, principally because he did not attempt, after he had offended, to appease the Lord, as his father David had done, who humbled himself after his offence, and did away with his transgression by asking pardon of the Lord. May God's grace enable you to do likewise. These things I write to you at present: other matters will be communicated to you verbally by the bearer, a religious man, of great reputation, and one in whose fidelity you may place as much reliance as if I myself was speaking to you. But above all things should I wish to be present and converse with you by word of mouth. Farewell, for ever my lord."

This letter was conveyed to the king by Urban, a Cistercian abbat[1], but produced no effect, and a second and third of similar import were dispatched after it, but still without effect. Not so, however, that with which the correspondence closed, and in which the archbishop, after a long explanation of the difference between the spiritual and temporal jurisdictions, concluded with this forcible denunciation :—

"Hear then, my lord, if so please you, the counsel of your liege, the admonition of your bishop, the castigation of your father. Have no familiarity or communion for the future with schismatics, nor enter into any contract with them. All the world knows how devotedly you embraced the pope's cause, and how much the pope and the holy Roman Church have loved you, and listened to you next to God. Do not then, if you value the salvation of your soul, withdraw from that Church its due. Nay, rather permit her to enjoy liberty in your kingdom, as she does in other kingdoms. Remember the profession, which you made and placed in writing upon the

[1] Herb. de Bosham.

altar at Westminster, to preserve the Church's liberties, when you were consecated and anointed to be king. Restore the Church of Canterbury, from which you received your promotion and consecration, to the state in which it was in the days of our predecessors, with all its possessions, castles, manors, and farms, and all other property that has been taken away from any of my men, whether clerks or laymen, and allow us to resume our duties in the aforesaid Church, without trouble or molestation. If your majesty will consent to this, I am prepared to serve you with all obedience as my beloved lord and sovereign, as far as lies in my power—SAVING THE HONOUR OF GOD AND OF THE ROMAN CHURCH, AND MY OWN ORDER. But if you will not do these things, know for a certainty that you shall feel the severity of God's vengeance!"

This letter inflamed the king's anger the more, as it arrived just as he had received other intelligence, equally startling, of the archbishop's movements.

A letter from the pope, already quoted, signified to the archbishop that he should delay launching the thunders of the Church upon his enemies until the ensuing Easter[6]. That period was at last come, and the archbishop lost no time

---

[6] See page 324, letter xxxii.

in availing himself of the permission which he had received.

In the first place he went on a pilgrimage to Soissons, where for three nights he performed vigils and other holy exercises: after which he proceeded, accompanied by several of his clerks, to Vezelay, where the festival of Easter was at this time to be celebrated with unwonted splendour. On the great day of the festival he preached an able sermon to the assembled people, and afterwards having explained to them the persecution which he had suffered from the king of England, he pronounced solemn excommunication against John of Oxford, for having intruded into the deanery of Salisbury, and also for communicating with schismatics, by acting as the king's ambassador at the court of the emperor. He then excommunicated several other persons by name, for having continued, in spite of his warnings, to keep possession of the property of the Church, and suspended the bishop of Salisbury, for having inducted the above-named John of Oxford into the deanery of Salisbury, without the consent of certain canons of that Church, who were exiles in his company, and to whom belonged the right of electing the dean. It had been his intention to excommunicate the king also, but from this he was deterred by hearing of his serious illness.

Whilst these events were proceeding, the king and bishops on the other hand were alarmed by the denunciations contained in the archbishop's final letter: an appeal from the king to the pope was decided on: the bishops hastened to Pontigny, that they might deliver the appeal in time to prevent the sentence on his majesty, which they anticipated, for by the canon law an appeal after excommunication was not valid. When, however, they arrived, the archbishop was already gone to Soissons[7]. The king soon heard of the excommunication of his officers, and of the denunciations against himself. The bishops of England received the same notification from their metropolitan: they assembled on the 24th of June, to determine what steps to take, and having appealed in form to the holy pontiff, they dispatched a severe letter of expostulation to Pontigny. The archbishop replied in the same strain, and appeared to ascribe all the severity of their proceedings to Gilbert Foliot, the bishop of London. This drew from Foliot a long and ably written letter, in which he reviews all the events of Becket's pontificate, and puts the whole appearance of the question at issue as much as possible to his disadvantage. The archbishop

[7] Herbert de Bosham says he had intimation of the appeal, and withdrew from Pontigny purposely to prevent notice being served on him.

replies briefly, without condescending to enter into all the details of the bishop's letter. Whilst rhetorical common-places occupy the greatest part of the lengthy letter of Foliot, that of his rival equally abounds with those which are drawn from Scripture and religion. These angry proceedings will be more fully developed by the following letters, all of which were written between the months of May and August, in the year of our Lord, 1166.

LETTER XXXIV.

"POPE ALEXANDER TO THE BISHOPS OF KENT.

" To succour the oppressed and injured is the duty of our holy office: especially in the case of ecclesiastics who endure exile in defending the Church's liberties; and we are bound to protect them, as far as in our power, from suffering any diminution of their rights. The clerks of our venerable brother, Thomas of Canterbury, have incurred the anger of the king in the defence of the Church, and been deprived of their possessions. Your discretion cannot be ignorant of this, the more so that you must have seen it with your own eyes. Wherefore, because it is intolerable that by this violence they should suffer the loss of their benefices, we command you, my brethren, by these our apostolical letters, to compel all who have, by the king's orders, taken possession of those benefices in the absence of their owners, the clerks aforesaid, under pain of anathema, and without appeal, to make immediate restitution; and we require you to show yourselves neither remiss nor lukewarm in executing these our orders. Given at the Lateran, the fifth day before the calends of May." [Ap. 27.]

LETTER XXXV.

" THOMAS, BY THE GRACE OF GOD, HUMBLE MINISTER OF THE CHURCH OF CANTERBURY, TO HIS VENERABLE BRETHREN THE BISHOP OF LONDON AND THE OTHER BISHOPS OF THE PROVINCE OF KENT, SO TO PASS THROUGH TEMPORAL GOODS THAT THEY LOSE NOT THOSE WHICH ARE ETERNAL!

"My beloved brethren, why do you not rise together with me against the malignants? Why do you not stand up with me to oppose those who work iniquity? Do you not know how that God will scatter the bones of those who strive to please men? They shall be confounded, because the Lord hath despised them. Your discretion knows well that evil, when not resisted, is approved, and truth, when not defended, is crushed: and, as Gregory says, he is consenting unto wrong, who does not step forward to correct that which requires amendment. For this cause it is that we have too long borne with our lord the king, and the Church of God has gained no alleviation from our sufferance. For the rest, it is dangerous any longer to tolerate the excesses which he commits in his treatment of the Church and of ecclesiastics; particularly as we have endeavoured, by messengers and by letters, to turn him from the error of his ways. And since he has heard, but not listened to me, we have invoked God's Holy Spirit, and condemned and annulled that charter which contains his constitutions, or rather depravities, by which the peace of the Church has been so disturbed. Moreover, we have excommunicated all who advised them, or have observed them, or aid in their promulgation, and by God's authority, and our own, we have absolved all the bishops from the promise which bound them unlawfully to their observance. For who can doubt that Christ's priests are the fathers and masters of kings and princes, and of all the faithful? Is it not pitiable folly for the son to exercise power over the father, or the scholar over his master, by whom he believes that he may be bound and loosed both in earth below and in heaven above? Wherefore, that we may not fall into this error, we have condemned that writing, and the depravities which it contains, namely, 1. That archbishops and bishops shall not leave the kingdom or answer to an appeal before the pope, without the licence of our lord the king. 2. That bishops shall not excommunicate tenants in chief, or lay their lands under an interdict without the king's licence. 3. That bishops shall not punish men for perjury or breach of faith. 4. That clerks shall be summoned before the secular tribunal. 5. That laymen, whether the king or others, shall decide questions concerning churches and tithes: together with other laws of the same nature.

"Furthermore, we denounce as excommunicate, and do hereby excommunicate by name, John of Oxford, because he has fallen into a damnable heresy, by making oath to schismatics, whereby the schism in Germany, that had well nigh expired, has revived, and because he has communicated with Reginald the schismatical bishop of Cologne, and because he has usurped the deanery of Salisbury contrary to the mandate of the pope and of ourself. And as this deed is unlawful and detrimental to the Church, we have utterly annulled it, and have commanded the bishop of Salisbury, as soon as he sees our letters, to hold him no longer as dean.

"Also, we have excommunicated, and do hereby excommunicate, Richard of Ilchester, because he has fallen into the same damnable heresy, by communicating with the same Reginald, the schismatic of Cologne, and by contriving evil against God's Church, in conjunction with the schismatical Germans, and particularly against the Church of Rome, by the treaty which he has contracted between those Germans and the king.

"We excommunicate also Richard de Lucy and Joceline de Baliol, who were the authors and fabricators of those depravities aforesaid.

"Also Randolph de Broc, who has seized, and holds in his possession, the goods of the Church of Canterbury, which are the inheritance of the poor, and because he detains in custody our men, both clerks and laymen.

"Also Hugh de Saint Clare and Thomas Fitz-Bernard, who also seized and holds possession of the goods and possessions of the church of Canterbury without our consent.

"We have, moreover, pronounced the same sentence of excommunication against all who shall hereafter lay hands upon the possessions of our Church, according to that sentence of pope Lucius: 'All plunderers of the Church, and alienators of sacred property, we do anathematize and condemn, and pronounce to be guilty of sacrilege:' and not only themselves, but all who abet them; for the same punishment awaits the agents and their abettors: and Scripture says in another place, 'He who consents unto sinners, or defends another in his sins, shall be accursed before God and man, and shall be corrected with the most severe correction.' And again: 'If any one defends a sinner, let him be punished worse than he who sinned.'

"In truth, we have delayed to pass sentence on the person of our lord the king, waiting if perhaps he may, by God's grace, repent: but we will pass it ere long, unless he does repent. For this cause it is, that we command your fraternity, and enjoin you in virtue of your obedience, that whereas we have excommunicated the aforesaid persons, you also, as is your duty, shall also hold them as excommunicate, and denounce them as such, according to that decree of pope Honorius: 'Let all bishops certify to the neighbouring bishops, as well as to their own clergy, the names of those whom they have excommunicated, that they may be fixed publicly upon the doors of the church, and all who come may see them, and thus they may be excluded from entering in, and all men may be without excuse.'

"Moreover, we command you, my brother of London, in virtue of your obedience, to certify these our letters to all our brethren, the bishops of our province. Farewell in Christ, and pray for us without ceasing!"

LETTER XXXVI.

"TO THEIR VENERABLE FATHER AND LORD THOMAS, BY THE GRACE OF GOD ARCHBISHOP OF CANTERBURY, THE SUFFRAGAN BISHOPS OF THE SAME CHURCH, AND OTHERS THROUGHOUT THEIR DIOCESES, DUE SUBJECTION AND OBEDIENCE!

"Whatever disturbances, father, your unexpected departure to so great a distance has produced among us, we had hoped, by God's grace, and your own humble-mindedness, might have been appeased. It was consolatory to us, after your departure, to hear it reported on all sides, that in your solitary and exiled condition you indulged no vain imaginations, and were forming no schemes against our lord the king, or his kingdom, but bore with modesty that indigence which you had freely taken upon you. It was said, that your attention was given to study and prayer, and to redeem with fasting, watching, and mourning, the time which you had lost, and that by these spiritual occupations you were carving your road, by the path of accumulated merits, to the resting-place of perfection. We rejoiced, that by such studies you were zealously preparing the way to the renewal of peace and all its blessings, and hoped that you might, by these means, call down the divine grace into the heart of our lord the king, that his royal mercy might relax from anger, and forget the injuries brought about by your departure. Your friends and well-wishers found access to his majesty so long as these reports were heard of you, and he received with kindness the petitions that were made to restore you to his favour. But now we have heard from certain, and we recall it to our recollection with much anxiety, that you have sent him a denunciatory letter, in which you omit the usual salutation, and use neither counsel nor petition whereby to obtain his grace, but your words and sentiments are alike hostile, and you threaten, with expressions of the deepest severity, to launch an interdict against him, and cut him off at once from the communion of the Church. Should this sentence be as rigidly executed, as it has bitterly been denounced, so far from hoping to restore tranquillity after our late convulsions, we fear that they will be kindled into a flame, ending in a lasting and irreconcileable hatred. Prudence is a holy virtue, and looks well to the end of all things, and is ever careful to conclude with success what has been commenced in wisdom. We would therefore pray your discretion to consider what will be the result; whether by such a course the desired end can be obtained. They have already dashed the hopes of peace which we had conceived, and plunged us into the depths of despair. The sword has been again drawn, and the fight recommenced, nor can we any longer find grounds for interceding in your behalf. In charity, therefore, we dictate to you advice as to our father, not to add toil to toil, injury to injury, but to cease from these threats, to study patience and humility, to commit your cause to the Divine compassion, and the merciful consideration of our lord. By this conduct you will heap coals of fire upon the heads of many. Thus charity will be kindled up, and, by God's grace and the counsels of the good, piety alone will obtain that which threats have failed to accomplish. It is better to be praised for voluntary poverty, than to be marked in public by all men with the stamp of ingratitude towards your benefactor. The minds of all men are strongly impressed with the favours which our lord the king conferred upon you, the honours to which he raised you from so low a state, and the familiar intercourse to which he admitted you; so that all his dominions, from the northern ocean to the Pyrenees, were subjected to your administration, and the public looked upon all as happy who obtained favour in your sight. That your renown might not be shaken by the storms to which all human affairs are subject, the king wished to anchor you fast in the things which belong to God and to his Church. Thus, against the advice of his mother, and the voice of the whole kingdom, whilst the Church too, as far as it was able, mourned and murmured at the act, he used every means to raise you to your present eminence, hoping that he should thenceforth reign in peace and security, supported by your power and assisted with your advice. If then he has found one that smites, where he had looked for safety, what think you will the public, one and all, say of you? Will they not bear in mind this extraordinary mode of requiting the favours which you have received? Spare your good fame, we entreat, have respect to your own glory: and study rather to vanquish by your humility, him who is your master, by your charity, him who is your son. If our admonitions are unable to influence, yet the love and fidelity of the supreme pontiff and of the holy Roman Church, ought to have power to move you. There ought to be little difficulty in inducing you to attempt nothing that may increase the difficulties of your holy mother, the Church, already too severely burdened; nothing whereby the disobedience of many may be aggravated by the loss of the remainder who still continue in obedience. Suppose that by your means and by your exasperation our lord the king, (which God forbid!) with so many nations and kingdoms which God has given him, should desert our lord the pope, and refuse for the future to follow him, because perchance he may not aid him against you. You know what entreaties, what gifts and promises have been used to induce him to do this. As yet, however, he has stood firm as a rock against them, and magnanimously trodden under foot all that the world can offer. One thing, however, remains to be feared, lest his own anger prompt him to do that for which treasures or wealth and all that is valued among men have been offered in vain. If all this should happen through you, lamentation will be yours, and the fountains of your eyes may for ever flow, for it will be out of your power, out of reason, to dry them up. Take counsel then in time, if it so please your highness, counsel that may benefit the cause of our lord the pope and the holy Roman Church; and mark! it will be of use to yourself also in every way, if it be adopted. Perhaps those who are about you hold their heads on high, and will not allow you to adopt this course: they advise you to try your strength with our lord the king, and to exercise your power and prerogative against him and his. This power is a snare to one who is in error, but most formidable to him who will not atone for his error. We do not say that our lord the king has never erred, but we say and assert with confidence that he has always been ready to atone to his Lord for what he has done amiss. He has been appointed king by the Lord, and he provides in every thing for the peace of his subjects. It is to preserve this peace to the Churches and people committed to his charge that he wishes and requires the dignities granted to his ancestors to be maintained, and secured to himself. If, on this point, any contention has arisen between you and him, and the supreme pontiff, with fatherly piety, hath admonished him through our venerable fathers, the bishops of London and Hereford, he has not elevated his head to the clouds, but in every matter, wherein either the Church or any ecclesiastical person hath shown himself aggrieved, the king hath always answered humbly and mildly that he has never coveted that which belongs to others, but that he will submit to the judgment of the clergy of his kingdom; and he has always shown himself ready to fulfil what he has thus promised. Compliance is sweet to him, when he is admonished to correct what he has done amiss towards God. Nor does he limit this to mere words of atonement, but is ready to give whatever justice may demand. Inasmuch then as he is ready to do and to give all that is required, and neither in the slightest particular shuns the judgment of the Church in aught that concerns the Church, nor shows the least disposition to withdraw his neck from the yoke of Christ, by what justice, by what law or canon can you assail him with an interdict, or (God forbid the deed!) hew him off by the spiritual axe from Christian unity? It is praiseworthy not to be borne away by passion, but to be guided by prudence and discretion. Wherefore it is the common petition of all of us, that you will not, by too hasty measures, slay and destroy, but provide with paternal solicitude that the sheep committed to your charge may enjoy life, peace, and security.

"We all of us sympathize in what has been lately done—some think preposterously—against our brother, the lord bishop of Salisbury and his dean, against whom you have hurled the sentence of suspension, and condemned before inquiry had been made into their fault, following, as it seemed to us, the heat of passion rather than the course of justice. This is a new mode of giving judgment, unknown hitherto, as we had hoped, to the laws and canons, to pass sentence first and afterwards to hear the cause. That you may not attempt to exercise or to extend this prerogative against our lord the king aud his kingdom, against us, and the Churches and parishes committed to our charge, to the injury of our lord the pope, and the disgrace and detriment of the holy Roman Church, and to the no slight augmentation of our own confusion, we stand upon the remedy that we have, and appeal against you. And whereas we have already, in the face of the Church, appealed to our lord the pope, against the sentence which we feared; we here also appeal a second time to the same in writing, and we fix as the term for the appeal the day of our Lord's ascension, praying most devoutly that you may adopt more salutary counsel, and spare this expense and toil to both of us; and so to shape your cause that a remedy may be found for it. We bid you, father, farewell in the Lord."

LETTER XXXVII.

"TO THE CLERGY OF ENGLAND.

"THOMAS, BY THE GRACE OF GOD, HUMBLE MINISTER OF THE CHURCH OF CANTERBURY, TO HIS REVEREND BRETHREN IN GENERAL, BY GOD'S GRACE, BISHOPS OF THE PROVINCE OF KENT, IF INDEED THE LETTER BE THEIR JOINT PRODUCTION, HEALTH AND GRACE TO ACT AS THEY HAVE NOT YET ACTED.

"YOUR joint letter, my brethren, which has just reached us, but which we cannot easily believe to have proceeded from your joint wisdom, has filled us with astonishment. Its contents seem to convey more of irony than of consolation: and I would that it had been dictated by pious zeal and feeling of charity rather than the suggestions of the will. Charity seeks not that which is its own, but that which is Jesus Christ's. It was the duty of those in your office, so says the Gospel, if you would rightly discharge the duty and faithfully fulfil the mission of Him whose likeness you bear, rather to fear Him who is able to cast both soul and body into hell, than him who can kill the body only; to obey God rather than man, our Father rather than our master: following the example of Him who became obedient to the Father, even to death. He died for us, leaving us an example, that we may follow his steps. It is ours then to die with Him, to lay down our lives in redeeming His Church from the yoke of slavery, and the oppressions of him who grieves her, the Church, which He hath founded, whose liberty He procured with His own blood; lest, if we act otherwise, we deservedly incur that evangelical censure: 'He who loves his own soul more than Me, is not worthy of Me.' You ought to have well known that if what your ruler commands is just, you are bound to obey his will; if unjust, to answer, We must obey God rather than man. One thing I have to say to you, if I may say it without offending you: I have long kept silence, waiting if perchance the Lord should so inspire you, that you should again take courage, after you had once turned your backs in the day of battle; that even one only of you would go up against the enemy and present himself as a wall of defence for the house of Israel, even if he only made a show of contending against those who do not cease daily to reproach the army of the Lord. I waited, but there was no one to go up: I was patient, but no one stood forward: I was silent, but no one spoke: I dissembled, but no one made even a show of resisting. For the rest, there remains to me to urge my complaint, so that I may truly say, 'Arise, O God, and judge my cause. Avenge the blood of the Church, which has been embowelled, and faints with oppression. For the pride of those who hate its liberty is continually ascending, nor is there any remaining that doeth good, no not one.'

"Would to God, my beloved brethren, that you[2] had the same zeal in defending the liberty of the Church, as you have shown towards its confusion, in your letters of appeal, falsely, as we believe, so called. But her foundations are upon a rock, nor is any man able to upturn, though he may shake them. Why do you endeavour to confound me, and in me to confound yourselves and me together? I have taken the whole danger upon myself, I have borne so many

---

[2] It is always difficult to determine in the manuscripts between *nobis* and *vobis*. The printed text has nobis in this place, but vobis appears to be the true reading.

reproaches, so many injuries, and have suffered proscription in behalf of all of you. It was expedient that one man should be afflicted for the Church, that so she might be released from slavery. Consider the matter in single-mindedness, examine it well, and weigh well the result, that you may set aside the majesty of royalty, and regard to persons, of whom God is no accepter, and that you may be brought to understand the true nature of what you have done, and of what you are about to do. May God remove the veil from your hearts, that you may perceive your duty. If there be any one among you who can say that since my promotion I have taken away from him an ox or an ass, or his money: if I have judged unjustly the cause of any one, or to the injury of any one among you have procured advantage to myself, let him now speak and I will restore fourfold. But if I have offended no one, why do you leave me to fight alone in the cause of God? You are fighting against yourselves in that cause so vital to the interests of the Church. Do not so, my brethren: do not, as far as lies in your power, confound both yourselves and God's Church, but turn to me and you will be safe. For the Lord hath said, 'I will not the death of the righteous, but rather that he should be converted and live.' Stand manfully with me in the battle, with shield and sword rise up to aid me. Gird yourselves with the sword of God's word, which is all-powerful, that we may be the better able to strive in the discharge of our duty against those who accuse us, against those who work iniquity, and assail that liberty which is the existence of the Church, without which she cannot flourish nor keep down those who would possess as their inheritance the sanctuary of the Lord.

"Let us make haste then, lest the anger of God descend upon us as upon negligent and slothful shepherds. Let us not be taken for dumb dogs, that cannot bark: let it not be said of us by those who pass by, 'From the elders of Babylon iniquity hath gone forth.' If in truth you listen to me, know that the Lord will be with you, and with all of you, in all your ways, to give peace to his Church, and to defend her liberties. If you will not listen to me, let God judge between me and you, and at your hands will be required the troubles and confusion of his Church. For whether the world will or no, she must stand firm in the word of the Lord, whereon she is built, until the hour come, when she shall pass from this world to the Father. God will judge why you have left me alone in the battle, with no one of all those who were dear to me, to go up with me to the fight: insomuch that each of you may think or say, Woe to him alone, for if he falls, he has no one to raise him up. But my hopes are laid up within my own bosom; for he is not alone with whom the Lord is: when he falls, he shall not be dashed to pieces, for the Lord sustains him in his hand.

"But let us come to the point, my brethren: has it escaped your memory how I and the Church were dealt with, when I was still in England? what was done at the time of my departure, after my departure, and in these latter days, and especially at Northampton, when Christ was judged in my person before the tribunal of the prince? when the archbishop of Canterbury was constrained by the injuries done indiscriminately to himself and the Church of God to appeal to the Roman see, and to place under the protection of God and the Roman Church, all the possessions which belonged to him, or rather which belonged to the poor, for they are the patrimony of our crucified Saviour, not given for our use, but entrusted to our stewardship? Although the Divine mercy has sometimes allowed the archbishop of Canterbury to be exiled unjustly, yet who ever heard of his being tried and condemned, compelled to give bail in the king's court, above all by his own suffragans? Where did they find this adverse authority, or rather perversity of the law and of the canons? Does not this act of enormity produce shame in all of you—shame leading to confusion—confusion to repentance, and repentance to retribution, both before God and man? To these great injuries wrought against God and his Church, and against me fighting in God's cause, I was unable to submit with a safe conscience, to remedy them without danger of my life, or to dissemble them without risk of my soul's salvation: wherefore I chose rather to turn aside for a while, that I might dwell with greater benefit in the house of the Lord than in the tents of sinners, until their iniquity should be complete, the breasts of the wicked laid open, and the thoughts of their hearts be revealed. Thus the injuries that were done to me were the cause of my appeal. This was the occasion of my departure, which you say was so unexpected; and if you, who know what was intended against me and how I was dealt with, would but speak the truth, you will admit that I was obliged to keep my departure secret, if I wished it not to be prevented altogether. But the Lord rules our misfortunes and turns them to good: He had regard to the honour of the king and his party, that nothing might be done against me which would redound to his dishonour or to the dishonour of his family. And it turned out well for those, who were eager for my death, and who thirsted for my blood, who aimed at the eminence of the see of Canterbury and at my destruction, with an avidity which, I grieve to speak it, is said to have surpassed even their ambition. We have appealed and have been appealed against, and whilst the possessions of the see of Canterbury, of myself and of my adherents, remain as they ought in safety, we have been engaged in prosecuting our appeal.

"If, as you say, things have been disturbed by my departure, and in consequence of my departure, let him take the blame who gave occasion for this disturbance: the fault lies with him who does the deed, not with him that retreats from it; with him who inflicts, not with him who shuns an injury. The author of mischief is he who has given cause for it. What more can I say? We presented ourselves before the court, and explained the injuries done to the Church and to ourselves, the cause of our coming, and the motive of our appeal: there was no one to answer us in anything: we waited, but no one brought anything against us: no judgment was reported against us until we came before the king. Whilst we were still waiting, as is usual, in the court, if by chance anything should be objected to us, our officials were forbidden to obey us in anything of a temporal nature, or to minister to us in any way against the command, or without the knowledge of the king. It was you, they say, my brother of London, with Richard of Ilchester and the archbishop of York, who advised this sentence. After this, they hurried to our lord the king, and the advice which they gave him will recoil on the head of the adviser. Without a trial, and for no reason, after we had already appealed, and whilst we were still remaining at the [papal] court, the Church was plundered, we and our adherents were plundered and proscribed, clerks as well as laics, men and women, women with infants in the cradle. The goods of the Church, which are the patrimony of our crucified Saviour, were added to the exchequer: part of the money was converted to the king's use, part to your use and to the use of your Church, my brother of London, if we have truly been informed. We now claim it, if you have had it, at your hands, enjoining you by virtue of your obedience, that within forty days after the receipt of this letter, whatever you have received from thence, or have converted to the use of your Church, you restore the whole thereof within the period above-named, without excuse and without delay. For it is unjust and contrary to all right, that one Church should be enriched out of the spoils of another. You must well know that of things taken from Churches, that man is ill qualified to exercise lawful authority, who practises violence and injustice.

"Under what perverse code of laws or preposterous canons shall those who commit sacrilege and invade the goods of the Church, shelter themselves, unless they restore what they have taken away? Shall they have recourse to an appeal? This would be introducing novelties, contrary to all justice, into the Churches. Consider the consequences of your proceedings. Unless you take good heed, they will be turned against yourselves and your Churches. The Church of God would be hardly dealt with, if a sacrilegious robber, invading its possessions, and the possessions of his neighbours, should be able to protect himself by an appeal. It is in vain to implore the aid of justice, when you have yourself neglected her and outraged her commands. Is it adding toil to toil, injuries to injuries, if we have been unable to bear such enormities as these and others, which have been wrought, and still are wrought in the Church, because when aggrieved we appealed and left the court, because we ventured to complain of the injuries done to the Church and to ourselves, because we do not hold our peace on all these subjects, because we are preparing to correct them? Sore, indeed, is a man's distress, when he is denied the consolation even of complaining. You, my friends, whose minds are more elevated, and endowed with greater prudence than the rest, since the children of this world are more prudent than the children of light, why do you deceive your brethren and those who are placed under you? Why do you lead them into error? What authority of Scripture has conferred on princes this prerogative in spiritual matters, which you are seeking to confer on them? Do not, my brethren, confound the rights of the monarchy and the Church. Their powers are distinct, and one of them derives its authority from the other. Read the Scriptures, and you will find how many kings have perished for usurping to themselves the sacerdotal office. Take heed to yourselves in your discretion, lest the weight of the Divine arm fall on you for such a crime. If it so fall, you will not easily escape.

"Consider, too, our lord the king: you are courting his favour at the expense of the Church: take care lest he perish, (which God forbid!) with his whole house, as those have perished who have been detected in such iniquity. Unless he desist from his attempts, with what conscience can we withhold punishment, or dissemble his misdeeds? Let him do so who has the power to cast a veil over sin, not I, lest such dissimulation recoil upon my own soul.

"You hint in your letters, or rather you say openly, that I was raised to this dignity amid the clamours of the whole kingdom, and the groans and the sorrow of the Church. Know you what truth says? The mouth that knowingly speaks falsehood, slayeth the soul. But the words of a priest ought ever to be accompanied by truth. Good God! would not one of the common people blush to say what you have said? Consult your own consciences, look at the form of election, the consent of all who were concerned therein, the consent of the king expressed through his son and through his emissaries; the consent of his son himself and of all the nobility of the kingdom. If any one of them spoke against it, or opposed it in the least, let him speak who knows, let him proclaim it who is conscious of it. But if any individual thereby had a downfall, let him not say that his private molestation was an injury done to the whole kingdom and to the Church. Remember, moreover, the letters of the king and your own letters, how you all, with much urgency, demanded the pall, and obtained it for me. This is the truth of the matter. But if any one has felt envy, or been actuated by ambition, if so peaceful, so lawful, and so unanimous an election hath grieved any one's mind, and led him to practise machinations by which things have become disturbed, may God induce him, as we would, to confess his error, may he not be ashamed to acknowledge the disquietude of his mind in the face of all men.

"You say that the king raised me to honour from a mean estate. I am not indeed sprung from royal ancestors; but I would rather be the man to whom nobility of mind gives the advantages of birth, than one in whom a noble ancestry degenerates. I was, perhaps, born beneath a humble roof; but by God's mercy, that knoweth how to deal graciously with his servants, and chooses the humble to confound the brave, even in my humble condition, before I entered into God's service, my way of life was sufficiently easy, sufficiently honourable, as you yourselves know, even as that of the best among my neighbours and acquaintances, whosoever they might be. David also was taken from the goats to become the ruler of God's people, and was exalted by his courage and glory because he walked in the ways of the Lord. Peter was taken from fishing, to become the head of the Church, and, by shedding his blood for Christ, he was thought worthy to receive a crown in heaven, a name of honour upon earth. I pray that we also may do likewise: for we are the successors of Saint Peter, not of Augustus. God knows with what eagerness the king himself wished my promotion. Let him consult his own intentions; they will best answer him; and we too will respond to the requirements of our duty, more faithfully by God's mercy, in our severity, than is done by those who flatter him with falsehoods. For better are the stripes of a friend, than the deceitful embraces of an enemy.

" You throw out against us an imputation of ingratitude. But there is no mortal sin which entails infamy on a man, unless it has proceeded from the intention. Thus, if one commit homicide unwillingly, though he is called a homicide, and is one, yet he does not incur the guilt of homicide. We apply the principle in this way: Though we owe obedience by the divine law to our lord the king, if we are bound to pay him respect by the royal prerogative, if we have checked him or warned him as a son with paternal love, if after warning we have grieved that he did not listen to us, and by the force of duty exercise towards him censure and severity, we believe that we are acting rather on his behalf, and for his good, than in opposition to him; that we deserve praise at his hands, rather than blame, or the reproach of ingratitude. Certainly, benefits are often conferred on men against their will, and that man's safety is better regarded who is deterred from the perpetration of a crime by force even if he cannot in any other way. Besides, our Father and patron, Christ himself, exonerates us from the stamp of ingratitude. By his Father's prerogative we are bound to obey Him, and if we neglect this, we shall be justly punished by being disinherited. A father can disinherit his son for a just cause: for He says, 'If you do not tell the wicked of his iniquity, and he die in his sin, I will require his blood at your hand.' If, therefore, we do not convene him who sins, if we do not reprove him when he will not listen to us, and coerce him when he is pertinacious, we offend against the precept, and are justly disinherited as guilty of disobedience. By his prerogative of being our patron, we are held to revere and to obey Him, because we are his freed men, for whereas we were slaves of sin, we are become freed unto righteousness through his grace. As, therefore, we are bound to no other, but saving our allegiance to Him, if aught be done vexatiously against Him to the injury of his Church, if we do not punish the crime by exerting in his cause that solicitude which is incumbent on us, He will deservedly withdraw from us the benefits which He has heaped upon us, and thus we indeed show ourselves ungrateful.

"You name to us the danger which will accrue to the Roman Church, the loss of her temporalities. This danger falls on us and on ours, but nothing is said of the danger to the soul. You hold over us a threat, that our lord the king will withdraw, (God forbid it!) from his allegiance and devotion to the Roman Church. God forbid, I say, that temporal gain or loss should ever cause our lord the king to fall back from his allegiance or devotion to the Church! This would be criminal and damnable even in a private man; how much more so in a prince who draws so many after him. God forbid that any of the faithful should ever entertain this thought, much less speak it, however humble he may be, not to say a bishop! Consider in your discretion, lest the words of your mouth should tempt any one, or even several, to the risk and damnation of their souls, like the golden cup of Babylon, smeared within and without with poison, of which he that drinks fears not the poison when he sees the gold; thus a desire to do this deed may spread abroad, and yours will be the deed. For He who is not deceived, brings the secret deed to light, and unveils wicked machinations.

"The Church hath ever increased and multiplied under tribulation and blood-shedding. It is her peculiarity to conquer whilst she is injured, to possess understanding when she is refuted, to succeed when she is deserted. Do not mourn for her, my brethren, but for yourselves, who are earning for yourselves a name, but not a great one, by such words and deeds, in the mouths of men. You provoke against you the anger of God and of all mankind: you are preparing a halter for the innocent, and inventing new and ingenious arguments, to subvert the liberty of the Church. My brethren, by God's mercy, you are labouring in vain. The Church will stand, though often shaken, in that firmness and solidity wherein she was founded, until the general consummation of all things, when that son of perdition shall arise, who will not, we think, arise from the west, unless the order of things as spoken of in the Scripture shall be perversely changed.

"If, however, it be a question of temporal matters, we should rather fear the loss of souls than of temporalities. Scripture says, 'What doth it profit a man to gain the whole world and lose his own soul.' We, therefore, utterly cast from us the danger to us and to ours: for he is not to be feared who kills the body, but He who kills both body and soul.

"You reprove us for suspending our venerable brother, the bishop of Salisbury, and excommunicating John, the schismatic ex-dean; for inflicting punishment, as you say, before hearing the cause, or following the usual course of canonical judgments. We answer that the sentence of both was just, the suspension of the one, and the excommunication of the other. If you knew the whole course of the matter, or rightly attended to the order of the judgments, we think you would alter your opinion. Such is the extent of authority, as you ought to know, that in manifest and notorious crimes a hearing is not required. Consider diligently what was done by the bishop of Salisbury about the deanery after the prohibition, which our lord the pope and ourselves made under pain of excommunication: you will then be able to judge whether the suspension did not ensue after an act of manifest disobedience. Wherefore the blessed Clement says, ' If all of every degree, whether princes of inferior or of superior rank, and all the rest of the people, do not obey their bishops, they shall not only be branded with infamy, but cast out from God's kingdom and the company of the faithful, and banished from the threshold of God's holy Church.

"As regards John of Oxford, we reply, that different persons become excommunicated in different ways; some by the law which denounces them as excommunicated, others marked by a sentence, and others again by communicating with those who are excommunicated. Now John of Oxford fell into a damnable heresy, by communicating with schismatics, and with those whom our lord the pope had excommunicated, and so contracted in himself the taint of excommunication, which pollutes like a leprosy, and involves the guilty and those who consent unto them in the same punishment. And whereas John, thus excommunicate, usurped the deanery of Salisbury contrary to the commands both of our lord the pope and of ourselves, expressed under pain of anathema, we have denounced him and excommunicated him, and hold him as utterly excommunicate. We have, moreover, annulled, and do hold as null, whatever has been done during his deanship, and connected with his deanship, as also our lord the pope has already annulled it by authority of the eighth synod, of which this is the import: 'If any one openly or secretly shall converse with one who is excommunicated, or join in communion with him, he at once contracts in himself the pain of excommunication.' The council of Carthage also says, 'Whosoever communicates with one who is excommunicated, if he is a clerk, shall be deposed. Take care, therefore, in your discretion, that none of you communicate with him.' For pope Calixtus says: 'Let no one receive any that have been excommunicated by their priests, before he has made full inquiry on both sides, nor communicate with them in prayer, or in meat or drink, or with a kiss, or with words of salutation.' For whosoever shall communicate knowingly with the excommunicated, in these and other particulars which are forbidden, shall, according to the institution of the Apostles, lie under similar excommunication. This is the canonical regulation, not repugnant, as we believe, to the canons, but supported by their authority.

"And do not wonder that he was condemned, though absent: for you read of the man who committed open fornication with his step-mother: he was neither confronted by witnesses, nor made confession of his crime, for all were acquainted with it, though no one charged him with it, as was the case with John of Oxford, who is unduly defended by the royal authority. Paul cast out that man from the communion of the faithful, and delivered him over to Satan, that by the death of the body his soul might be saved, as we also have done by John of Oxford. But in these days many such grave and enormous offences are perpetrated amongst you in my absence; and though absent in the body, my authority is ever present with you, nor can I with a safe conscience, nor ought I to pass them by uncorrected. You, my brother of London, ought to have known that sentence of Gregory the Seventh, 'If any bishop shall for money, or intercession, or favour, consent to a priest or deacon committing fornication, or the crime of incest, in his diocese, or shall not punish it by virtue of his office, he shall be suspended from his office;' and that of Leo, 'If any bishop shall consecrate to the priesthood an improper man, although he shall be safe from being deprived of his own rank, yet for the future he shall lose the right of ordination, nor shall he be present at any sacrament which he has unworthily discharged.' You, my brother of London, have doubly offended, as we have heard for certain, against the meaning of those canons; wherefore we enjoin and command you, by virtue of your obedience, if what we have heard be true, within three months after the receipt of these letters, to submit yourself to correction and satisfaction for this great transgression, with the advice of your venerable brothers and fellow-bishops, lest others by your example fall into the same error, and we are compelled by your negligence to propound a severer mandate.

"To the fear of censure from us you oppose an appeal, not of remedy, but of impediment, as we take it, that we may not inflict ecclesiastical discipline on those who do amiss and invade the possessions of the Church, nor proceed against our lord the king and his kingdom, or against your own persons and Churches, in the same way as we have already proceeded, as you say irregularly, against the bishop of Salisbury and his dean. Far be it from us to have done or to do anything irregularly against him or his kingdom, or against you and your Churches. But what if you have offended in the same way, or in a similar way with the bishop of Salisbury; can you, by this appeal, suspend our authority, so that we shall not exercise the severity of discipline against you and your Churches, if the enormity of your offence requires it? Consider whether this appeal be lawful, and reflect upon the nature of it. We know that every one who appeals does so in his own name or in the name of another. If in his own name, it is either against a censure already passed, or one which he fears will be passed upon him. We are certain that no censure has been passed on you by us, thank God, which requires that you should have recourse to an appeal: nor do we believe that there is any cause between us at present which especially concerns you. If you have appealed from fear that censure will be passed upon you or on your Churches, consider whether your fears are such as ought to be entertained by men of courage and fortitude, whether it be an appeal which ought to suspend the authority and power which we have over you and your Churches. It is thought by the well-informed, and we also think the same, that it is of no weight, both because it is destitute of form, and because it is inconsistent with reason, and utterly unsupported by all justice.

"If you have appealed in the name of another, it must be in the name of the king or of some third party. If not of a third, it must be in the king's name. Wherefore you ought to have known in your discretion, that appeals were introduced to repel injuries, not to inflict them, to relieve the oppressed, not to oppress them more. If then a man appeals, not from confidence in the justice of his cause, but for the sake of creating delay, and that sentence may not pass against him, his appeal should not be listened to. For what will be the condition of the Church, if, when her liberty is subverted, her possessions taken from her, her bishops expelled their sees, or not peacefully reinstated in full possession; the robbers who plunder her and invade her rights, shall appeal against their sentence and find safety in their appeal? What destruction will this be to the Church! Reflect on the consequences of your words and deeds! Are you not Christ's vicars? Do you not supply his place on earth, to correct and punish malefactors, and cause them to cease from persecuting the Church of God? Is it not more than enough that they should assail the Church, without your standing forward in their behalf, to the destruction of the Church and of yourselves? Who ever heard anything so strange? It will be proclaimed and published in every people and nation, that the suffragans of the Church of Canterbury, who should live and die with their metropolitan in defence of the Church and her liberty, and submit to any sacrifice for the same, are desirous, at the king's command, as much as in them lies, to suspend his power and authority, that he may not exercise the severity of discipline on those who offend against His Church. One thing I know full well; you cannot sustain the part of both sides, both of the appellant and of him against whom you appeal. You are the appellants, and the appeal is against yourselves. Is not the Church one, and are not you part of its body? This is truly a Cadmæan conflict, that the members of the Church are waging against their Head, which is Christ. I fear, my brethren, though God forbid that it should be so, lest they say of you, 'These are the priests, who have asked, where is the Lord? and holding the law, have known me not.' Moreover, we believe that in your discretion you cannot be ignorant, that appellants are only heard when it is their own interest at stake, or they are deputed to maintain the cause of another. Is it to your interest that those who offend against the Church should not be restrained? Surely not, but rather the contrary. But if the man who subverts the liberty of the Church, invades and seizes her goods and converts them to his own use, is not heard in his own defence when he appeals, surely those cannot be heard who appeal on his behalf. Neither our lord the king can derive support, nor you advantage from the appeal which you have made in his favour. If he can neither appeal, nor instruct another to do this in this cause, neither can you receive from him instructions to appeal for him. We add further, that you can in no way take up the matter for him in this cause. For no bishop can maintain the part of another against himself, particularly to the injury of the Church, of which he is the defender, and above all, when the Church in general is assailed. If, therefore, the appeal concerns you not, and you cannot undertake it by commission, nor defend the cause of another, your appeal cannot be heard, nor is it good in law.

"Is this your devotion, is this the consolation and fraternal charity which you show to your metropolitan, who is suffering exile in your cause? God forgive you for such a want of tenderness! Are you ignorant, my brethren, what a great gulf is established to the destruction of the laws and canons between us, so that none of you can pass over to us without risking loss of life or mutilation of limb, though any one of us may, if he pleases, cross over to you[4]? We wonder, therefore, what order you preserve, when there is no order observed towards us as regards Churches or ecclesiastical persons, but wrongs and a state of terror, such as, I pray, may not last for ever. Both ourselves and our adherents are

[4] There is, probably, some corruption of the original text in this passage.

plundered. Some of them have been redeemed, as well clerks as laics, that had been taken since our appeal made at Northampton, and your appeal against ourselves. Moreover, since that appeal, as you term it, a general edict has been issued, that all of us who are found on English ground shall be taken prisoners; that none of you or of our other friends shall dare to receive our letters or our messengers. This then is the respect shown to an appeal, during the continuance of which, if it be a just appeal, no fresh step should be taken. Look ye to this. How can you expect us to receive your letters and messengers, or to listen to what they say? But by this we do not mean, however we and ours may be dealt with, that we have ever done anything irregularly towards the person or the kingdom of our lord the king, or your persons and Churches, or by God's mercy will we ever do so.

"We had fancied, if you understood me rightly, that you would have shown your zeal for the Church, by blaming us for our too-long endurance, rather than by praising us for this delay of severity. For delay is dangerous; and too much patience is censurable rather than praiseworthy, having more of vice than virtue. Hence it is that we tell you in few words and affirm it unhesitatingly: our lord the king will have no reason to complain if, after being frequently and duly warned by our lord the pope and us, both by letter and by messengers, his refusal to make amends should draw down upon him severe censures. He is not wronged whom justice duly punishes: and to sum up all in few words, let it be clearly understood by you, that those who invade and plunder the possessions of the Church, are protected by no plea of justice, nor can appeal in any way avail them. If moreover, my brethren, you desire to be of use to the king, as is right of you, and as we also wish, God who is the searcher of hearts well knoweth, take heed to assist him in such a way as not to offend God, nor the Church, nor your own order ; to the end also that he may escape speedily and providentially from the danger to his own soul, which is awaiting him. Thus much have I urged, if perchance by the divine grace he may be advised by you to make amends to the Church: she will rejoice at the return of her son, for she has always been and still is ready to receive him with devotion and gratitude, and we too shall rejoice.

"But you say that he is willing and ready to make amends to the Church by your judgment, if any contention has arisen between him and us concerning the liberties of the Church, of which there can be no doubt, for it is well known to all the world. This proposition of yours is unreasonable and contrary to justice: how then can we do wrong by not entertaining it? Is that a sufficient reason why he should not feel the Divine wrath for turning a deaf ear to canonical censure, and for adding injury to injury? It is certain that you cannot act as judge between him and us. In the first place you are his opponents, or you ought to be, in defence of the liberty of the Church, which is committed to your care: look to it if you neglect this duty, for hesitation will bring you into danger. In the next place, we nowhere read of superiors being judged by their inferiors, metropolitans by their suffragans. Thirdly, there are some among you whom the Church and we regard with suspicion; I hope not all of you: the reasons for which are different, but for the present we forbear to mention them.

"I pray then, that our lord the king may listen to the petition of his faithful servant; and not despise the counsels of his bishop, the admonitions of his father: so may God bless him, and prolong his days and the life of his sons for many years to come. May he permit his own Church to enjoy peace and liberty under him as under a most Christian king, whilst the Roman Church is suffered to exercise in his dominions the same jurisdiction and liberty which she has a right to, and which she possesses in other countries. Let him restore to us and to the Church of Canterbury, the rights, liberties, and possessions which have been taken from us, in full security, that so we may serve God in peace and tranquillity, and he may employ our services as shall seem good to him, saving the honour of God, and of the Roman Church, and of our own order. Such are the royal dignities and good laws, which a Christian king ought to demand and to observe: in these he should take delight, and the Church flourish under him. Such laws as these are in accordance, not in opposition to the law of God, and he who observes them not, becomes an enemy to God; for the law of God is pure, converting the soul. For the Lord says of his own laws, 'Keep my laws:' and the prophet says, ' Woe to those who establish unjust laws, and writing, write iniquity, that they may oppress the poor in judgment, and do violence to the cause of the humble ones of God's people.'

" Let not our lord then be ashamed to return to a better state of feeling, to humble himself in humility and contrition of heart before the Lord, to make satisfaction to Him and to his Church for the injuries he has done it. For the Lord does not despise the humble and contrite heart, but embraces it in sincerity. Thus also holy David, after he had offended, humbled himself before the Lord, and asked for mercy, and obtained forgiveness. Thus also the king of Nineveh and all his city, when threatened with destruction, humbled themselves before the Lord in sackcloth and ashes, and by contrition of heart obtained a remission of their sentence.

"We write thus to you, my brethren, not that your faces may be put to confusion, but that when you have read our letter, and comprehended its import, you may the more boldly and freely do what duty bids you. May you henceforth so act that we may the sooner have peace, and the Church more ample liberty. Pray for us, that our faith may not fail in tribulation, but that we may say with the apostle, 'Neither death, nor life, nor angels, nor any other creature shall separate us from the love of God.'

"Farewell all of you in the Lord; may the whole English Church remember us daily in their prayers."

LETTER XXXVIII.

"TO HIS VENERABLE LORD AND FATHER IN CHRIST, THOMAS ARCHBISHOP OF CANTERBURY, GILBERT MINISTER OF THE CHURCH OF LONDON, HEALTH.

"MANIFOLD and lengthy, my father, is the subject of your profound and copious letter, and however anxious we are to prosecute the appeal to our lord the pope, you compel us, almost of necessity, to write again to your highness. For amid the shafts which you launch out at random on every side, you single me out from our whole fraternity as an object for reproach, and cover me with abuse, though I have done nothing to deserve it.

It is marvellous that a man of sober feeling, of a grave and reverend character,—a professor bound by his episcopal station and by his doctrines to have regard to truth,—should act so intemperately when the truth was told him; that he should not only have rejected the son who wished to advise his father, but have undeservedly ascribed his advice to a malicious feeling, of which he is himself unconscious. When, therefore, I am publicly charged with subverting the Church of God, confounding right and wrong, with insanely aiming to overthrow that mountain of the Church which is the pillar of the living God, with having been ambitious to possess what belongs to you, and when repulsed in my designs, with having vented my malice in disturbing the peace of God's Church and your own, and with having turned my back in fighting the Lord's battles, it is difficult for me to keep silence, lest I be supposed by the present generation to plead guilty to the charge, and posterity admit the accusation against me, because it has never been refuted.

"Now as cupidity is the root and origin of all evils, I will begin with that, lest those who are easily led by others, suppose that I am influenced thereby. The apostle says: 'What man knows the secrets of a man, save the spirit of man that is within him?' The secret thoughts of a man are known to no man, but only to the Lord of heaven. Things that are unknown cannot escape Him, nothing can be hidden from Him. The word of the Lord lives and is of power, it is sharper than the sharpest sword: nor is anything invisible in his sight. It is to Him, and in his presence that I speak: before his tribunal my reply is given, and I say boldly and fearlessly, and with truth, as my conscience dictates, that no impulse of ambition has ever for a moment excited me to covet that power and station which belong to you. Never have I felt envy that another should enjoy that honour. Never have I courted any one by gift, service, influence, or favour, that I might myself obtain it, or carve out for myself a guilty road to that eminence.

"Who can know this better than you, my father, who at that time were archdeacon of that Church, and not the chosen counsellor merely of the king, but his bosom friend, without whose aid it was absolutely impossible for any one to obtain promotion? What favour did I ever attempt to gain with you? Did I ever by gifts or services endeavour, directly or indirectly, to secure your good-will that I might obtain promotion by your intervention, which was, at that time, the only way? If this be true, it is but just to infer that I have acted with the same moderation towards others, who might be supposed to possess less influence than you.

"Thus, then, I sum up this business, and do not fear to take the burden of this accusation upon me; that I may have it laid up in store for me against the great day of account, if my conscience convicts me in the smallest particular of being guilty of this crime. No, my father, it was not my own rejection that grieved me in your promotion. I did not seek on that day to advance my own interests, but those of Christ Jesus, and to give glory in all things, not to myself, but to his name, and I grieved to see my endeavours baffled. When we saw the privileges of the Church subverted, right and wrong confounded, and the summit of that lofty mountain, of which you speak, humbled to the ground, when we saw that spouse of Christ shamefully deprived of the liberty which she had always before enjoyed, we groaned aloud in the Lord, and many of us immediately, by some influence of God's Spirit working in us, had a foretaste of the troubles which we are now suffering. We ought then to have remembered what is written, how difficult it is to bring to a happy issue what has been ill begun. For if we look back at the beginning, who is there so dull in all our part of the world, as not to know that you obtained the dignity of chancellor by sale for several thousand marks, and that by favour of this wind, you found a haven in the Church of Canterbury, to the government of which you were at last promoted—whether canonically or not—whether by your merits or otherwise, is known to many, and on the memories of all good men is written with the pen of sorrow.

"Our good father, the late archbishop Theobald, of excellent memory, had descended to the grave, and you, who had your eyes open to this contingency, came back with speed from Normandy to England. The king speedily sent that able nobleman and guardian of his kingdom, Richard de Lucy, whom you have now so meritoriously excommunicated; his instructions were, that the monks of Canterbury and suffragan bishops of that Church should elect you for their father and pastor without delay, otherwise they would incur the king's anger, and speedily find by experience that he regarded them in the light of enemies. We know what we are saying, and you know it too: for we anticipated that the Church was about to be smothered, and we in a manner raised our voice against it, for which we heard a sentence of proscription passed against us, and not only our own person, but our father's house, our friends and relations were doomed to banishment. Others also were made to drink from the same cup. It is written, 'The lion shall roar, who will not tremble?' and again, 'As the roaring of a lion, so is the terror of a king.' But what the king himself commanded with so much earnestness, what he urged on by such powerful embassies, and you, as was known to all, were so bent upon, whilst all your friends and creatures were using threats, promises, and blandishments to promote it, who was there that dared make opposition to it? who could resist this torrent of the will and of the royal mandate? The sword of state was in your hand, shedding terror on all whom you might view with an angry eye. It was the same sword which your own hand had plunged into the bosom of our holy mother Church, when you stripped her of so many thousand marks to pay the expenses of the expedition to Toulouse. That you might not use it again to smite, she obeyed your orders, and to avoid what she feared, feigned acquiescence in what she loathed. O how averse were the hearts of all good men from the deed! how repugnant were their wishes! but what had been enjoined on us by such fierce threats, was hastened to its completion. Thus you entered into the sheep-fold by another way, and not through the gate, and by this invasion, my father, you took away from the Church the liberty which she had enjoyed for ages, yea, her very life, as you yourself express it, and so you have made her lifeless. Good

God! what horror came over all on that day, when all prognosticated from what they saw the indication of the future, spoken of by the evangelist Saint Matthew, how the Lord said to the barren fig-tree, 'Let no fruit be borne by thee for ever,' and it withered away immediately. We ought on that day to have replied to the king's message, that we should obey God rather than man. Would that our minds had been alive on that day to the fear of Him who is able to kill the soul in hell, rather than to him who can kill the body only! But it was not so, and the sin calls forth our blushes—our blushes cover us with confusion—confusion will, by God's mercy, produce repentance, which in turn will lead to atonement, so that the tears will not cease to bedew our cheeks, until God turn the captivity of Sion, and console the mourners in Jerusalem, and bring back the eye of mercy upon her outcasts.

"In the mean time let us briefly describe the sequel, and see what was the fruit of your elevation. Since the accession of our religious king up to that day the Church had enjoyed tranquillity, save, as we have said, that she felt the weight of your hands for the equipment of the army at Toulouse; otherwise, under our good king, every thing was tranquil and happy. The throne treated the altar with due observance, and the altar supported the throne in every good work. The two swords were both on duty in the Church, both in devout obedience to the Lord Jesus, not opposing one another, nor acting in contrary directions. The people were one, and, as it is written, of one lip, zealous to punish crime and eradicate vice. There was peace between Church and State, which were united together in mutual good-will, and went hand in hand. In your promotion we looked for an increase of blessings, when lo, for our sins, every thing was thrown into confusion. It is a virtue to oppose vice when it arises; and to dash against the rock, which is Christ, the untoward productions of the mind. Your prudence, therefore, should have taken precautions against the differences which might arise between you and the king, lest they might increase, and so, from a small flame, should arise a large fire, which might consume many. But it turned out otherwise; and for causes which it is too long to mention, differences were augmented, anger excited, and deadly hatred engendered. This was the cause, this the first origin of our lord the king's determination to inquire into his royal dignities, and to publish them to the people. The observance of them was demanded from you, and from the suffragan bishops of your Church; but because some of them seemed calculated to destroy the liberty of the Church, we refused to give our consent to them, except to those which could be observed without detriment to the honour of God and of our own order. Our lord the king urged us to promise an absolute and unqualified observance, but he could not obtain from us what impugned both the liberties of the Church and our allegiance to our lord the pope. For this end were meetings held, and councils convoked: why need I mention what was done at London, or afterwards at Oxford?

"Let us pass in review what took place at Clarendon; where, for three whole days, the point was to obtain from us a promise to observe unconditionally the king's dignities and customs. We stood by you then; because we thought you were standing boldly in the Spirit of the Lord: we stood immovable, and were not terrified: we stood firm, to the ruin of our fortunes, to encounter bodily torment, or exile; or, if God should so please, the sword. What father was ever better supported by his sons in adversity? who could be more unanimous than we? we were all shut up in one chamber, and on the third day the princes and nobles of the kingdom, bursting into fury, entered the conclave where we sat, threw back their cloaks, and holding forth their hands to us, exclaimed, 'Listen, you who set at nought the king's statutes, and obey not his commands: these hands, these arms, these bodies of ours, are not our's, but King Henry's, and they are ready at his nod to avenge his wrongs, and to work his will whatever it may be. Whatever are his commands, they will be law and justice in our eyes: retract these counsels then, and bend to his will, that you may avoid the danger before it is too late.' What was the result of this? Did any one turn his back to flee? was any one's resolution shaken? Your letter, my father, reproaches me with having turned my back in the day of battle; with having neither gone up to the strife, nor placed myself as a wall of defence before the house of the Lord. Let God judge between us; let Him judge in whose cause we then stood: in his cause we were not bent by the threats of princes; let Him say who it was that fled, that became a deserter in the battle: for it assuredly was not that noble champion in God's cause, Henry of Winchester, nor Nigel of Ely, nor Robert of Lincoln, nor Hilary of Chichester, nor Jocelin of Salisbury, nor Bartholomew of Exeter, nor Richard of Chester, nor Roger of Worcester, nor Robert of Hereford, nor Gilbert of London. All these were found to stand firm; but there was no one found who dared to smite them: they accounted temporal things as dross, and exposed themselves without fear for Christ and for his Church. Let the truth then be told, let the light of day be thrown on what was then done in presence of us all. It was the leader of our chivalry himself who turned his back, the captain of our camp who fled: his lordship of Canterbury himself withdrew from our fraternity, and from our determination; and, after holding counsel apart for a while, he returned to us, and said aloud, 'It is the Lord's will that I should perjure myself: for the present I submit and incur perjury: to repent of it, however, as I best may.' We were thunderstruck at these words, and gazed one upon the other, groaning in spirit at the fall of one whom we had thought a champion of virtue and constancy. There is no such thing as yea nay with the Lord, nor did we anticipate that his disciple was so easy to be turned.

"When the head faints, the other members faint also, and speedily suffer from its weakness. Our lord of Canterbury himself acceded to the king's royal dignities and constitutions, when they were reduced to writing, and when he had himself promised to observe them, commanded us to bind ourselves by a like engagement. Thus was a finish put to the contention, and the priesthood reconciled with the throne. Thus Israel went down into Egypt, from whence we read that he afterwards came out with glory. And we also had hopes that when our lord the king's mind was tranquillized, we might restore things to their former state: but the old enemy was envious of our tranquillity whilst it was still recent, and we had hardly entered the harbour ere we were again compelled to put to sea. The promise that you would not leave the kingdom without the king's consent, was still fresh upon your lips, and the words of a priest should always be the companions of truth. But lo! within a few days you spread your sails to the winds, and essayed to flee the realm, though the king knew nothing of the matter. When the king heard of it, no one was more surprised than he, no one grieved more at this deviation of a priest from his plighted word. For he knew the scandal that would be created against himself, and the attack that would be made among foreign nations upon his reputation, hitherto unstained. What, indeed, could those who were unacquainted with the truth suppose, save that his unchristian malice had led him to expel Christ's priest? He would rather have been wounded in his person by your hand, than suffer this blemish upon his fame. But the wind was adverse, and you were driven back to port; yet thus in the king's power, did you receive injury from his hand or insult from his lips? Far from it; he received you with courtesy, and sent you back among your own people.

"This storm had hardly ceased to blow, and our minds were scarcely tranquillized, ere another convulsion shook us. You received a royal mandate to do justice to one who had a claim upon your Church. But this suitor waited in vain for justice, and returned disappointed to the king. His majesty espoused the suitor's part, and cited you to appear and render in his presence the justice which you had denied to his written mandate. To this citation you did not listen, but returned an answer that declared your disobedience. The king, whose power was thus outraged, convoked a council at Northampton. The people came together as one man: the nobles and elders heard the king, whilst, with becoming moderation, he described your disobedience to his summons. But you at once acknowledged the charge without waiting for the counsel of your bishops, and you gave as your reason, that the suitor John had sworn, not upon the gospels, but on a book of jests. All then agreed that this was not a valid cause for neglecting the king's summons, and that it was customary in such matters for a fine to be adjudged to the king, subject to his mercy. Your highness bowed to the sentence and gave bail for the full amount, without considering the canon, 'No bishop shall be cited before a civil or military judge in any cause, either criminal or civil,' and again: 'A clerk impleaded before a secular judge, shall not answer to the plea.' Nor that rescript of Gelasius to bishop Helpidius, 'How dare you write that you are preparing to set out for Ravenna, when the canons forbid your going for that purpose, without first seeing or consulting us⁵?'

"Would to God that the matter could have ended with this humble-mindedness, and that when the king claimed from you the money which you owed him, and sought nothing but his due, you had then been less ready to rise in indignation against it. What harm could it have done you to reply to this question? The king transferred you from the court to the government of the Church, and by so doing, as most men think, released you from all former obligations: but if this does not apply to debts, an exception might here have been taken, and if there were any points which could not well be reduced to calculation, compensation might have been made, for the king was actuated, not by avarice, but by anger, and so this civil question might most creditably have been settled.

"But you say it is an unheard-of thing that an archbishop of Canterbury should answer to such things in the king's court; and you may say that no one ever before heard of an officer of the king's court having so suddenly mounted

---

⁵ Two or three pages of uninteresting theological commonplaces are omitted here.

to so high a dignity—that he should one day be following his dogs and hawks, and the next be bending at the altar, and ministering in sacred things before all the bishops of the kingdom.

"Thus then you adopted a hostile course, for you entered the king's house carrying your own cross, and created in the minds of men a suspicion of foul conduct from the king. But his long-suffering declared how admirable was his integrity and his innocence: he was offended at your carrying the cross, but his offence exceeded not the bounds of moderation: he endeavoured to terminate his just claims within the bounds of justice. But you appealed from the judgment to the pope, and thus in the issue as in the outset his modesty and his toleration were conspicuous. The voice of paternal love once cried out, 'Save Absalom, save the boy Absalom,' and so also the voice of his heralds proclaimed aloud that the sword of public justice should overtake any one who dared to injure you. This was not all, for, as if your life were in danger, you fled by night in disguise, and escaped by sea out of the kingdom, though no one was pursuing you, and you chose out a residence for a time in a foreign country; from which you now attempt to steer that vessel of the Church, which you left without a pilot amid the waves. You call on us to turn to you to save ourselves, to encounter death with you in the cause of Christ's Church. Truly, if we consider what treasures are in store for us in heaven, we shall have no regard for the things of earth. For tongue cannot tell, nor intellect comprehend the joys of the heavenly city, to join the company of the angels, and with the blessed spirits to sing the praises of the Creator, to look upon his countenance, and free from the fear of death, to glory for ever in immortality. The sufferings of this world are nothing in comparison to the future glory which shall be revealed in the saints. Our momentary tribulations here will work out for us hereafter an exceeding weight of glory. All this, my father, I have long cherished in my bosom; all this has long been the subject of my aspirations. This head, which still rests upon my shoulders, should long have fallen by the sword of the executioner, to ensure the favour of God upon my earthly pilgrimage. But it is the cause and not the stroke which makes the martyr: to suffer persecution for holiness is glorious, for obstinacy or perverseness it is ignominious. It is victorious to die for Christ, but to provoke death is madness; and if we weigh your deeds as well as your words, my father, we shall not hastily provoke martyrdom. For you bent the knee at Clarendon; and took to flight at Northampton; you clothed yourself in the dress of disguise, and escaped beyond the frontiers of the land. What did you gain by this? Why, you showed your anxiety to escape that death, with which no one condescended to threaten you. With what effrontery then, father, do you invite us to meet death, which you, by such palpable means, so studiously avoided? What charity is it to place on us a burden which you threw off from your own shoulders? The sword hangs over us, from which you escaped, and which you try to repulse with missiles, never daring to advance to close encounter. Perhaps you wish us to flee also. Alas! the sea is closed against us since your escape, and every port blockaded. Islands are a king's safest prisons, from which it is difficult to depart, and almost impossible to do so privily. If we fight, it must be hand to hand ; if we join battle with the king, his sword will cross our own in the fight, and if we give a wound, we may expect another in return. Are your revenues so dear to you, that you would spill the blood of us who are your brethren to recover them? Yet even the Jews spurned the money which Judas brought back, because it was the price of blood. But you have another motive. Pause we here then, and consider what are your motives for counselling us to die. Blessed be God, it is no schism of faith between us, no question about the holy sacraments, nor of morals: our faith thrives with the king, the bishops, and their people. All the articles of our Creed are adhered to by the clergy of this kingdom. No one has failed in his obedience to the holy pontiff, the sacraments of the Church are respected by all, and all join devoutly in communion. In our morals, indeed, we all go astray daily: but no one boasts of his errors or defends them, but all hope by repentance to be washed clean from their acknowledged sins. The whole strife, therefore, is with the king, for certain constitutions of his ancestors which he wishes to be observed towards himself. Your highness has admonished him, but he will not renounce what long usage has sanctioned. This is why you have recourse to arms, and you are holding the sword ready to fall upon his hallowed head, though it was not he who propounded these constitutions but his ancestors, as the voice of the whole kingdom certifies. The tree which has been long planted, and shot its roots deeply, is with difficulty uprooted : and if we attempt by force to transplant it, it withers away. It must first be dug around and the earth be thrown out until the root is laid bare, and thus patience will effect what cannot be attained by violence. We should take example from the good men who have preceded us, and see how they acted. Your predecessor, Saint Augustine, eradicated many enormities from this kingdom, and when he converted the king, made him abandon many depraved laws and customs, not by heaping maledictions upon him, but by giving him his blessing, and by exhorting him to good works.

"In our own times John of Crema, who was sent into these parts by the Roman Church, changed many customs, in which all his life had been spent. This he effected, not by maledictions or by threats, but by sound doctrine and by holy exhortations: and as he had sowed in blessings, in blessings did he reap. If all these men had taken up arms, their success would have been small, if any.

"The pious king of France long desired to have a son; and when Heaven at last granted what he prayed for, many grievances, which antiquity had sanctioned, were nevertheless abolished at the suggestion, as they tell us, of the Church, which admonished, but never uttered threats against its sovereign. But who can enumerate the dignities, privileges, immunities, and possessions which pious princes have bestowed upon the Church of God? The time would fail me: suffice it to say, that such bounty is the noblest prerogative of kings. The humble obtain from them what is never conceded to the haughty. Money is to them trifling and of no value, yet whoever tries to take it from them by violence will find to his cost that the possessors can stoutly defend that to which they had attached so little value. You should have handled such concerns as these, not with the ardour of a novice, but with mature deliberation, and the advice of your brethren and others; you should have turned to the acts of the old fathers, and weighed the gains of the Church against her losses; and should not have taken a decided part, until you saw that there was no remedy remaining, and when at last your decision was given, you should have reflected who was the object of it, what were your motives, and what would be the evil or the good that would result to the Church from it. The object of your canonical censures is a sovereign, who even at this moment is hardly detained by the dearest ties of wife and children, and so many kingdoms that obey his rule, from taking up his cross and going a pilgrim to see the place where our Lord lay, thereby fulfilling that saying,—'He that carrieth not his cross and followeth me, is not worthy of me.' Yet this is he whose obstinacy of mind, whose cruelty and malignity towards God's Church, you lay so much stress on, and prepare to visit with excommunication. If you were to execute this threat, the Church of God would be wounded in her noblest part, and whole nations, not one or two individuals only, would groan beneath the stroke. Mercy must be blended with severity, that charity may step in and heal our wounds, for correction can never be salutary when the object of it has numbers associated with him. What physician ever gains applause by healing one sore, if he opens another still more dangerous? Is it the part of discretion, in order to effect an object that could have been better accomplished in another way, to desert one's flock, to rebel against the sovereign, to disturb the peace of the Church throughout the whole kingdom, and to neglect the salvation of the souls of the people? Saint Ambrose abandoned his possessions, but would not abandon his Church. Your prudence might have hoped for anything from a prince whom you know to be so zealous in the cause of Christ. What advantage could he expect from these earthly constitutions, when it was well known that the world and all it can offer had lost its charms for him? Ought we not to have waited till Christ's spirit was fully fledged in him, that so he might have resigned to us not only the constitutions in question, but many more with lavish hand have been showered upon us? In this I speak only what I know. Our lord the king would not have cared for those dignities and constitutions, but for two reasons only. He thought it would be a reproach to him if he should allow the crown to suffer loss and diminution of the honours which had been handed down to him by his ancestors: and secondly, though he might give up anything for his God, he would nevertheless blush to have it taken from him by violence. But he had already trodden underfoot the first of these motives, and the fear of God, his natural goodness of heart, the admonition of the pope, and the united prayers of many had already produced such an effect upon him, that out of reverence for Him who has exalted him above all his predecessors, he wished to call together the Church of God, and to alter and modify those constitutions by which they felt so much aggrieved. And if the humble-mindedness which began to show itself in you had but lasted, the Church would at this moment have been in the possession of widely extended tranquillity and rejoicing. For all that you had aimed at was already gained by entreaty, but all was again defeated by the disturbance which you began. For whilst he was preparing to lead his army against the Britons, who had not yet bowed to his sovereignty, but were indomitably lifting up their heel against him, you sent him those terrible letters, savouring neither of the affection of a father, nor the modesty of a bishop; and all that had been done by the admonition of the holy pontiff, and the entreaties of so many persons, was at once destroyed by your threats.

Thus you have again made our king and kingdom a scandal to the world worse than it was before.

"May God avert the evil which we fear, if this state of things continues; at least, may it not happen in these our times! to ensure which desirable consummation, for the honour of God, the benefit of the Church, and your own, my father, if so please you, for the sake of peace, and putting a stop to the scandals and disturbances which are so rife amongst us, we have appealed to our lord the pope, that we may check, at least for a time, that fury which impels you on against the king and his kingdom. And it will be well if you contain your zeal within moderate bounds, lest by rejecting our appeal, you be found to despise the authority of the pope as well as the rights of kings. May it please you to remember that our Lord made Zaccheus descend from the sycamore tree before He would enter into his house, and thus should you also condescend and strive to pacify the king whom you have offended, by offering to give him satisfaction, even though you may have suffered at his hands. Our Lord told his disciples to imitate the example of a child, who though wronged is not angry, and soon forgets an injury, but compensates for all by the innocence and happiness of his life. An extraordinary model of perfection we have in Him who pardons those who punish themselves, who orders us to love our enemies and persecutors, and to forgive our brother, not for seven, but for seventy times seven offences. What might not be expected from such humility at the hands of our lord the king? Such a course would have been like the straight way, leading directly to peace: when you once enter upon it, my father, you may hope to arrive at peace, and to fill with joy and gladness that which is now covered with the clouds of sorrow; whilst from our religious and beloved king you will gain all that you are aiming at, and even more than all, through the grace of God's Holy Spirit filling his mind, and bringing it even nearer and nearer to the knowledge of Himself!"

LETTER XXXIX.

"JOHN OF SALISBURY TO BARTHOLOMEW OF EXETER.

"Although my letter is destitute of that form of salutation which friends generally use towards one another, yet my prayers are fervently offered to God, that He may prosper your ways in all things. The salutation has been omitted, not from any deficiency or coolness in my regard towards you, but from motives of prudence, that queen and mistress of all wise actions. I need not tell you my motives, for every body knows them. Everything around us is so beset with spies and snares, that good and honest people do not dare to express their thoughts freely to one another, either by word of mouth or by letter. Iniquity is daily forming paltry schemes against innocence: conscience is constantly goading it on, and so all men and all things around them abound with treachery and suspicion. So be it then, they deserve it, the wicked should never be at peace. Justice daily assails her enemies, and rarely without gaining the advantage: the fears of the wicked are generally realised, and the just man shall be freed from tribulation, because the mouth of the Lord has spoken it. The fury of the storm is battering God's Church, and the impious seem for a time to prevail against it: but Christ, whom they are persecuting, will so repay them according to their deserts, that the scale of vengeance will finally preponderate: indeed, the punishment will be so great that they will not appear to be weighed in the balance, but rather to be crushed by its weight. I do not mean that injustice will be done them, but that punishment of unwonted magnitude will fall on those whose sins are without bounds. I do not wish any one to think that I am speaking of what will happen some time hence, though even if it was so, I am borne out by the authority of the Divine oracles, which foretel things to come hereafter;

for the judgments which I am describing have already begun, and sentence seems already to have been delegated to the executioners.

"That tyrant of Teutonic race lately was in the height of his pride, and seemed to overbear foreign nations, and the Greek empire was fain to offer him, not alliance, but submission. But lo! the fear of him has vanished, and he can now hardly manage the princes of his own Teutonic empire. He was once foremost to declare war against other nations, and now he is glad to accept a truce from his own subjects. For as he complains himself, from the moment of his attempting to separate the Gallican Church from its allegiance, and lead it into heresy, all his successes have faded from him, and fortune, that once favoured him, now seeks to depress him. It is the hope of all faithful Christians, that God's honour will soon be justified by his further abasement, until Christ, whose spouse he persecutes, humbles him under her feet.

"And have you no examples at home of God's judgment against those who vex his Church? Look at the king of England, what power he possessed, whilst he was little in his own eyes, and only made a show of fidelity and reverence towards God's Church: he succeeded in all he undertook: his arrow never missed its mark, nor did his buckler ever fall or his spear swerve aside in battle. Like a lion he crouched over the spoil; who dared to stir him up? his very look alarmed his enemies. The neighbouring princes bent to his will, whilst the more distant sought his friendship. He was adored by his countrymen, honoured by foreigners, and talked of among all mankind. All good men loved him, especially the clergy, who honoured him above measure, revered him to the utmost, and agreed in loving him beyond the love of woman. Why need I multiply words? He enjoyed all things in abundance, and had no fears or anxieties save those which his very enjoyment gave him. But how has he received all these gifts of God? To say nothing of the wrongs which from ignorance, or pretence of claiming his rights, he had done to different Churches, I will mention the siege of Toulouse, for which he compelled all the Churches to contribute their quota, contrary to their privileges and ancient dignities: nor would he allow them so much as to express their dissatisfaction at this contribution, or rather exaction, though it was so unjust: for he reproached them which did so as acting unworthily, and held them in no esteem. What has he gained by his wealth, or by these injuries and exactions? Have they not been thrown into a leaky vessel, so as to benefit his enemies and not their owner? Has not fortune left him since that very day, and the number of his triumphs retrograded?

"But some one here will say, Those exactions are to be ascribed to his chancellor, who now is archbishop, or at least wishes to be so: it was he who led the king into all those evil deeds. This is what envious men will say, but I know better. I know well that he never gave his sanction to license, but submitted to necessity: though his being the agent of iniquity at that time, renders it all fair that he should suffer for it now; and that he, whose agent he was, and whom he preferred to God the Creator of all things, should now be the person who inflicts his punishment. For, as we read in Wisdom, 'By what a man sins, by the same shall be his punishment.' Thus Cain, the first homicide, fell by the hand of another. Canaan reduced others to slavery, and was himself condemned to perpetual captivity. Pharaoh with his host was sunk beneath the waters in which he had drowned the Hebrew innocents: besides many more examples of the same kind.

"But the same now does penance for the crime which he acknowledges, and if with Saul he once vexed the Church; he is now ready with Paul to sacrifice his life in her defence. Who then shall deny that judgment has proceeded forth from God's house, when already so many kings are crucified before the light of day, that God's justice may be revealed in the sight of the nations? Are not these two the leaders of the people,—the one in spirituals, the other in temporals? Is not the law of ministry and of dispensation committed to their hands? These are the two cherubims whose wings overshadow the law and the propitiation, and which look one towards the other, whilst both look towards the propitiation, &c. Let a man cast his eyes around, and see what enemies God has raised up against the king, since he has lifted his heel to depress God's holy Church, and he will admire, and if he be wise, will bow down before the judgment of God, who has committed his punishment, not to the emperors and kings of the earth, but to the Britons, the most remote of men: and so those who once bent at his footstool, now oppose him in bloody strife. Let frail flesh then no longer glory, but laud the name of the Lord for.ever and ever! Thus we read,—robbers and slaves, not princes, punished the ingratitude of Solomon. No one will prosper in the world unless by repentance he turn to God. There have arisen in these our days foolish men, who have given foolish advice to our king. He is harassed by anxiety of one kind and another; but above all he is burdened by the war which he has undertaken against the Church of Christ, and which, like a labyrinth, involves him daily deeper in its windings.

"He lately summoned his nobles to Chinon, together with those of his advisers who took pleasure in encouraging him in evil: conjuring them with promises and threats and protestations, to assist him with some device against the Church, and complaining, with sighs and groans, of the archbishop's conduct towards him. According to those who were present at the time, he asserted, with tears in his eyes, that the said archbishop would take from him both body and soul; and in conclusion, he called them all a set of traitors, who had not zeal nor courage enough to rid him from the molestations of one man. On this his lordship of Rouen rebuked his majesty with some warmth, yet gently, in his own way, and with the spirit of meekness; whereas the cause of God required a sterner course.

"What so especially embittered his majesty on this occasion, was a fear which he had conceived from letters sent to himself and his mother by the aforesaid archbishop. I enclose you copies of them. He feared, and with justice, that an interdict was to be pronounced against his territories, and himself anathematized without farther delay, under the immediate sanction of the pope. While he was in this strait, the bishop of Lisieux suggested as a last resource, that the impending sentence might be warded off by an appeal. Thus, by a strange fatality, it came to pass that his majesty, while contending for those very usages by which he sought to avoid the right of appeal, was compelled himself to sanction it for his own protection.

"At the breaking up of the conference, the bishops of Lisieux and Seez went out from before the face of God and the king, to seek his lordship the archbishop with all haste, that they might be in time with their appeal, and thus suspend the sentence till the Sunday after Easter 1167. The archbishop of Rouen, too, accompanied them, not (as he protests) to join in the appeal, but, if possible, to mediate a reconciliation. But our archbishop, who was now girding himself as for the battle, had made a sudden journey to Soissons, where are the three shrines, that of the blessed Virgin, whose memory is cherished there, and another of the blessed Drausius, to whom men resort before a duel, and the third of the blessed Gregory, the founder of the English Church, whose body rests in that city. To these saints he wished to commend himself against the approaching struggle. But the blessed Drausius is that most glorious confessor, who, according to the belief of France and Lorraine, imparts the certainty of victory to all who watch a night before his shrine. The Burgundians, too, and Italians fly to him for succour before any perilous encounter. Here it was that Robert de Montfort watched before his combat with Henry of Essex. Thus, by God's grace, it came to pass that the assiduity of the state bishops was frustrated. For when they arrived at Pontigny, they found no archbishop to appeal against, and returned at once, much mortified at the expense and trouble which had procured them nothing.

"But the archbishop, when he had watched three nights before the shrines of the abovenamed saints, the day after Ascension day, hastened to Vezelay, intending the following Sunday to pronounce sentence against the king and his party. It so happened, however, by God's will, that on the aforesaid Friday, when he was in the Church of St. Mary, he received a well authenticated account of the severe indisposition of the king of England, which had prevented a conference between him and the king of France, that had been solicited by him with much earnestness. This had been certified on oath by Richard, archdeacon of Poitiers, and Richard de Humet, whom his majesty had sent to excuse his nonattendance, and was signified to the archbishop by a messenger from the king of France; for which reason the sentence against his majesty was deferred, as your correspondent had before ventured to advise.

"John of Oxford, however, he publicly denounced as excommunicate, and excommunicated him on the authority of the Roman high priest—I quote his own words—'for having fallen into a damnable heresy in taking a sacrilegious oath to the emperor, and communicating with the schismatic of Cologne, and usurping for himself the deanery of the Church of Salisbury, against the commands of his lordship the pope.' These causes he alleged from the pulpit, in the hearing of the whole concourse of diverse nations, who had flocked together at Vezelay on the day of the festival. In the same place likewise, after alleging various and just causes, he excommunicated Richard, archdeacon of Poitiers, and Richard de Lucy, Jocelin of Balliol, Randolf de Broc, Hugh de St. Clair, Thomas Fitz-Bernard, and all who for the future shall put forth their hands against the goods and property of the Church of Canterbury, or ill-use or interfere with those for whose necessities they have been set apart.

"The king, on whom he had already called for satisfaction by letters and messengers, as his royal dignity and the custom of the Church required, he now invited with a public summons to the fruits of penance, and menaced with an anathema, unless he speedily returned to wisdom, and atoned for his outrages against the Church. This, however, he will not resort to, except most reluctantly. I know none of his household who urges the passing of this sentence.

"That document, moreover, in which are contained the perverse devices of malignants against the Church, which they call the usages of our ancestors, he has publicly condemned; including in a general anathema all who shall henceforth act on its authority, and expressly the following clauses, which the Church of Rome selected for especial condemnation.

"'That no bishop shall excommunicate a tenant in chief without the king's licence.' 2. 'That no bishop shall decide causes of perjury, or breach of faith.' 3. 'That clerks shall be subjected to the lay tribunals.' 4. 'That laics, whether the king or others, shall take cognizance of tithe causes.' 5. 'That appeals, for whatever cause, to the Apostolic See, shall not be lawful, except by licence of the king or his officers.' 6. 'That no archbishop, or bishop, nor any other dignitary, shall attend a summons from his lordship the pope, without the king's licence:' besides others of the same kind, opposed alike to the divine law, and to the constitutions of the holy fathers.

"All the bishops, moreover, he absolved from the promise they had given, to abide by that document against the institutions of the Church; and these things he announced by letter to the archbishops and bishops, as the Church of Rome had directed him.

"Such has been the employment of the archbishop.

"The king, as I doubt not has come to your knowledge, despatched a very worthy man, M. Walter de Lisle, to England, from the conference of Chinon, with letters to warn the islanders of the appeal, and cause the ports and passes to be watched attentively, and suspend the clergy from their obedience; though the appeal has not yet been made, and the archbishop can be found without any difficulty.

"I doubt not that this contrivance displeased the aforesaid Walter, as well as other encroachments made upon the Church, for he fears God. The king has also sent for his lordship of Chichester and others, by whose prudence he hopes to strengthen his own malice. If they were wise, they would spare themselves and theirs in this matter.

'Pœna reversura est in caput ipsa suum.'

"As to the rest: his lordship the pope prospers in the city. It is said that Cremona has most certainly rebelled against the German, and eight other cities with it. The bishop of Tusculum and

Cardinal Hubald are dead. William, king of Sicily, is likewise dead, and his sons have succeeded him; one to the kingdom, and the other to the dukedom of Apulia. When on his death-bed, he caused 40,000 sterling to be paid to John of Naples for the pope's use. His son too, who succeeds to the throne, has sent as many. The king of France supports the archbishop of Canterbury in every thing, and honours him more than a brother. The news of the English court, where many changes are taking place, is, I conclude, better known to your lordship than to us.

"May your fatherly goodness prosper, and be strong in the Lord; and commend us to the prayers of the saints, that they may comfort us in our tribulation.

"We shall be allowed to return to our native land, when it pleases Him who has been pleased that we should be exiled. As long as it is his good pleasure that we should remain, we will submit with cheerfulness to his will, and endure any suffering with fortitude, which He will give us. May the same grace which has thought us worthy to suffer, give us patience to endure our sufferings. You have my best wishes and prayers for your Church and your whole family, and all who minister to you in your necessities."

END OF VOL. I.

LONDON:
GILBERT AND RIVINGTON, PRINTERS,
ST. JOHN'S SQUARE.